The Face of Exile

The Face of Exile

autobiographical journeys

By Judith M. Melton

University of Iowa Press Ψ Iowa City

University of Iowa Press, Iowa City 52242

Copyright © 1998 by the University of Iowa Press

All rights reserved

Printed in the United States of America

Design by Richard Hendel

http://www.uiowa.edu/~uipress

The poem "Fleeing" from *O the Chimneys* by Nelly Sachs is
reprinted by permission of Farrar, Straus & Giroux, Inc.

Printed on acid-free paper

Library of Congress Cataloging-in-Publication Data

Melton, Judith M.

  The face of exile: autobiographical journeys / by
Judith M. Melton.

    p.   cm.

  Includes bibliographical references and index.

  ISBN 0-87745-649-6

  1. World War, 1939–1945 — Refugees — Europe.

  2. World War, 1939–1945 — Personal narratives.   I. Title.

  D808.M45   1998

  940.53'086'91 — dc21   98-24440

98 99 00 01 02 C 5 4 3 2 1

For Jerry

Contents

Preface, *ix*

Introduction: The Experience of Exile
and the Autobiographical Impulse, *xi*

part one   DISRUPTED LIVES

1 Escape to Life, *3*
2 The Fall of France:
Narratives of Escape and Internment, *15*
3 The Persecution and Flight of the Jews:
Narratives of Survival, *28*
4 After the War: Coming to Terms with Exile, *50*

part two   RECONSTRUCTIONS

5 Crossing Boundaries:
Theoretical Dimensions of Exile Autobiography, *63*
6 Childhood and the Mystery of Origins, *84*
7 The Intellectual Response, *112*
8 A Personal Mythology, *144*
9 The Currency of Language, *160*
10 Reconstructing the Self:
Identity and Reflections of the Postmodern, *174*
11 The End of the Journey, *198*

Notes, *201*
Bibliography, *209*
Index, *219*

Preface

The completion of this book has been a long-term project. My interest in those who fled Europe during the rise of Nazism began in the early eighties when I was team-teaching a humanities class on Europe in the twenties and thirties. It was intensified when my colleague Alan Schaffer urged me to attend a conference at the Smithsonian Institution entitled "The Muses Flee Hitler" which delineated the influence of artists and intellectuals who had emigrated to this country in the thirties on American intellectual trends. The discussion of famous exiles at this conference reminded me that my graduate education in the field of languages reflected this phenomenon since so many émigrés found refuge in language departments across the country. Later, when my interest in the critical study of autobiography escalated, I recognized that a great number of émigrés had written autobiographies. It seemed very pertinent to follow exiles through their autobiographies. The journey was fascinating.

I gratefully acknowledge the work of those autobiographical scholars who helped me understand the shifting boundaries of the genre of autobiography. The theoretical writings of James Olney, Paul John Eakin, Albert Stone, Paul Jay, Felicity Nussbaum, Eugene Stelzig, and Shari Benstock have been very important for my perspectives on exile autobiography. I particularly want to thank the many friends and colleagues who pointed me to autobiographies which illustrated many of my theses. Paul John Eakin's work on Saul Friedländer in *Fictions in Autobiography* led me to Friedländer's interesting autobiography. I very much appreciate Lilian Furst's willingness to send me the manuscript version of her autobiography, *Home Is Somewhere Else*. Her autobiographical testimony added much to my review of children who were caught up in the upheaval of the thirties. I am also indebted to the uncovering of Charlotte Salomon's very unusual autobiography by Mary

Lowenthal Felstiner recounted in her excellent book *To Paint Her Life: Charlotte Salomon in the Nazi Era*.

Gratefully I thank the editors and staff at the University of Iowa Press for their generous support and help. Particularly, I want to thank Holly Carver, Paul Zimmer, and Edie Roberts for their advice and encouragement.

I also want to thank all those who offered me encouragement and assistance during the drafting of this book. Robert A. Waller, dean of liberal arts, always believed in the project and supported me with a semester sabbatical in 1991 and very much needed time away from the office in summers during my years as department chair. With pleasure I acknowledge those who read earlier and later versions of the manuscript: Judith Stanton, Don McKale, Margit Sinka, Patti Connor-Greene, Barbara Zaczek, Rebecca Hogan, Fred Shilstone, and Rob Roy McGregor. I especially want to thank my husband, Jerry E. Griggs, for his unstinting support and critical judgment. Thanks, too, to all those who patiently heard about these exiles and their stories over the years.

The Experience of Exile and the Autobiographical Impulse

Every expression of exile is absolutely authentic.
The testimony of an untalented man and that of
a genius are genuine in equal measure.
>   Werner Vordtriede,
>   "Vorläufige Gedanken zu einer Typologie der Exilliteratur"

It could indeed be said that exile is the
archetypal condition of contemporary lives.
>   Eva Hoffman, *Lost in Translation*

In his book of essays, *Extraterritorial*, George Steiner character-izes exile writers such as Vladimir Nabokov as appropriate sym-bols of the twentieth century, an age of social and political catas-trophe:

> A great writer driven from language to language by social upheaval and war is an apt symbol for the age of the refugee. No exile is more radical, no feat of adaptation and new life more demanding. It seems proper that those who create art in a civilization of quasi-barbarism which has made so many homeless, which has torn up tongues and peoples by the root, should themselves be poets unhoused and wanderers across language. (11)

Nabokov is only one of many exiles who have conveyed the traumatic experience of losing connections to home, homeland, cultural identity, or native language. John M. Spalek and Robert F. Bell, exile literature scholars, estimate that there are approximately four hundred autobiographies written by exiled intellectuals as a result of the rise of fascism in Europe. Writers, artists, scientists, and scholars of many fields — art, architecture, psychology, philosophy, music — found themselves seeking asylum in foreign, sometimes distant countries. Some members of the intellectual community of Germany, a great many of whom were Jewish, felt compelled to leave when Hitler first came to power. Other European groups at risk left Europe for safer harbors when Hitler began his lightning strikes against neighboring countries.

The most vulnerable group was the Jews. The Nazis began to persecute them systematically in 1933 and intensified actions against them after the passing of the Nuremberg laws in 1935. But intellectuals of political persuasions differing from the Nazi stance were also in danger and quick to leave. Bertolt Brecht, known for his leftist views, left Germany the very day Hitler seized power on January 30, 1933. Thomas Mann, an outspoken advocate for the democracy of the Weimar Republic, heeded the pleadings of his son Klaus and daughter Erika not to return to his home in Munich following the lecture tour he was on after Hitler became chancellor. These famous exiles, like hundreds of others, began their odyssey in advance of the spreading Nazi power. Brecht sought asylum in Denmark and Finland before fleeing across Russia to California. Mann took refuge in Switzerland before emigrating to the United States, first to Princeton and later to Pacific Palisades in California. Many intellectuals found refuge in France in the thirties, only to flee a few years later in the face of the occupying Nazi army.

Ultimately many of the intellectuals fleeing from Hitler enriched the intellectual life of their host countries. In America alone, Albert Einstein, Walter Gropius, Arnold Schoenberg, Hannah Arendt, Billy Wilder, Herbert Marcuse, to name only a very few, added significantly to the scientific, artistic, educational, and cultural life of the United States.[1] In 1980, the Smithsonian Institution held two seminars entitled "The Muses Flee Hitler: Cultural Transfer and Adaptation in the United States, 1930–1945," which surveyed the scope of the influence of European exiles on the culture of the United States. The fleeing intellectuals, artists, and scholars made a significant impact on widely diverse fields. Their distinctly European intellectual predilections brought fresh conceptual perspectives to American cultural and scholarly endeavors. Arnold Schoenberg brought his atonal music to California, Hans Hofmann brought abstract painting into representational schools of art, and Walter Gropius and Ludwig Mies van der Rohe brought the Bauhaus style of architecture to the United States. The extent of exiles' influence on American traditions, culture, and scholarship has still not been determined.

But if many of these refugees eventually found a home in their host country and assimilated into its intellectual and cultural life, it was not without experiencing the trauma of exile, of losing comfortable, reassuring ties to their homeland. Coping with life in a new country and a strange culture and language simultaneously with the loss of one's homeland brought on shock and sometimes despair. Many, like Brecht, wandered for long years before finding a safe haven in California. As Heinrich Heine, a nineteenth-century German exile, noted, "But exile, exile, that is a terrible thing" (Exner, *"Exul Poeta"* 289). Like Heine and other historical exiles, these modern ones tasted the bitter bread of this "terrible thing" called exile.

Exile is an age-old concept. Ovid, Dante, and Petrarch have described their experiences of separation from their places of birth. Being banished from one's homeland brings about feelings of disorientation, alienation, psychological discomfort, and pain. Paul Tabori, who has given a definitive account of the experience in his book *The Anatomy of Exile*, emphasizes that exile is a part of ancient history. He cites as the first exile Sinhuhe, an Egyptian who went into exile to escape punishment in 2000 B.C., but individuals in Greece and Rome and other early empires were frequently politically banished. The banishment of the Jews is also a well-known episode of people in exile. Both Tabori and H. Stuart Hughes, however, emphasize that it is not until the twentieth century that social and political upheavals such as the Russian revolution and the rise of fascism created waves of refugees, making exile a way of life. Political banishment continues today for people from the Middle East, South America, and Africa.

Charles Connell divides exiles into three categories: those "banished from their native countries by the sovereign authorities," those "compelled to leave their motherlands by force of circumstances," and those who "voluntarily change . . . 'their homes and pleasant thresholds' to seek abroad that which, for one reason or another, their own lands could not provide" (9). In the first instance, exile was a punishment such as Ovid or Dante experienced. For the second group, fear, anger, or economic reasons compelled the exile to seek refuge elsewhere. The last group is more or less made up of self-imposed exiles such as the community of American writers in Paris in the twenties. Connell, however, stresses that all these groups experience homesickness at one time or another.

Paul Tabori defines an exile more specifically as a

> person compelled to leave or remain outside his country of origin on account of well-founded fear of persecution for reasons of race, religion, nationality, or political opinion; a person who considers his exile temporary (even though it may last a lifetime), hoping to return to his fatherland when circumstances permit — but unable or unwilling to do so as long as the factors that made him an exile persist. (37)

Those not in exile call exiles by many names (refugees, displaced persons, émigrés, or immigrants), but no matter what the name, all have in common the loss of their homeland and feelings of alienation.

Connell's and Tabori's somewhat analytical definitions of exile dealing with lexical and semantic differences do not suggest the mental and physical anguish of this traumatic experience. In his essay "The Mind of Winter," Edward W. Said characterizes exile "as the unhealable rift forced between a human being and a native place, between the self and its true home" (49). Particularly for the autobiographer, how one is exiled may not be as important as the experience itself — coping with feelings of loss, disrupture, and uprootedness. Michael Seidel notes, "Many writers have gained imaginative sustenance from exile," including "Ovid, Dante, Swift, Rousseau, Madame de Staël, Hugo, Lawrence, Mann, and Brecht." The experience is nevertheless a traumatic one that changes the very fabric of the life of the one being forced into exile (x). Said states that the "essential sadness of the break can never be surmounted" (49). Said, Tabori, and others such as Erik Erikson and H. Stuart Hughes stress that exiles can be motivated to do heroic tasks and achieve great deeds in exile, but Said insists that "the achievements of any exile are permanently undermined by his or her sense of loss" (49). He continues, "Modern exile is irremediably secular and unbearably historical. It is produced by human beings for other human beings; it has torn millions of people from the nourishment of tradition, family, and geography" (50). This disabling experience that has jolted so many people in the twentieth century from the sustaining environment of their native land has become a metaphor for alienation in our time.

Both Said and Steiner note the metaphorical dimension of exile among twentieth-century writers. Steiner, as noted above, sees exiled writers such as Nabokov, Pound, and Beckett as pertinent symbols of the twentieth-century mind. Said asserts that the "canon of Western culture is in large part the work of exiles, émigrés, refugees" (49). Seidel characterizes this dimension of exile as "a metaphor for the alienated or marginalized modern consciousness, whereby individuals are alienated not only from the place they inhabit but from the things they do or the things they are" (xi). Franz Kafka is the writer par excellence who illustrates this alienated and metaphorically exilic condition of modern man, but the voices of Nietzsche, Rilke, Beckett, and others have added dimensions to this melancholy metaphor. Henri R. Paucker in his essay "Exile and Existentialism" compares exile writers, particularly Klaus Mann, Hermann Broch, and Robert Virgil, with the French existentialist writers Sartre, Camus, and St. Exupéry, noting particularly how the exiled writers illustrate the excluded existential hero. Most recently, feminist critics Mary Lynn Broe and Angela Ingram have appropriated exilic metaphors to describe the marginality of women writers in the Western tradition.

While the trope of exile has become a recognized motif in modern literature, the present study of autobiographies written by exiles concentrates on individuals who have experienced the physical rupture of being exiled during the social and political upheavals caused by the rise of fascism, whether that stems from political change and political and religious persecution, fear of violence, or some other catastrophic social change. Weathering the schism of exile psychologically is a wrenching experience, as autobiographers reveal. Initially, exile brings shock, disorientation, confusion, or even numbness. Later, as the individual rebounds somewhat, disorientation and a feeling of loss nevertheless continue, so much so that the experience haunts some for the rest of their lives. It is also significant that so many exiles are motivated to write autobiographies. Even today exile autobiographers continue to focus on events leading up to World War II and its aftermath. People who were children during the war years and whose lives were disrupted when their parents went into exile are still impelled as adults to write about this traumatic experience. Eva Hoffman's 1989 autobiography, *Lost in Translation*, is one that most clearly dissects the exilic experience. But autobiographical narratives were published almost as soon as Hitler rose to power, for many felt the immediate need to confront the experience. Others, however, only penned accounts of their exile during a more reflective time of their lives, after the war or toward the end of their careers. Thus, many accounts were written in the fifties and sixties, and personal narratives continue in the nineties.

When does a person no longer feel that he or she is in exile? What does assimilation mean? What are the definitions of refugee, immigrant, émigré? Tabori and other scholars of exile literature raise such questions. German exile literature scholars generally designate 1933 to 1945 as the period of Germany's exile literature. But as Spalek and Bell point out, this arbitrary dating leaves out the younger generation of exile writers (xii).[2] At the end of the war, exiles asked themselves some of the same questions, revealing the fundamental changes they had experienced. If people return to their native land or leave their adopted country permanently, when are they no longer considered exiles? It is traditionally accepted that the trial of exile ends when individuals regain entry to their native country. The number of autobiographies written late in the lives of so-called former exiles indicates that even though they recover from this disruptive experience, they are changed by it and feel that the experience warrants attention in a narrative form. Indeed, my own research suggests that placing arbitrary dates on the exile experience of Europeans during the fascistic period is not prudent, because many of the most intriguing autobiographies have been published only in recent years. Mircea Eliade, for example, subtitled the second volume of his autobiography *Exile's Odyssey*, although he had been in the United States for twenty-five years and had achieved recognition as one of the leading historians of comparative religions. Golo Mann, one of Thomas Mann's younger sons, described his and his family's exile experiences in his autobiography, *Reminiscences and Reflections: A Youth in Germany*, published in Germany in 1986. Even a brief survey of autobiographers writing about exile experiences indicates that Said is right: the experience permanently changes the exile.

To answer the question of why so many exiles chose to write their autobiographies it would be well to examine some views of the exile experience in a writer's career. Claudio Guillén observes, "A certain kind of writer speaks of exile, while another learns from it" (272). Guillén sees two basic authorial responses. In the first, the author feels compelled to narrate the experience itself. As he explains, "[It] is the direct or near-autobiographical conveyance of the actual experiences of exile itself by means of emotions reflecting the experiences of or attitudes developed toward them" (Guillén 271–272). In this mode, poetry, "often . . . elegiac modes," is customary. In the second, the author mines the experience for meaning, creating "the imaginative presentation of relatively fictional themes, ancient myths or proposed ideas" (Guillén 272). He terms the second "counterexile" and sees in this instance "responses which incorporate the separation from place, class, language or native community, insofar as they triumph over the separation and thus can offer wide dimensions of meaning that transcend the earlier attachment to place or native origin" (Guillén 272).

Guillén names the first response the Ovidian response, drawing on Ovid's autobiographical writings that lament his exile, and further states, "I cannot suppose that the direct expression of the sorrow, which is the Ovidian mode, is the most important response" (272). Clearly, Guillén values the "imaginative" response, the one resulting in literature, as the more important response and discounts the purely autobiographical. His prejudice against the autobiographical form is shared by many literature critics in the nineteenth and twentieth centuries. Only recently have critics claimed literary value for the genre of autobiography, and, as recent critical discussions of the genre have shown and as will be discussed in chapter 5, the parameters of the form and/or genre are not clear cut. For some, such as James Olney, autobiography can be any form of writing that conveys the experiential and psychological dimensions of the author. For the purpose of this study, all autobiographical responses to such an intensive experience as exile are deemed important whether categorized as autobiography, memoirs, elegiac poetry, autobiographical novels, or any other form of artistic medium. Embedded in Guillén's second category, the imaginative response, is also an assumption that the author should have "transcended" the experience in some way (272). I maintain, however, that transforming the experience from memory and emotion to narrative of any kind is itself a valued and powerful imaginative response. The writing process itself creates a transformation for the exile, helping him or her to overcome the psychological trauma of the experience.

While acknowledging the validity in the motivations noted above for exile autobiography, this study offers additional motivations. First, I show that many writers felt the impulse to testify to their experiences, to show the rest of the world what was happening to them and their homelands. The first section of the book presents such autobiographies, self-defined witnesses to history. In the second part of the book, I focus more on the psychological expressions of exile. In these works, many times autobiographers write to heal their dislocated selves. Writing an autobiography becomes a means of healing, of reconnecting, or of regaining identity. H. Stuart Hughes asserts, "A geographical and emotional displacement has often provided the shock that has set the mind off its familiar course and turned it toward introspection and social or psychological probing" (2). Guillén touches on the same motivation when he speaks of another very famous exile, Li Po, who wrote a series of elegiac letters lamenting his exile in the Chinese provinces. As Guillén says of the letter "To Tung Tsai-chiu," it "can be readily approached by the Western reader in Ovidian terms, i.e., of the literature of exile itself; these are . . . epistles . . . dominated by the themes of friendship and its ability to heal the wounds of separation in space and time, by the exercise of memory and the tendency to, or need for, autobiography and self-reconstruction" (274).

Exiles are separated not only from their homelands but also from the enculturations of that place — family, friends, status, or language; in short, from the life enculturations that helped form their identities, a part of themselves they took for granted. An individual forced to part from these psychological supports experiences a rift of being. As the focus of the ensuing chapters in part II makes clear, an overwhelming motivation for the autobiographical narrative is to heal this psychic rift, to help the author reconnect to lost psychological supports — homeland, belief systems, childhood, a sense of cultural identity, native language, or, in some cases, the creation of a place to come to terms with a new identity.

Fred Weinstein suggests that everyone needs a sense of continuity for psychic health: "[p]eople everywhere need to maintain a sense of continuity, a sense of self-sameness over time. . . . Any individual must be able, through memory, to use time as an ordering principle for the succession of events that constitute his or her history" (26). The human being's need to preserve order, to stave off discontinuity, explains the emotional fragmentation of the physically and mentally displaced. Elie Wiesel's lament about this experience is particularly apt: "[exile] envelops all endeavors, all explorations, all illusions, all hopes, all triumphs, and this means that whatever we do is never complete. . . . [E]xile means to be displaced, I am here and I am not here. The content and form do not espouse one another. When a person is in exile, nothing fits" (Lipsey 27). Writing an autobiography, reestablishing connection with a lost world, salvages the feeling of loss and discontinuity for the exile. Whether this writing takes the form of a work clearly delineated as a personal memoir or falls into the category of imaginative literature, the writing process itself transforms and helps heal feelings of disruption. Under such circumstances, the autobiographical impulse becomes a natural one. Weaving the story of their disrupted lives into a concrete work helps restore exiles' sense of continuity by recapturing the extensions of their former existence, re-creating their yearned-for past, or resolving the emotional devastation they have experienced.

Thus, as we shall see, such writers as Nabokov, Gregor von Rezzori, Elias Canetti, Golo Mann, and Eva Hoffman re-created vivid, personal pictures of childhood experiences in places that have now politically and culturally disappeared. Stefan Zweig, whose long list of works expresses hope for a unified and enlightened Europe, tried to re-create a lost epoch in his exile autobiography, *The World of Yesterday*. He developed an extended image found only in his mind. In contrast, Thomas Mann and Czesław Miłosz created highly intellectualized responses to the irrational and violent behavior they saw trampling the cultural tradition of humanistic idealism.

Part I of this study, "Disrupted Lives," shows the immediate and disastrous dislocation of peoples in the face of social and political change. These witnesses to history provide a panorama of escape, flight, and resettlement. In part II, "Reconstructions," the initial chapter focuses on the theoretical dimensions of exile autobiography. The remaining chapters delineate comparative themes such as the re-creation of childhood, the dissolution into personal myth, the discontinuity and resulting self-rupture of failed and outmoded belief systems, responses to dissolving intellectual supports, and the loss of identity and native language. In the examination of such writers as Carl Zuckmayer, Elias Canetti, and Vladimir Nabokov, among others, I hope to illuminate how the autobiographical writing process itself can become a place of refuge. Whether the exile autobiographer wrote during the chaotic period of early exile, during a more reflective period in the decades after the war, after the cause of exile had dissipated, or during an even more removed decade, writing autobiographical works provides a link with the past, a reconnection to a former, for the most part comforting, existence. The writing itself becomes a bridge to self-reconstruction and self-regeneration.

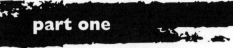

part one

Disrupted Lives

chapter one

Escape to Life

For we went, changing countries oftener than our shoes.
    Bertolt Brecht, "To Those Born Later"

I am now living on the small island of Lidingö.
But one night recently
I had heavy dreams and I dreamed I was in a city
And discovered that its street signs
Were in German. I awoke
Bathed in sweat, saw the fir tree
Black as night before my window, and realised with relief:
I was in a foreign land.
    Bertolt Brecht, "1940"

In 1939, Erika and Klaus Mann published a collaborative work in English, *Escape to Life*, whose express purpose was to bring to the attention of the world in the late thirties how the lives of those persecuted by the Nazis were being and had been dislocated. The authors portrayed the experiences of a large group of artists, authors, and scholars, many of whom later chronicled their own experiences in autobiographies. This book provides background into the confusion and disorientation of the early exiles. For the most part they moved only to neighboring countries in the early years, France, Switzerland, or Austria, countries where they were already at home. These early migrations, however, turned out to be only the beginning of many years of uncertainty and anxiety.

In the prologue to *Escape to Life*, Klaus Mann noted that "the circumstances we grew up in, and are living in today, have robbed us of any confidence in the stability of things" (Mann and Mann 10–11). The authors described the flight and exile of the famous who experienced this anxiety. In addition to essays on their father and uncle, Thomas and Heinrich Mann, they told about the emigration of such notables as Bruno Walter, Franz Werfel, Stefan Zweig, Lotte Lehmann, and Luise Rainer. Underlying the narrative is a call to arms of all antifascist thinkers. Yet the community of exiles failed to unite politically against the Nazis. Although all opposed fascism and the Hitler regime, the leftist writers and those who upheld the democratic views of the Weimar Republic could not agree in their basic polemics against Nazism. Moreover, some such as Zweig and even Thomas Mann in the beginning of his exile were loathe to support some exiles' initiatives which publicly denounced Germany and the Germans. From the beginning, Klaus Mann, one of the more outspoken exiles, led many of the political battles in the exile community.[1]

Outrage and righteous indignation describe the tone of *Escape to Life*. The authors note that "[i]t is painful for a man to leave his country at dead of night, with a suitcase packed in haste, trembling lest the hirelings of a hated, hostile government should catch him at the very frontier, stop him and drag him back again" (Mann and Mann 35). Again and again the authors recount how so many barely escaped prison or death and how some did not. They write poignantly of the writer Carl von Ossietsky, the outspoken pacifist and antifascist who won the Nobel Peace Prize in 1935 while in a Nazi prison. Noting that Hitler stole Ossietsky's prize money and prevented him from acknowledging his award to the wider world, the authors quote the sick and tortured man: "[i]n prison, in a concentration camp, or in hospital, which is simply another kind of prison, I shall be more of a nuisance and a danger to my enemies than as an exile" (Mann and Mann 25). In a later chapter, they briefly describe a number of writers and thinkers who were either murdered or committed suicide, such as Professor Theodor Lessing, assassinated at his writing desk in Marienbad.

Using quotations, letters, mock interviews, and other techniques, the authors allow their subjects a voice in the narrative as well. These techniques imbue the book with a sense of the immediate. For example, a supposed diary of a young German student exile in Princeton introduces such extraordinary figures as Albert Einstein, the art historian Erwin Panofsky, and the archaeologist Ernst Herzfeld. A letter Klaus wrote in 1938 to Erika reveals him listening to the radio and beginning to understand that Austria was falling into the hands of the Nazis. Many of their descriptions are based on conversations they had with exiles in European capitals still safe as they were writing the book: Paris, Zurich, Amsterdam, Prague. In Zurich in 1938, for example, they interviewed Franz Werfel and his well-known wife, Alma Mahler-Werfel, before their flight from France in 1940.

The authors also tell stories of many writers and intellectuals who committed suicide rather than face exile. They speculate that Kurt Tucholsky, the acerbic writer and journalist, took poison in Sweden partly out of fear of being murdered. They ridicule and censure those who sided with the Nazis for personal gain or for personal views. One object of their scorn, of course, was Gustav Grundgens, the famous actor and Erika's first husband, who remained in Germany and profited during the Third Reich. His story is the acknowledged model for Klaus's novel *Mephisto*. They also attacked the dramatist Gerhart Hauptmann, one of the elder statesmen of German letters who remained in Germany and made concessions to the Nazis. At the same time, they praise German writers such as Oskar Maria Graf who were outraged that their books were not burned by Goebbels in the famous book burnings in May 1933.

Before ending the book with a plea to the exile community (which they describe as a family), the authors depict the changing fortunes of exiles in their new homes in Europe and the United States. They reference writers, artists, actors, opera singers, film and theater directors, poets, and scholars. In short, they try to convey to the Western world the pain and anguish that so many famous German and Eastern European exiles were experiencing. Acknowledging in the final chapter that "hope seems faint," they warn the exile community and the rest of the world that all must remain "unknown warriors" in the fight against Hitler (Mann and Mann 368, 371).

Escape to Life is an avowedly political book. It was rushed into print in order to gain sympathy (and resources) for those fleeing the Nazis. While it did alert the free world to the changes in fortune for many famous artists and writers, the writing was essentially completed before the major events of 1938 had transpired, events which set off a new wave of refugees. The years 1938, 1939, and 1940 became particularly dangerous for those at risk in Europe. Throughout the years from 1933 to 1938, many Germans and German Jews debated leaving their countries. Many had not yet left by 1938. Leaving a home and a country was not an easy decision, and many hoped that they would not have to make it. But whole new groups of émigrés began their journeys in 1938 because of escalating political events directed at Jews and antifascists.

First, Hitler successfully annexed Austria in spring 1938. This new political configuration caused many antifascist Austrians and earlier exiles from Germany to seek new refuges. Shortly thereafter, in October 1938, Hitler occupied the Sudetenland and then in March 1939 Czechoslovakia. The Czechoslovakian government had been very open to the first group of exiles, providing them with Czech citizenship and passports. But after Nazi troops occupied the country, émigrés there as well as Czech citizens began seeking asylum in other countries.

After the invasion of Poland, Britain and France finally declared war on 3 September 1939. This positive step against Hitler's aggression, however, brought new problems for those who had found refuge in France, an age-old haven for political exiles. Those who had lived comfortably for a number of years under French hospitality suddenly found themselves with a new status — enemy aliens. Lion Feuchtwanger, a best-selling antifascist writer, writes lovingly of his "well-furnished house" and the beautiful area of Sanary sur Mer, where he settled after leaving Germany. Most, however, were drawn to Paris, the long-time city of exiles, where they established a fairly large community. In Paris the exiles enjoyed freedom, if they did not always find financial security. But it was a life apart, a sort of émigré ghetto, as Koestler termed it: "[T]he great mass of refugees in France lived cut off from French contacts and led a kind of ghetto existence. They read their émigré papers, frequented their émigré clubs and cafés, lived immersed in their émigré universe, and its inevitable feuds and intrigues" (*Invisible Writing* 247).

But even this somewhat comforting way of life changed abruptly after the invasion of Poland. All male German nationals in France were immediately interned. Feuchtwanger speaks of this bleak period: "Protests in England got me out of the internment camp after a few days, with apologies from the French government" (15). He adds, however, that the exit visa to England he requested at that time was not issued. Following this brief disruption of their freedom, most exiles were released but continued to be harassed.

In the spring of 1940, Hitler and his troops began a campaign to conquer and occupy the countries to the north and west of Germany. In quick succession, Nazi troops marched into Norway, Denmark, Holland, Belgium, and Luxembourg, each invasion presenting new trials for refugees.

When Hitler turned his attention to France, all German nationals, men and women, were interned. The net was very wide, for other foreigners as well as those Germans with passports from other countries were incarcerated. Exiles had difficulty understanding this change in French policies, given their recent years in France and France's reputation of freedom and laissez-faire behavior toward foreigners. Suddenly being treated as enemy aliens was psychically damaging as well as physically constraining. Though they considered themselves committed antifascists, the authorities incarcerated them out of fear of their collaborating with the Nazis. Feuchtwanger recounts what he said to himself when he landed in the camp at Les Milles: "At this very moment, now, people in every country in the world sit reading my books about the barbarism of the Nazis, filling their hearts with wrath at those barbarians; but here am I lying in wretched confinement, beyond the human pale, suspected of being a confederate of those barbarians!" (72–73).[2]

The autobiographical accounts of the initial panic, flight, and settlement in a new country illuminate the paths that exiles used to escape from harm during the thirties in Europe. The autobiographers dealing with that period and the war years emphasize those characteristics necessary to survive such devastating life changes — perseverance, resourcefulness, and adaptability. Bringing these accounts together provides a mosaic of a time when the world seemed to be shifting on its axis. To survive and be able to tell about these experiences notifies the rest of the world about the terrible forces loose in Europe. But if such autobiographies can be seen as providing discreet glimpses of historic events, as historical documents they are problematic. They are anecdotal testimonies and display the authorial shaping of narrative discourse. They become, as Albert Stone suggests, "individual versions of history" ("Modern American Autobiography" 95) and thus only partial views of events. Nevertheless, they are provocative and offer certain insights into the displacement of people once Hitler began his conquests of power. In the following chapters I want to review some of these exile autobiographies as examples of personal narratives which have a sharply defined purpose — to document escapes. Specifically, in chapter 2 I discuss three autobiographies which focus on events during the fall of France. In chapter 3 I focus on escape narratives of children, particularly riveting accounts of luck and courage. Through these narratives the trials of those seeking escape not only give readers a wider understanding of the social disruption of the period but also illustrate a form of autobiography closely associated with historical interpretation — the memoir.

Memoir and History

Autobiography characterized as memoir was the dominant form of life writing in the early history of the genre. In this form, the "individual is perceived, respectively as the actor in or the witness to history" (Eakin, *Touching the World* 142). The emphasis on the development of the self and the autobiographer's subjectivity, what Paul John Eakin calls "life-self writing," emerged only in the nineteenth century (*Touching the World* 142). Readers in the past looked to memoir to experience history. The "autobiographer was expected to subordinate imagination to the attempt to communicate trustworthy, verifiable, subjective messages" (Stone, "Modern American Autobiography" 100). The memoirs of important players of historical events — generals, prime ministers, statesmen — were and are eagerly read for their views on the events in which they participated. Historians, however, have always reacted skeptically to such memoirs for several reasons. First, memory is notoriously unreliable, and, as Stone notes, such autobiographical narratives are more "a record of the author's reactivations than of the actor's original behavior and perceptions" ("Modern American Autobiography" 97). Second, historians recognize, as do many literary critics, that memoirs, too, are subject to the constructions of narrative modes. As Lawrence L. Langer states in reference to Holocaust testimonies:

The content of a written survivor memoir may be more harrowing and gruesome than most autobiographies, but such a memoir still abides (some more consciously than others) by certain literary conventions: chronology, description, characterization, dialogue and above all, perhaps, the invention of a narrative voice. This voice seeks to impose on apparently chaotic episodes a perceived sequence, *whether or not that sequence was perceived in an identical way* during the period that is being rescued from oblivion by memory and language. (41)

For the historian, such memoirs provide important information and authentic subjective responses to historical events, but additional documentary sources are needed to verify actions and facts. For the student of autobiography, the artful shaping of the "memory and language" also warrants scrutiny. The historical grounding of the work becomes less important, particularly when autobiographical critics prefer to focus on the apparent or hidden implications for the self displayed in the autobiography.

Yet autobiographical narratives as channels to history are important in a variety of contexts and for both literary critics and historians. Stone asserts that autobiography cannot be seen only as imaginative literature or as documents of social history:

I remain uneasy over the tendency to treat autobiography chiefly as a branch of imaginative literature and thus to stress artistic creation over the equally complex processes of historical re-creation, ideological argument, and psychological expression. *Life* is the more inclusive sign — not *Literature* — which deserves to be placed above the gateway to the house of autobiography. (*Autobiographical Occasions* 19)

Autobiographies as windows to history are valid but problematic. They must be understood as "overdetermined" expressions of the autobiographer's autonomy, but they nevertheless bring into focus the historical, social, and cultural environment in which the author lived (Stone, "Modern American Autobiography" 95–119).

In *Touching the World*, Eakin consciously refocuses attention on the connections of history and autobiography, although like most autobiography critics he rejects the traditional memoir. He selects for discussion autobiographies "in which the role of the witness or shaper and maker of the history observed is openly, even aggressively, disclosed" (Eakin, *Touching the World* 179). Here he emphasizes the autobiographer's "relation to history." His stress is on the complex relationship between the autobiographer who lives *in* history and the narrative the autobiographer constructs regarding that history. The autobiographer's definition of self expressed in the resultant autobiography is "intrinsic" to the historical moment and becomes the central focus of the autobiography. Eakin's examples include Patricia Hampl's *A Romantic Education* and Michael Arlen's *Passage to Ararat*. Eakin suggests that these writers create autobiographical identities through their interactions with history.

An earlier critic, Francis Russell Hart, articulated some traditional forms of autobiography in regard to history. He notes the interplay of the forms confession, apology, and memoir:

> "Confession" is personal history that seeks to communicate or express the essential nature, the truth, of the self. "Apology" is personal history that seeks to demonstrate or realize the integrity of the self. "Memoir" is personal history that seeks to articulate or repossess the historicity of the self. Confession as an intention or impulse places the self relative to nature, reality; apology places the self relative to social and or moral law. Memoir places the self relative to time, history, cultural pattern and change. ("Notes" 491) [3]

Pointing out that these three modes frequently overlap, Hart distinguishes these divisions of autobiography partially on the basis of the autobiographer's intention. His definitions are helpful in drawing connections between autobiography and history. The memoirist writes primarily to recapture the historicity of the self, not to "confess" flaws or to delineate an ideological position. Of course, as pointed out above, the memoir has been abused. Readers today easily recognize the self-serving memoir as a cliché. Such memoirs are rightfully rejected in serious discussions of history or autobiography. But memoir as a form of witnessing to historic events still retains power.

In a later essay "History Talking to Itself: Public Personality in Recent Memoir," Hart reclaims the memoir for our time: "Other autobiographical modes flourish at other times: confession abounds in times of soul-searching, apology in times of confrontation. But ours is a time of survival, and memoir is the autobiography of survival" (195). Hart asserts that "memoirs are *of* a person, but they are 'really' of an event, an era, an institution, a class identity" ("History" 195). Drawing upon memoirs written in the seventies such as Studs Terkel's *Talking to Myself: A Memoir of My Time*, Michael Harrington's *Fragments of the Century*, or Michael Herr's *Dispatches*, Hart notes that the autobiographers of such memoirs personalize history. They give personal accounts of events and, in the case of Terkel, conversations with committed fighters for principles, but the private realm is excluded. These are individual accounts of public events. They provide a personal approach to some of the modern era's more thorny social questions — the justification for the Vietnam war, the dissolution of the "socialist cadre," or the trials of those committed to social causes.

In the second half of the century, testimonies (or oral autobiographies) of surviving witnesses to historic events have become important resources for historians. The vast collections of oral (and some written) testimonies of Holocaust survivors are well known. This very complex and hard to understand episode of this century's history can be more intensively studied with the benefit of such testimonies. Audio, video, and computer technologies have aided in collecting them.[4] Oral testimony as well as journals, diaries, and other written resources have also become important tools for studying eras of people's history where the customary documentary sources are not present — black history, for example. The history discipline now embraces the field of oral history. Historians under stringent guidelines conduct interviews with witnesses to historical events for use along with other sources to expand knowledge of a certain era or episode of history. For social historians in particular who are more interested in delineating the history of the everyday and the private individual, oral testimony becomes a valuable resource indeed.

But like memoir, oral testimonies are based on recall, resulting in the same inherent problems in using them as sources — the weakness of memory and the interference of present-day attitudes. But as Langer notes, oral narratives generated on video, for example, do not strike the viewer so significantly as "self-consciously *represented* reality" as do survivor accounts which have been written and thus consciously shaped. Nevertheless, he also notes that the interviewees almost "unavoidably introduce some kind of teleology, inventing the incidents with a meaning" (Langer 40). For the historian, archival journals and diaries, for example, have the advantage of spontaneity, which oral narratives do not. But it should be remembered that published journals can also be products of biased or self-serving revisions, thus diminishing the advantage of spontaneity. For historians, accuracy and validity are important questions concerning oral history. The historian Alice Hoffman offers practical suggestions to counter these concerns. She admonishes interviewers to ascertain accuracy of oral testimonies in two ways: look for consistency in a person's version of events (does the person tell the same story the same way) and compare documents and other interviewees' versions of the same events (Hoffman 70). These techniques also apply to the validity of written memoirs.

The tasks of the historian and the literary critic are, of course, very different, although they may use the same texts. For the historian, memoirs or oral autobiographies become one of many sources the historian uses to interpret as accurately as possible an era or an episode of history. The accuracy of the texts is balanced by the additional use of archival documents, which broaden the context of the testimonies. The autobiography critic focuses on

the form and narrative strategies of the text. But as autobiography
critics such as Stone, Eakin, and Hart have shown, the connections between history and autobiography are also pertinent. For
my study, a positive reading on memoir as Hart, Stone, and Eakin
have suggested becomes valuable because in examining the forces
of exile through autobiography I am also extremely interested in
the interplay of history and autobiography.

The Exile Memoir

Exile autobiographers inevitably have a sense that they are witnesses to history. They chose exile in response to external political
events. The anguish and hardship they faced were a part of mo-
mentous political change. Although they were alienated, they did
not act in isolation. They shared their frustrating experiences with
others in the exile community. They faced loss of freedom, loss of
livelihood, unanticipated flight, and, in the case of the Jews and
political enemies of the Nazis and other fascist regimes, persecution. From our vantage point in history, we now know that those
who evaded the Nazis did so with luck, perseverance, and courage.
But at the time, it was difficult for the exile community and the
rest of the free world to understand what was happening. The exiles who cataloged their experiences in the early forties wrote autobiographical texts with a sharply defined focus. As in *Escape to
Life*, the authors wanted the world to know what was happening
to them. Authors Arthur Koestler and Lion Feuchtwanger, who
were caught up in the invasion and capitulation of France, immediately published accounts of their trials. They tell remarkable stories, but no more remarkable than the stories of the escapes of
German, Austrian, and Polish Jews. These "focused memoirs"
highlight the sudden abruptness of a life change or dramatic, even
dangerous escapes. Although many escape or survival narratives
were written years after the war, the autobiographers fashioned
their narratives to emphasize the immediacy and the drama of
their experiences.

In the second half of my study, I focus on autobiographies
which dissect the implications of exile, highlighting the multiple

identity changes those autobiographers have undergone. They show connections to history, for the reconstructed identities portrayed are intimately bound up with the dynamics of that historical moment when the autobiographer chose exile. But in this first part, I emphasize "focused memoirs" written to capture the terror of exiles' flight and escape. The early, more political ones, such as *Escape to Life*, contrast with ones published after the war in that the politics of exile is not so imperative. Nevertheless, they highlight themes such as flight, escape, survival, and integration into a new culture. They are texts which emphasize how historic events — wars, political uprootings, and enforced ideologies — can abruptly redirect a person's life. Examining these "focused memoirs" allows us as readers to better understand the relationship of autobiography to history, but it also gives us insight into the subjective responses of the personal crisis of going into exile.

chapter two

The Fall of France:
Narratives of Escape and Internment

The continent is lousy with dictators.
    Arthur Koestler

Choosing exile or escape from the Nazis meant a break with all stability and social comfort. Those who made the break took a step into chaos. Those who later chose to chronicle this period narrate experiences that many shared. Flight through France during the first days after the capitulation of the French government and the subsequent occupation by the Nazis of Paris and northern France finds prominence in several autobiographies. Arthur Koestler and Alfred Döblin, for example, characterize their very different experiences of this event. Likewise, internment of refugees in France becomes a significant subject in the exile autobiographies of Feuchtwanger, Koestler, and others. Delineating some consistent themes — flight, escape, survival, and integration — will be the focus of the next three chapters.

While these autobiographies provide many of us an introduction to the significant social changes brought about by Hitler's aggressive conquest of countries surrounding Germany, they make transparent the autobiographer's conscious rendering of these events. Autobiographers who see themselves as witnesses to these startling events tell needed stories. The task for us is to understand their representations within the context of autobiographical narration as well as grant them special providence as unwilling participants in these dynamic events.

Specifically, I have chosen autobiographies which detail events during the upheavals in France in 1940–41, those written by Jews fleeing persecution from the Nazis, particularly escape narratives from children's points of view, and those who speak to the difficulties of integrating into a new culture. By focusing on thematic comparisons, I hope readers can be introduced to the fear, anxiety, and social dislocation during this period through the autobiographical storytelling of the ones forced to participate.

Terror in France: Flight

In June 1940, when France collapsed, Hitler and his troops occupied northern France, followed by Hitler's triumphant entrance into Paris. Those who were targets of Hitler's persecution — Jews, exiles, and political agitators — started a trek south. Thousands of French and international refugees found themselves on country roads moving very slowly toward the area in the south that was to become Free France. Renée Fersen-Osten recounts her early memories of this mass migration of people.

> It was called the EXODUS — the French of the north moving toward the south, which was not yet occupied by the Germans in 1940. They fled in hope they would escape the occupation and find refuge in the south. . . . I remember the heat, being very crowded inside the car. I remember Maman driving, stopping all the time, squeezed between the thousands of cars in front and in back of us. Many people were on foot, carrying bags on their backs. Many were dragging little children by the hand. Some were carrying them on their backs. I remember feeling sad, sad because they had to walk. . . . There were big army trucks all around with lots of soldiers dressed in khaki uniforms like Papa's. (Fersen-Osten 25)

This small child (probably about five at the time) was en route with her mother, sister, grandparents, and neighbors. Her father, a soldier just dismissed from the French army, had not yet caught up with the family. When they got to the border, the family without papers had to crash through the barriers.

> Maman started the engine. She turned slowly to the left, and suddenly she made a full turn, back to the gate, full speed, crashing through it like a bullet.

Passing the soldiers,
the shotguns,
the lights,
the signs,
Going . . . going . . . speeding . . . speeding . . .
Maman went like the speed of lightning, never looking back,
not even at us, as the bullets were fired all around, hissing and
burning. (Fersen-Osten 27)

This dramatic escape across the border allowed this Jewish family
traveling illegally to find asylum in the village of Cardesse at the
foot of the Pyrenees. Even though the father joined them, their
refuge in this small village was short-lived. The two sisters were
placed in a convent in Toulouse, and the parents were sent to
Auschwitz. Only the grandmother spent the war years living in
Cardesse.[1]

Although Fersen-Osten did not publish her book, *Don't They
Know the World Stopped Breathing?* until 1991, when she was in her
fifties, she recounts her experiences of being hidden from her
point of view as a child. Interspersed with poems and vignettes of
daily life in the convent, she describes her family's trials brought
on by Hitler's wide-reaching policies against the Jews. Later in the
convent, lessons about past heroes cannot compare with her own
memory of her mother's heroic act.

Alfred Döblin, the well-known German novelist, offered a very
different reaction in his autobiography published in 1968, *Destiny's
Journey*, to the flight through France. Döblin was fifty-five when
he sought refuge in France in 1933. There, he continued to write
and countered the politics of Nazism by returning to his long-
term study of Jewish history. When France collapsed, the sixty-
two-year-old Döblin, by then a naturalized French citizen, started
a journey that ended in depression and destitution. Döblin had
sent his wife and his twelve-year-old son, Etienne, out of Paris earlier. When the Nazis were threatening to occupy Paris, he left the
city with a friend who worked for the French government and
whose entire office was being transferred to safer quarters. The
group left in trucks but shortly changed over to freight cars.

Döblin's diaristic account of his flight plunges the reader into his disturbing and debilitating experiences, a time when he lost control over the most mundane activities of his life. He did not adapt well to the deprivations he began to experience almost immediately after leaving Paris. The whining tone of his writing emphasizes his irritability over the minutiae of inconvenience as well as the increasing scarcity of food and material comforts. Shortly after leaving Paris, he felt himself to be among the "observers and travelers no longer" but one of the "masses." This was the first "stage of the metamorphosis."[2] Later, while traveling in the freight cars, he characterized the transformation of their lives even more bleakly, describing his fellow refugees as "unworthy but tenacious weeds of the species 'human'" (*DJ* 33). He progressively sank into a lasting depression which colored his perceptions as well as led him to dissociate himself from his former identity. As he says, "My will had been taken captive in a way that often infuriated me, had thwarted my conscious 'I,' forced it into a corner. It wasn't crippled. I was totally involved. But behind my urge to travel there was a dull defiance, an unfathomable seriousness, sorrow" (*DJ* 50). Or later, "Where I was, I wasn't. I always wanted to be 'elsewhere.' My entire nature had changed" (*DJ* 52). He began to refer to himself in the third person: "He attaches deep significance to practically everything — pardon me, he selects only the bad things — that happens to him" (*DJ* 80). But he didn't believe that he was a paranoiac; instead he was a normal person, suffering "the madness of a loss of connection" (*DJ* 83).

Döblin is experiencing what psychologist Robert J. Lifton terms "psychic numbing," a phenomenon exiles frequently experience. When psychic disruption becomes too great, the mind, according to Lifton, stops creating symbols and becomes deadened to external stimuli. Döblin's near breakdown occurred in Mende, where he spent several weeks in a refugee camp. The normality of his former life had completely broken down. He no longer even had control over his thoughts. "My thoughts have taken on a stumbling, oscillating, pendulum-like character. I have no way of stopping them. My thoughts no longer even have the character of thought, they are like pistons in an engine" (*DJ* 120). Later, shortly before he is reunited with his family, he recognizes that some normality is returning, but he remains dissociated.

> Looking around the hotel room in Béziers, I had already felt that I had left the shore, the wilderness behind, and was being sent back into the world of cities. I began to recognize things from my former life. The globe of my memory began to fill. But my emotions didn't respond. There was no *I* to respond to the memories. The last weeks had passed as if I had been ill and they didn't leave me as I had been before . . . How far away all of that was, what had happened before June 10. . . . A normal express train stood at the station, and left on time. It stopped only where it was supposed to. It didn't detour and didn't go back from where it had come. (*DJ* 148)

Döblin and his family were luckier than most. He eventually found haven in the United States, where one of his older sons resided, but even then he did not shake off the depression brought on by his misfortunes.

Internment

When France entered the war, the French government began a roundup of so-called enemies of the state. All foreigners, but especially those who were political activists, were sought. So, as both Koestler and Feuchtwanger note, antifascist exiles and communists as well as foreigners sympathetic to the Nazis were interred together. As mentioned earlier, there were two general internments. The first coincided with France's entrance into the war. The second came when France capitulated and the Nazis marched into France.

As Koestler was a well-known journalist and a professed communist he was interned during the first round in 1939 and sent to the notorious Le Vernet, known as the camp of the undesirables. The camp already housed many political prisoners, such as members of the International Brigades who had fought in Spain,[3] and the groups sent from Paris included habitual French criminals and those internationals, like Koestler, who were seen as political agitators. Koestler pointed out that almost all international internees had spent years in political prisons, including many who had been released from German concentration camps such as Dachau, Wolfenbüttel, and Buchenwald. In his somewhat cynical way, Koestler saw the European continent as a place where great numbers of people felt themselves to be outcasts, either because of an accident of birth or because they were "doomed for their metaphysical creed or rational conviction regarding the best way to organize human welfare" (*Scum* 94). In his view, being severely persecuted and harassed had given even the most dedicated idealists a strong inferiority complex: "Men of exemplary courage and daring, after having been labelled 'refugees' and beaten out of three or four countries, went about as if carrying an invisible leper's bell. Eminent scholars and dignitaries shed tears of happiness when taken to a 'democratic' jail after their escape" (Koestler, *Scum* 94). Thus, internees transferred from Paris were greatly relieved to learn that they were being interned and not imprisoned, even though the conditions at Le Vernet were unimaginably disabling.

With very little food — according to Koestler even less than at Dachau — and forced labor, although without the savagery of the guards as in Nazi concentration camps, the men in the camp quickly became transformed:

> Detention, drudgery, the unspeakable material conditions, and the continuous chain of humiliations did this slow work on our minds. Perhaps the worst of it was the complete lack of privacy. To live for months on end in 22 inches of space, in the buzzing beehive of the barrack without an hour of solitude, without ever being able to come up for air, affected even robuster proletarian nerves. I had a feeling that the contents of my brain had melted to a sort of amorphous jam which did not allow the formation of any consistent thought. The mills of misery ground slowly but surely, both our bodies and our minds. (*Scum* 133–134)

Remembering that many of these internees were the "progressive *élite* of the intelligentsia" and thus not used to physical labor, Koestler reminds the reader how physically draining camp life was. "But for people unskilled in heavy manual labour and under-fed to the degree of acute and chronic hunger, the routine [forced labor] became plain torture. An undramatic, everyday torture which transformed our crowd within a few weeks into grey-faced, hollow-eyed, apathetic wrecks" (*Scum* 104). With the help of the British, Koestler was released and returned to Paris but had to flee when France capitulated to avoid a second internment.

After the French armistice, all Germans, men and women, were interned. Internment camps for men were set up both in the north and south of France. The women's camp, Gurs, was established in southwest France close to the Pyrenees. The camp's locations were critical, for when France capitulated on 22 June 1940, the exiles in the occupied zone were at greater risk of falling into the hands of the Nazis. As a part of the armistice, Article 19 demanded that all German nationals be "surrendered on demand." During the in-creasing disorder following France's collapse, it was difficult for their French guards, frequently sympathetic to their plight, to pro-vide them protection. Before the end of the "phony war" only about fifty prisoners, Koestler included, were released from Le Vernet. This was also one of the first camps that the Gestapo vis-ited looking for those anti-Nazis to be "surrendered on demand."

The well-known German novelist and antifascist Lion Feucht-wanger had been detained during the first round but was allowed to return to his home in Sanary sur Mer. During the second roundup, he was interned in Les Milles. In his memoir, *The Devil in France*, published in 1942, after he was safely in New York, Feuchtwanger pointed out the absurdity of his situation as well as showed how resilient a human being can be under very adverse circumstances. In this early view of the chaos in France, he stressed the psychic and physical breakdown of life in an internment camp and the sheer insanity of people battered by chaotic political forces.

When Feuchtwanger was notified that he was to be interred in Les Milles, he and others from Sanary sur Mer appeared at the po-lice prefecture to discuss how to get to the camp. They finally went a couple of days later by taxicab, a fitting introduction to this crazy but frightening and dangerous episode in Feuchtwanger's life.

The camp at Les Milles was located in a former brickyard, and the two thousand — later burgeoning to three thousand — men suffered all the problems customary in housing large numbers of humans in such inadequate places — vermin, bad food, depression, total lack of privacy, and poor hygiene leading to dysentery. The inmates were made up of German and Austrian émigrés as well as German nationals married to French women. The number also included French foreign legionnaires. Men from all walks of life — scholars, dentists, writers, mechanics, soldiers of fortune, restaurateurs — and from ages sixteen to seventy were packed into ill-adapted housing with insufficient food, cut off from their families and all news.

> In that brickyard a brick building was our shelter, and bricks were otherwise to become the distinguishing feature of those days in our lives. Brick walls, reinforced with barbed wire, shut off our enclosures from the beautiful green fields beyond. Broken bricks were heaped in piles on every hand. We used them as seats to sit on, as tables for our meals, as partitions to separate our straw piles, one from another. Brick dust filled our lungs and got into our eyes. Brick racks made of laths lined the walls of our building and cut into the inadequate space allowed us and the inadequate light. We were often cold, and at such times many of us would have liked to crawl into one of the great kilns, in order to enjoy a little of the warmth that the word "kiln" suggested. (Feuchtwanger 3–4)

As at Le Vernet, camp life — poor food, inadequate space, lines in front of the filthy latrines — wore down the internees, but they adapted even though they became "deadened," another example of the effect of psychic numbing.

> It was amazing how soon we all adapted ourselves to circumstances in the camp. Hard as it was for many to make the shift from their ordinary manner of living to the primitive conditions that prevailed at Les Mille[s], after a few days they were behaving as though they had been there for years.

The fact is we all "went flat," we were deadened. Discomforts and indignities, our own or others', that would have enraged us a short time before we now accepted resignedly with a shrug of the shoulders. Before long we were not even noticing them. (Feuchtwanger 75)

After the fall of France, the French commanders of Les Milles knew that the safety of the internees was not secure. They decided to load most of them, about two thousand, into a train to be sent to Bayonne. But the venture was ill conceived, since no one knew the circumstances in the country surrounding Bayonne. After wandering around the countryside for five days, the train returned to Les Milles. Most internees, including Feuchtwanger, went on to the camp at Nîmes, farther to the east.

The camp at Nîmes took on a rather bizarre cast, according to Feuchtwanger. It was set up with white French tents, the "so-called 'marabouts' of the French Colonials" (Feuchtwanger 183). As the French government and army dissolved, the guarding of the camp inhabitants became more and more lax. Camp entrepreneurs rapidly created a lively black market. Feuchtwanger escaped to the town of Nîmes for a few days and lived with sympathetic French families but soon thought it better to return to the camp. He found it completely changed.

It was now a big fair. Cafés, sales booths, one after another in unbroken sequence, lined the streets of the tent city. Hawkers roamed the streets from five in the morning till one in the morning calling their wares: "Condensed milk forbidden. Obtainable nowhere in France except here of me." "Fried chicken with fresh cucumber and tomato salad in ten minutes at Tent 54." "Three fountain-pens, as good as new, at unheard-of bargain prices." (Feuchtwanger 229)

Eventually Feuchtwanger, in a dramatic rescue by relief workers, was taken to Marseilles and reunited with his wife. They subsequently obtained passage to New York.[4]

Assignment: Rescue in Marseilles

Feuchtwanger, Koestler, and Döblin, like other refugees who made it to the unoccupied territory or who managed somehow to escape the internment camps, were then trapped in southern France. They sought any way possible to emigrate to the United States, Mexico, South America, Britain, or other refuges. Obtaining the right papers was agony. The Americans, for example, were not well disposed to accept immigrants. As David S. Wyman recounts, the American people did not want to allow large groups of refugees into the United States. Powerful senators and congressmen, ever mindful of the voters' views as well as their own political agendas, prevented the American government from opening up the quota system to allow in more refugees. Wyman gives three reasons for these political views: widespread anti-Semitism; fear of refugees taking jobs away from Americans; and "nativistic nationalism," the attitude of America first. These strong political attitudes created an atmosphere in the United States that hampered a number of private and governmental groups that were trying to find solutions to the refugee crisis during these years.

The lives of thousands of refugees in unoccupied France during the remainder of 1940 and the first eight months of 1941 depended on being in the right consulate and the right French authorities' line at the right time or on having some contact with the right relief group. Anna Seghers, the German communist writer, describes this life in her novel *Transit*. The novel portrays the endless obstacles encountered when obtaining the correct papers. The main character spends his time listening to rumors in cafés or going to various consulates seeking visas. He becomes inured to the process and is never able to leave Marseilles, even though opportunities present themselves. Such stories apparently did happen. Feuchtwanger sums up the absurdity and grotesqueness of the refugees' plight:

> One who has passed his life as an inhabitant of a country that has never been shattered by domestic revolution, by war, or by foreign military occupation, knows nothing of the role that an

identification paper or a rubber stamp can play in a man's life. It is usually a ridiculous scrap of paper and a still more ridiculous rubber stamp apathetically applied by a nondescript clerk. Yet how many thousands, tens of thousands, millions of human beings go chasing after just such scraps of paper, just such rubber stamps. How many thousands of intrigues, how much money, how much nerve, how much life are wasted by thousands and thousands of human beings in getting possession of them. How many swindlers get a living by purveying, now legally, now illegally, just such stamps, just such scraps of paper. How much happiness, how much unhappiness may come from the legitimate or illegitimate possession of them. (83)

Refugees in France needed at least three separate types of visas to escape this trap. They needed an exit visa from France, transit visas for travel through intermediate countries, and a visa for the country of their destination. So if the refugees were going to the United States by ship from Lisbon, they needed a visa from the U.S. consulate, an exit visa from France, and transit visas from Spain and Portugal. Those going to Mexico needed the above and possibly transit visas from the United States and Cuba. Obtaining these precious documents was made more difficult because each visa was dated. An individual might obtain all the necessary papers but one, but the delay could cause all the other papers to go out of date, forcing him or her to begin the process again.

Nevertheless, international refugee committees were working overtime to help refugees find a place to settle. Relief organizations such as the American Friends Rescue Committee, the Emergency Rescue Committee, the Unitarian Service Committee, and the Red Cross were extremely helpful in easing the economic and psychological difficulties of refugee life during this distressful period.

The Emergency Rescue Committee, set up in southern France by a group of Americans and particularly supported by German and European exiles already in the United States, became a virtual lifeline for well-known writers and artists as well as the not-yet famous. The committee, created and funded to bring to America important writers, artists, and intellectual leaders as well as those seeking political asylum, was veritably overrun by those in flight. A young American, Varian Fry, was sent to France to rescue talented European writers and artists. Influential intellectuals in the United States contributed to his efforts. According to Cynthia Jaffee McCabe, Fry and his "small, devoted staff" helped approximately one thousand "carefully screened émigrés" to leave unoccupied France, "legally or illegally" (79–80). Equipped with a list of noted Europeans needing to escape, Fry left the United States in early June 1940. Expecting to return by August 1940, he remained in France for thirteen months and "was forcibly escorted across the French border in September 1941" (McCabe 90). His valiant attempt brought out of the reach of the Nazis artists and intellectuals such as Heinrich Mann, Franz Werfel and Alma Mahler-Werfel, Marc Chagall, Jacques Lipchitz, and Marcel Duchamp, among a host of others.

Fry set up his refugee service in his hotel, Hôtel Splendide, aided by those who became his staff. He learned very quickly that he didn't need to seek out the émigrés; they came to him. From eight in the morning until late at night, he interviewed refugee writers and artists and listened to their tales of escape and harassment.

> They began coming the next day. Many of them had been through hell. Their nerves were shattered and their courage gone. Some of them had been in concentration camps, escaping only at the last moment as the German troops marched through France. They had joined the great crowds of people streaming south. Sometimes they had walked hundreds of miles to get away from the Nazis. (Fry 13)

Fry ultimately found several routes to help refugees flee the Nazis — over the Pyrenees through Spain to Lisbon; by ship to the coast of Africa; and by ship from Marseilles to Martinique and then to the United States, Veracruz, or ports in South America.

> Legally, I saw hundreds of refugees, in addition to those named on my lists. Illegally, I worked at getting the people I had been sent to rescue out of France. In many cases, this meant getting

them false passports or forged visas. While we waited for their papers, I showed these people my lists and asked if they knew the whereabouts of any of the other people whose names were on them. (Fry 23)

Fry and his staff encountered many times the problems Feuchtwanger noted that refugees experienced while trying to obtain the right identification papers. While trying to rescue artists at risk, Fry was often misled by those wanting to make a profit. They were often forced to depend on some of the more shady black market characters and even professional criminals in Marseilles, sometimes with great success. Only a few individuals conned or betrayed them. Although Fry managed with the help of many to rescue almost a thousand individuals, he nevertheless lost some to the Gestapo and the concentration camps in Germany.

Fersen-Osten, Döblin, Koestler, Feuchtwanger, and Fry have in common their experiences of this difficult period in France. They had dramatic stories to tell, and they offer very different personal versions of their terror and deprivation. But these "focused memoirs" all convey the abrupt changes people can experience during political upheaval.

The dismayed Döblin sums up the exile experience in these turbulent years in his description of exile gatherings at the poste restante in Lisbon, one of the final stops before the exiles were able to experience a release from their terror.

This *poste restante* corner in Lisbon, in Portugal, in this outermost corner of Europe, was the tragic meeting place for many in the unhappy year of 1940, a year that had exposed the frivolity and thoughtlessness of the false calm of the past. Entire nations were being enslaved, families scattered. Europe was doing penance for its sins and omissions. And we refugees, subjects of this Europe, were standing here in Lisbon and waiting for the life buoy to be tossed to us from the other side of the ocean. (Döblin, *DJ* 218)

chapter three

The Persecution and Flight of the Jews: Narratives of Survival

Places. Places without people. These are the dry bones of memory.
The fields of Europe are full of them.
   Shlomo Breznitz, *Memory Fields*

A deadly trap. Get out, said the Nazis and then made it impossible for
anyone to go.
   Frederic Zeller, *When Time Ran Out*

The Anschluss in March 1938 and Kristallnacht in November galvanized the German and Austrian Jewish population to prepare to emigrate. Any Jews who had hesitated to leave prior to these periods of terror immediately began moving west if they had the means and the money. Following the march of the German army into Austria, the Illegalen, the Austrian Nazis who had joined the local Nazi party illegally, began systematic harassment of the Jews. They confiscated Jewish assets based on lists they had compiled prior to the Anschluss. Almost anyone who wanted a business, apartment, car, or any other possession could seize it from a Jew. Jewish men from ages seventeen to seventy were arrested at random and sent to concentration camps. The sanctions and laws against Jews that had been developed in Germany over a five-year period of Nazi power were put into effect immediately. Nazis and others harassed Jews on the street without fear of reprisal. Witnesses give accounts of Jews being forced from their homes to wash political slogans from the sidewalks. These slogans had been scrawled on the sidewalks during the intensely political weeks leading to the plebiscite that Kurt von Schuschnigg had canceled.

Eight months later, on November 9, the Nazis set off a wave of terror against the Jews in Germany. Following the assassination of a German diplomat, Ernst vom Rath, by a young Jew, Herschel

Grynszpan, the Nazis retaliated by instigating planned attacks against Jews in Germany and Austria. Angered by the treatment of his Polish Jewish parents, whom the Nazis had expelled from Germany, Grynszpan killed Rath in Paris. Under the guise of protesting the Parisian incident, storm troopers systematically destroyed Jewish businesses and synagogues in Germany and Austria. They rousted the Jews from their homes and detained them. Many were simply beaten on the streets. Historically, the event has been named Kristallnacht (Crystal Night) because one could hear glass breaking in cities and towns all over Germany. These events compelled more and more people to leave just when leaving Germany and Austria had become increasingly difficult.

Most research, publications, and testimonies by Jews about the Nazi period have concentrated on the Holocaust, the systematic killing of an estimated six million European Jews. Wide-ranging studies have compiled the details of this devastating episode during World War II. Historians and scholars have sought testimony from survivors of as well as participants in the events of the Holocaust. Until recently, however, those Jews who with luck and enterprise escaped the Nazis have not been as extensively documented. Dorit Bader Whiteman's book *The Uprooted: A Hitler Legacy: Voices of Those Who Escaped before the "Final Solution"* (1994), sheds light on the Jews' journeys into exile.

Whiteman based her book on collected testimony from surviving escapees. Initially, she set out to produce an empirical study by "asking all the participants identical questions that would subsequently be analyzed in order to make statistical comparisons" (Whiteman 5). But she quickly changed her plan, as had earlier scholars who studied testimonies of life in the death camps (Des Pres) and who analyzed attitudes of German Jewish refugees in England (Berghan). She came to view "the history of the escapees as if it were an enormous picture cut into jigsaw-like pieces."

Each person's story, telling of unique or even monstrous calamities, is a small but important part of the total. Every story contributes to a different aspect of the whole picture, which will never be complete. I believed my task . . . was to give a sequential account of the escapees' experiences and their consequences, as seen through their own eyes, and, while organizing the different stories, to examine them for both unique and communal aspects. (Whiteman 5–6)

These types of descriptive studies may be seen as "collective autobiography," the multivoiced autobiography of a collective event. Using eyewitness accounts, both written and spoken, the editor presents the autobiography of an event, just as an oral historian uses interviews as sources for interpretation of historical events. The editor shapes the fragmentary accounts into a narrative. Whiteman based her comments on 190 respondents who answered her questionnaire or who wrote individual accounts of their experiences. She chronicled their communal experiences. Establishing the terror and fear they experienced in their homes and homelands, she documented the inordinate amount of bureaucratic harassment they endured obtaining the "correct" permission to leave. They experienced severe frustration trying to emigrate to a new country or even to reside temporarily in a new country while trying to be admitted to a second country. She outlined the routes Jews pursued in seeking asylum from the Nazis and highlighted their resourcefulness in coping with actions taken against them. Finally, she delineated her respondents' emotional reactions to this uprooting. For the reader, the voices recounting the shocking actions perpetrated against the Jews and their tenacity in overcoming these events paint a vivid portrait of human endurance during one of the most appalling episodes in our history.

Detailing the brutality the Jews experienced at the hands of the Nazis, Whiteman underscored the inevitable result when one group of people loses the protection of the law. Their lives and their possessions are imperiled without any recourse to justice. After Kristallnacht, Jews whose families had been in Germany or Austria for generations searched for a way out, but by this time it was not easy. Austrian and German Jews could only take ten marks out of the country, and multiple permissions had to be in order. The Jews became prey to opportunists who promised help and provided none or to officials who purposely harassed them.

For most, the avenues of escape were closed, and they were subsequently sent to the death camps. Yet a few still managed to escape the ever-tightening net. Herbert A. Strauss in "The Movement of People in a Time of Crisis" estimates that of the 525,000 German Jews defined by their religion, about 300,000 may have left Germany and about 125,000 were able to leave Austria. However, 30,000 were caught in the roundups in occupied countries such as France, Belgium, or Holland and were deported to death camps. These numbers do not include the Jews who were defined by their descent and not their religion. Strauss believes that no reliable statistical information exists on these German and Austrian Jews (49).

Whiteman traced several paths the Jews took to escape. We have already seen the route through France. Others fled to Palestine (if they could get in) or to the United States. Frequently they remained in transit countries such as England for lengthy periods. Others traveled to the distant countries of Australia or South America. Family members frequently split up and fled to different countries so that as many as possible could get out. Some endured the war in particularly dire circumstances in the Shanghai ghetto. Wherever they went, the trip was arduous.

Children's Narratives

Some of the most poignant yet stirring accounts of these events are the narratives of those who escaped as children. The overt actions against the Jews described above forced Jewish parents to consider radical solutions to save their children. In many instances, by 1938–39 it was too late for Jewish families to leave, but it was not too late for some of the children. Legal and illegal children's railroads began operating. The drama of these escapes has been captured in several autobiographies written by adult survivors and by research projects such as Whiteman's. The testimonies of children tell powerful stories indeed.

If the governments of other countries were unwilling to admit large numbers of refugees, at least some children could be saved, or so thought the myriad relief workers such as the Quakers, who began pressuring these governments. At the same time, the desperate situation in Germany and Austria for the Jews caused parents to realize that sending their children abroad was best, as painful and traumatic as that could be. One avenue of escape was provided by the Germans and became known as the Kindertransports (Children's Transports). With the help of the Germans and many European groups, German and Austrian children were sent by train to countries outside of Germany. David S. Wyman in *Paper Walls* estimates that by September 1939, when the war broke out, England had accepted more than 9,000 children: "Holland had received 2,000, Belgium 1,500, France 600, Sweden 250, and the United States 240" (98).

In her excellent overview of these transports, Whiteman notes that Kristallnacht acted as a catalyst for residents of other countries. Whiteman's British respondents portrayed the human side of being on a Kindertransport. Britain agreed to admit up to ten thousand children temporarily. Relief workers worked feverishly during the remaining months before the war to bring the German and Austrian children out. Nazi regulations stipulated that the children should be healthy and under eighteen years old and have a guarantor in England. In Germany, volunteers had to resolve the logistical problems of bringing enough certified children together at one time to make up a trainload of four to six hundred children. Relief workers were required to obtain permission from the Nazi officials for each child and to cooperate with the authorities in organizing the transports. Each child's papers and photographs had to be collected and sent to Britain. On the British side, valid placements had to be found. When all the permissions and bureaucratic problems were resolved, then the distraught parents accompanied their children, many very young and wearing tags around their necks, to board the trains. According to Whiteman, not one former *Kind* remembers the "journey to England from beginning to end" (157).

The SS allowed only a few adults to accompany the children on the trains. These chaperons had to return immediately to Nazi Germany so that future transports would not be canceled. Because of such restrictions, older children had to take care of the younger, even infants and toddlers. Hans, sixteen years old at the time, recalled what the partings at the train stations were like.

> There is a harassing memory of the assembled youngsters about to be handed over to the staff of the refugee committee. Babies in their cradles and small children of tender age were surrendered by their parents, knowing that this was the only way to save their children's lives. There were parents fainting and children screaming when we realized that this might be the last time we might see each other. (Whiteman 151)

In England, the children were taken into family homes, orphanages, and summer camps retooled as children's homes. For some the temporary havens lasted years, but for others they were only stopping points. Although parents assured their children that their family would be reunited, many, many children's parents did not make it out of the Reich.

Whiteman's project provides readers with heart-rending descriptions of Jewish families' flights from Germany. Nevertheless, it is important to remember that her respondents sent her their stories. As the editor, she shaped them into a narrative and ordered them according to theme and chronology. Her work offers the modern reader views of significant life upheavals during this trying period, but she is the artful shaper of the story. She did not draw on published or even unpublished autobiographical accounts, although surely some of the narratives she used manifested well-known narrative strategies — chronology, dialogue, characterization, and so on. The many published memoirs detailing these events provide more insight into Jews who evaded the Nazis. Some of the most interesting are those which recount the experiences of children and teenagers who escaped the Nazi roundups.

Scenes of Nazi Brutality

To show the fear and brutality experienced by ordinary people who had become the targets of the Nazis, I will excerpt passages from several published autobiographies that portray how difficult life became for the Jews. These Jewish memoirs focus on the pain

and terror the Jews lived with as the Nazis carried out their persecution. Yet their choice of metaphor, prose style, and rhetorical
ploys remind us that the writers are rendering these experiences
through composed, self-conscious autobiographies.

Some of the most extraordinary narratives center on episodes
of Nazi brutality that young Jews experienced. Frederic Zeller,
in his autobiography, *When Time Ran Out: Coming of Age in the
Third Reich*, published in 1989, was a teenager living in Berlin on
Kristallnacht. After hearing on the radio about the assassination
of the German diplomat in Paris by the young Jew Grynszpan,
Zeller's father thought there might be trouble and went to spend
the night with friends. Zeller, his mother, and his sister were in the
apartment when it started:

> Mother woke me quietly. . . . "Dress quickly and come to the
> window."
>
> Almost at the same moment I heard a tremendous crash
> and shattering of glass in the street below and woke up in-
> stantly. . . . Now I saw them. On the other side of our narrow,
> curving street. The open truck. Nearly a dozen storm troopers,
> some of them in the truck hauling big cobblestones over the
> side, down to others in the street. Almost simultaneously sev-
> eral men turned, staggered clumsily in an uneven row, the
> heavy cobblestone against their chests. They hobbled the few
> steps to the remaining two big windows of the Hochmann
> store and heaved the stones right through the plate glass. There
> were a quick series of crashes that sounded like explosions.
> Large chunks and hundreds of small pieces of glass shattered,
> fell and slithered over each other partly onto the pavement,
> partly into the store. Like an after-quake, there was a second fall
> of jagged glass. The empty, lamp-lit street looked like a stage
> set; the stationary truck, the slowly moving, robot-like, uni-
> formed men, seen from above, the glittering, shimmering glass
> all over the pavement . . . it all seemed unreal. (Zeller 162–163)

Following this introduction to the violence that night, Zeller then
went out to warn neighbors and to help many protect their stores
from looting. He walked through the neighborhood and discov-

ered the synagogue on fire. "There were a couple of fire engines standing by. Small groups of firemen stood at ease, watching the fire, their hoses ready — in case a neighboring house caught fire" (Zeller 163). After the lawlessness of this night of terror and destruction, Zeller and his family began in earnest trying to escape Germany. He and his sister made it to Holland, as we will see.

In his autobiography, *Memory Fields: The Legacy of a Wartime Childhood in Czechoslovakia,* published in 1993, Shlomo Breznitz recalls a brutal incident in the small Czech town of Zilnia. Breznitz, along with his sister, were hidden in a convent in this town at the time his parents were sent to Auschwitz. One Sunday morning, he and his friends were playing in the snow around the small town square after mass. Families out to enjoy the bright Sunday morning sunshine filled the square, but the drumming of the Hitler Youth corps marching into town shattered the peaceful scene. Carrying clubs, they stamped their feet and shouted cadences to underscore their chant, "Jesus war ein Judenkind! Jesus war ein Judenkind!"[1]

Suddenly, the distant sound of drums, getting closer. I tensed up, waiting. People started moving from the open part of the square to the darker, more protected areas under the columns. . . . The leaders of the Hitler Youth column could be seen entering the square . . . As I listened, the familiar hollow feeling in my stomach reasserted itself. I imagined all these healthy and well-dressed youngsters combing the city for Jews. Clubs at the ready, they would desperately try to find a Jew — any Jew, even a Catholic Jew — in order to pursue their deadly game.

"Jesus war ein Judenkind! Jesus war ein Judenkind!"

They kept on coming, the healthy and well-dressed Hitler Youth. Milling around the prelate's house, perhaps waiting for the rest to catch up, . . . the snake [of young boys] was transformed into a mob . . . When I finally managed to get up [on the church wall to see], it was just in time to see the door of the prelate's house breaking under the onslaught of boots and clubs. . . . The crowd gasped, watching the prelate in his Sunday robes being dragged out of his house and into the street . . . And so it was that I witnessed the attack on the prelate from a safe distance. I never saw him again, nor did I dare ask about him. (Breznitz 114–119)

Fearing for his own life, this young boy witnesses instead the cruel assault on the man who had helped to place him into the orphanage for safety.

Many writers describe similar incidents. From such episodes readers not only see the breakdown into lawlessness of that period but understand the real terror that engulfed those being persecuted.

Hiding in Plain View

Breznitz and Renée Fersen-Osten give accounts of young Jewish children being placed in Catholic orphanages to survive the war, a frequently used ploy to protect Jewish children. Some older Jewish teenagers survived the war and Jewish persecution by disguising themselves as gentiles. Two such autobiographies are *The Lost Childhood* by Yehuda Nir and *Counting My Steps* by Jacov Lind. Some exiles spent the war years still trapped in areas of Europe controlled by the Nazis. The accounts by Jews in hiding are amazing and sometimes miraculous. Many Jews from German and Central European countries such as Romania and Poland struggled for survival during the war years. These war survival stories become yet another bleak and many times frightening stage in the long-term struggle to leave one home and establish another. The exiles who centered their autobiographies on these incidents provide gripping accounts of survival during the war.

In *The Lost Childhood*, published in 1989 when he was seventy-two, Yehuda Nir gives one of the most riveting accounts of surviving the Nazi occupation of Poland.[2] Nir was twelve when Poland was invaded in 1939 and his middle-class Jewish parents attempted to escape Poland. During the early years, when the Russians occupied their hometown, Lwów, they remained in their apartment. When the Germans entered in 1941, Nir's father was captured and killed (although Nir and his mother and sister did not know this until much later), leaving him, his sister, and his mother to find ways to survive. They decided to go into hiding by withdrawing to a small resort town. Nir, fourteen years old when they went into hiding, did not leave their quarters for almost two years because he was afraid of being exposed as a Jew. Eventually they obtained papers showing them to be Polish and moved to Warsaw, where all three worked.[3]

Women could more easily assume "Aryan" identities. Nir's mother and sister "spent hours memorizing the catechism and all the Catholic prayers commonly used in the church" because the Gestapo used them to test anyone they suspected of being Jewish (61). Nir, like all Jewish men, was the most at risk, since gentiles in Poland at that time were rarely circumcised. Breznitz, Zeller, Lind, and Nir all mention this fear of exposure. Nir portrays this fear in a passage describing a time when he was a boarder with a Polish woman's family in Warsaw.

The first crisis at Mrs. Krawczyk's came a week after my arrival. It was Saturday night, time for the weekly bath in a tin tub placed for that purpose in the center of the kitchen. In order to save on hot water, Mrs. Krawczyk decided that I would take a bath together with Edek [her son]. Until then I had acted extremely shy when we were dressing or undressing, so Edek could not see my circumcision. Now came the moment of truth. There were no two ways about it; I had to take off my clothes in order to take the bath. I was procrastinating, and Mrs. Krawczyk was getting impatient. I was supposed to be the model child, wasn't I? I was frantic. But moments later I had a plan. There was no electricity; the house hadn't been wired when the war broke out, and a glass petroleum lamp on the table was our sole source of light. I decided to risk my landlady's wrath and break the lamp "accidentally," of course. Hearing the breaking glass, Mrs. Krawczyk came running into the kitchen. She was furious, suspecting Edek at first. I apologized profusely, and while she went to buy a new lamp I proceeded to undress in the total darkness and join Edek in the bathtub.

I planned to make him more self-conscious in the future, so that in the following weeks we would take our baths separately. (Nir 90–91)

Nir is much relieved when he later secures a job at a German dentist's office and can live there as well, thus living alone.

Identifying Jewish men by their circumcisions was widely practiced by the Nazis. Nir's sister, Lala, drew upon this practice to save her and her mother when they were picked up by the Gestapo after a Polish woman had turned them in. They had up-to-date but forged papers, but the Gestapo were nevertheless obliged to investigate. When the questioning was almost over Lala broke the tension: "You know, this is the first time in my life that I regret not being a boy." The Gestapo officers looked surprised. "If I were a boy," she continued, "I could just pull down my pants and prove to you I'm not a Jew." The amused men let them go (Nir 68).

In a recent film *Europa, Europa* made in 1991, the young protagonist is haunted by this fact of his Jewish heritage. His family sends him and his brother east to avoid capture, but he quickly gets separated from his brother. Finding refuge in a Russian school, he is eventually captured by the Germans but survives by claiming to be Aryan. He interprets Russian for them and even becomes something of a mascot for the German officers. They eventually send him back to Germany to a Hitler Youth school. Here, the problems of his circumcision become paramount. At one point, he even tries to create a foreskin by placing a metal ring around the tip of his penis and bringing some of the back skin forward. Needless to say this caused great pain and even infection, but for a short period he felt safe. After years of hiding his circumcision, the end of the movie finds him and his brother together again in a refugee camp. Helping his brother outside to urinate, he shows to the audience that fear of discovery is no longer a threat. The most intimate acts will no longer betray him. Ironically, Jacov Lind, the German writer, was spared because of his circumcision. On his way to Israel, he was stopped by the French as a possible escaped Nazi. He proved he was Jewish by taking down his pants.

Lind's account of his survival during the war provides yet another example of the resourcefulness of individuals. He published his frank autobiography *Counting My Steps* in 1968 when he was fifty-three. It is the story of a brash young Jewish boy who survived under the Nazis' noses. Born in Vienna, Lind was thirteen in 1938 when the Nazis took over Austria. He and his younger sister were sent by train (a Kindertransport?) to Holland to join other Zionist Jews. There, he lived with several foster families and once in a commune of Zionists. On 10 May 1940 the Germans invaded Holland. At first, the Dutch were not concerned, but Lind knew that he was in much greater danger. He reacted by shouting at the dinner table, "Let's go! Let's go! Let's take a boat to England. Immediately!" (Lind 69). His sardonic voice narrates the changes in this small country. "Things started to happen. The Germans turned a sleepy, fat country into a place of thrills and marvelous adventure" (Lind 70).

His real trials began when the Nazis began rounding up Holland's Jews. He decided emphatically not to go to the transit camp Westerbork, thus probably saving his life. He managed not to be caught in the roundup by steeling himself to break away from his protective foster Jewish families. He was ruthless in his resolve:

> I hate the Jews . . . To survive this calamity I have to hate them; if I do not wish to die as one of them, I have to learn to live with the sentiments of the rest of the world. The rest of the world either hates the Jews or is indifferent to them. Those who love the Jews suffer . . . I couldn't afford indifference. I have to hate because I love life. I love to remain among those who breathe. (Lind 79–80)

On the day of the last big raid, he and the Granaats, his foster family, hid in the attic of their home. When the Nazis called out that all should come out or they would be sent to "special punishment camps," the Granaats and a Romanian family also in the attic went back downstairs. Lind did not. He remained on the roof until it was quiet and then spent the night in the sealed apartment, leaving the next morning. Disguised as a Dutch Nazi, he fled back to the town of Gouda, where he had previously stayed with Zionists, and succeeded in getting papers as Jan Gerrit Overbeek. He survived the war first in Holland as a farm laborer and later as a sailor on a barge. Crossing into Germany as part of the barge's crew, he fled the boat during a bombing attack. He survived; his barge mates didn't. Safe on shore, he says:

> I climb slowly up to see some more of this world. Two, three more explosions. Then total silence. The I. G. Farben is burning, people run in all directions. There are ships in mid-river, a train passes a bridge. There are ships moving upstream and downstream. But of the *Hugo Stinnes 30* [his boat] there is only the rear end left, and the two boats next to it seem to be sinking. What did happen in these forty-five minutes? A long high-pitched sound, like someone shrieking down my ear. End of alarm. A new rebirth in June '44. I am lucky. Imagine! . . . and can't imagine it. I am alive and want to wash my hands. I am alive and hungry and regret the sausage and the wine and the lunch that has gone to the fishes. Together with Theo and a few of his friends they will enjoy it. (Lind 125–126)

Seeing such events as "apocalyptic . . . therapy," he moves on.

Lind's irreverent autobiography contrasts sharply with Nir's more dramatic account. Lind's is the tale of a bold young man who survives an absurd world of death, war, and destruction by learning to be a chameleon, an issue I explore in chapter 10. Nir, too, becomes a chameleon, but his narrative contains less commentary and more dramatic storytelling. Although the two autobiographies have very different styles, each one's intensity captures the reader, for it is through such personal accounts that readers begin to understand how ordinary people survived this epoch.

Flight

The crucial year of 1938 caused widespread panic among Jewish families still in Germany and Austria. There were no longer any questions about wanting to emigrate, but leaving was very difficult. When families could not leave together, Jewish parents were more willing to have their sons and daughters find ways to safe havens. Three autobiographers — George Clare, Frederic Zeller, and Lilian Furst — recount their escapes as youths from these two countries during this fateful year.

George Clare was seventeen years old when Hitler annexed Austria.[4] He published his autobiography, *The Last Waltz in Vienna*, in 1980, when he was sixty years old and thirty-five years after the end of the war. He saw firsthand the harassment from the Austrians during those first terrible days after the Anschluss. The Austrian Nazis searched and looted his and his friends' and relatives' houses. He watched as they dragged his father, uncle, and a cousin from his home one evening and ordered them to clean the sidewalks in front of their elegant apartment. Clare and his parents left Austria for Berlin in the summer of 1938. There they expected to obtain visas from Ireland, which his father's business contacts were arranging. When he got to Berlin Clare was surprised to find that Jews in Germany still could participate in public activities.

> It seemed incredible to me, but it was perfectly true — in Berlin, in the capital of the Third Reich, in the very lion's den, Jews were still allowed in September 1938 to visit places of entertainment, coffee-houses; some even still owned pâtisseries, they could own cars and shop where they pleased. On the whole of Kurfürstendamm . . . I saw only one shop with the sign "no Jewish customers," so universally displayed in Vienna. (Clare 209)

During the worsening Czechoslovakian crisis, Clare's father, fearing that Clare would be drafted, urged his son to flee Germany. Latvia was the only country allowing visas to Jews, as Clare's family learned from Clare's girlfriend, whose family had just emigrated to Latvia. To reach safety Clare needed a Latvian visa and a Lithuanian transit visa. His Austrian passport was stamped "valid for one outward and one return journey," a statement that to émigrés and to Clare and his family meant a one-way journey. It was widely held that if Jews returned they would be arrested. In one hectic day Clare packed and found himself on the train from Berlin to Kaunas, the capital of Lithuania, and then on to Riga in Latvia.

When he arrived at the border between Latvia and Lithuania, Latvian guards confiscated his and another Austrian Jew's passport. The guards told them in halting German that their passports were not valid. Only Germans could come into Latvia.

> When he [the guard] mentioned a possible return to Germany my stomach suddenly began to turn over. Mandl's reaction was very much more visible than mine. He began to shiver and tremble and was in such a state that I had to help him with his luggage and even support him as he climbed down from the coach to the platform. After a couple of minutes he had recovered enough for the two of us, struggling with our luggage and followed by an armed escort, to move along the platform to the border police office. (Clare 215)

The two were sent back to Kaunas, where local Jews urged them not to remain there since they held only twenty-four-hour visas. Unlike the Latvians, who simply deported Jews, the Lithuanians turned them over to the Gestapo. Their contact bought them tickets to Königsberg and suggested that Clare wire his parents for money for the return to Berlin. At the German border, both expected the worst. Their passports were taken by a German customs official with a swastika in his lapel. Clare saw his thirty-five-year-old companion's face become a "wax-coloured death-mask" (218). But the official returned their passports. It turned out that the East Prussian passport control accepted the statement "valid for one outward and one return journey" to mean exactly what it said. In Königsberg they received the money from Clare's parents and returned to Berlin.

Clare survived this frightening experience and even returned to Austria to have his passport revalidated. As he comments, "The nightmare of my flight from the Wehrmacht was over. The nightmare of life in Hitler's Germany could continue" (Clare 219). Clare's father took an opportunity to go to France, so Clare and his mother waiting in Germany finally received the long-awaited visa the morning after Kristallnacht. They were legally able to fly out of Berlin immediately.[5]

After Kristallnacht, Frederic Zeller and his family redoubled their efforts to leave Germany, but they could not obtain the necessary papers. The Nazis were quickly closing down illegal escape routes. Just before Kristallnacht, the Zellers had been told about a "children's railroad" but learned during the anxious period after the events of November 9 that it had been discovered by the Nazis. In this illegal railroad, small numbers of German Jewish children were escorted through the border to a nearby town in Holland where relief workers met them. The guide returned to take a few more children a few days later. The cousins' names were given to the people running this escape route, but there were many children ahead of them.

Even though the railroad was discovered, the young Zeller convinced his parents and aunt that it might be possible for at least his cousin Susi and him to get through, if they had the names of Dutch contacts on the other side. Zeller laid down some rules for this bold attempt. He would not take Norbert because his younger cousin wouldn't mind the two older ones. Nor would he take his sister because she was too young. They could come later if the older two got through. Also, his parents were not supposed to accompany them to the station. The certain traumatic farewell would put the teenagers in danger. His aunt insisted that Norbert go, and although his father agreed not to go to the station, his mother would not stay home. Frederic relented and allowed his aunt and mother to come to the station to see them off.

On the train they met four other young teenage Jews who had decided to try the same escape route. They threw their lots in together. In Krefeld they were to change trains. The train stopped again at Kleve before crossing the border. Their destination was Nijmegen, the first stop in Holland. The Zeller cousins planned to spend the night in a hotel in Kleve where they could hide money. In case they were spotted and sent back to Germany, they could make another attempt after retrieving the money in Kleve. The other four had learned that previous escapees had made the cross by being in the front cars of the train when it pulled into Nijmegen. They jumped over a five-foot fence rather than go through the control. Frederic decided that the seven should follow the second plan. They organized themselves into three groups.

The teenagers transferred trains in Krefeld and then buried money in Kleve for a second attempt, if needed. As they entered the last train they learned that it would make two stops in Germany before reaching Nijmegen. Throughout their long train trip there were some risky moments when passengers questioned why several youngsters were traveling alone into Holland. The most nerve-wracking period came, however, on the last leg of the journey when an SS officer entered their compartment. Learning that they had no passports because they were Jewish, he left the compartment screaming that he would have them arrested.

> "Damn it, Saujuden [bastard Jews]," he screamed, "you have to have a Hitler Youth leave pass or else an official document that you're not eligible for service. Eine Schweinerei [How disgusting], you know very well that's the law! You have to have proof or you can't leave Germany. I'll have you arrested! Stay here and don't you dare move out of this compartment, I'll be right back! Heil Hitler!"
>
> We sat there looking at each other and not even attempting to hide our fear. We kept on waiting for him to return with reinforcements. But the train just went on ratatatting into the night. (Zeller 194)

When the train stopped for the last time in Germany, a customs official entered. He understood only too well what they were about and wished them success. The SS officer never returned. They made it to Nijmegen, where they were spotted but accepted by the Dutch officials anyway. A Jewish representative of the Nijmegen Jewish Refugee Committee welcomed them to Holland.

Zeller and his cousins were given refuge in Holland and placed in an orphanage. Later the three cousins were transferred to a refugee camp in Rotterdam. Zeller kept in contact with his parents as long as possible and continued to request that they send out his sister. He also wrote to her directly, telling her how to do it. About two months later, he received a telegram from the twelve-year-old girl saying, "Going Halle tonight, your beloved sister Lilian" (Zeller 226). Figuring out that Halle was her code word for Holland, he knew that she was making the escape. She took money from her parents' emergency fund and went to downtown Berlin. From there she sent both her parents and her brother telegrams and passed the day in Berlin by shopping and having her hair cut. Having been alerted to her plan by the telegram, her parents tried to catch her at the train station, but she took the train from Bahnhof Zoologischer Garten rather than Charlottenburg. She was picked up by Dutch relief workers as the others had been and was reunited with her brother in Rotterdam.

In 1994, Lilian Furst, a well-known comparative literature scholar in the United States, published an unusual autobiography when she was sixty-two entitled *Home Is Somewhere Else: Autobiography in Two Voices*. This unusual dual autobiography was written by Furst and her father, Desider Furst, who had died in 1985. Lilian Furst was seven years old when she and her family escaped from Vienna and Germany in December 1938. Her father wrote an account of the family's escape in the early 1970s, but she did not read it until after his death. When she did, she was inspired to add her own memories of these same events. Although Furst continues her account of their lives beyond her father's retirement and her own success in England and the United States as a scholar and teacher, the early chapters of their escape and initial setbacks in England are the most riveting.

Furst's father and mother were both dentists and had met as medical students in Vienna. In 1938 they were prosperous professional people. They remained in Vienna nine months after the Anschluss, although her mother's relatives had already emigrated to London and urged the Fursts to follow. The Fursts were able to obtain the exit papers they needed to get out of Vienna but did not have entry papers to another country. Her father learned that Britain was accepting forty refugee dentists. He applied but heard nothing. After Kristallnacht, the Fursts realized that they needed to leave the Third Reich illegally. They had obtained a place on a

Kindertransport for six-year-old Lilian, but her mother decided at the last minute that it would be better for the three to remain together at all costs.

They traveled during the Christmas holidays, hoping they would be less noticeable during the holiday travel. Their immediate goal was Holland or Belgium, and from there they hoped to go to Britain when and if the papers came through. In Cologne they learned from the Jewish network of two escape routes, one to Belgium through Aachen and one to Holland. They had the name of a contact in Aachen and went immediately to him, but Furst's father mistrusted him and did not like the escape plan. They returned to Cologne and found another route, traveling to Kleve on the Dutch border. From here they were told to take a taxi across the border. It was taken for granted that the Dutch would allow them in. In Kleve, however, they learned that this route, too, had been discovered. The taxi drivers were now under strict instructions from the Gestapo not to take illegal passengers across. Their contact advised them to return to Cologne immediately.

Once again in Cologne, they found a contact at the Jewish community center who was prepared to take the three Fursts and two others to Belgium the next day. Their flight into Belgium is recounted by both Lilian and her father. Here is her father's version:

> We were to be at a certain corner of the Eiffel Place at 2 P.M. the next day. We were there, and exactly at the arranged time a car stopped and in no time we were in and on the move. The three of us sat on the back seat facing the two youngsters. We were separated from the driver [and his assistant] by a glass pane. . . . They were very pleased that our German passports were valid; it made their task easier. Their main worry was the steadily falling snow, which might block the road over the Eiffel mountains, through which we had to travel. Their fear was justified; near the top we got stuck. We noticed a group of young men in uniforms. When they saw us stuck, they came over to the car with their shovels, dug us out, and cleared the way. . . . Fortunately, we were not asked to get out, and we tried to hide our faces by bending over. (Furst and Furst 66)

When they reached the border, Lilian was dropped off at a small inn because her parents didn't want her to be searched at the border. After the border necessities, they were taken to the crossing area.

> We met Mr. Müller outside, and after we had fetched our daughter from the inn he led us through a small forest. When we came out, we saw a railroad bridge in front of us. There we had to wait. By this time it was dark; only far ahead could we see some light. The Belgian [their driver] had disappeared. After about ten minutes we heard someone whistling, and Mr. Müller urged us to cross the bridge quickly. (Furst and Furst 67)

The Fursts were taken into Brussels and finally found their friends, having successfully but illegally left Nazi Germany.

Lilian's version allows us to understand the fear of the six-year-old girl during this scary border crossing. She notes that she is "still amazed at the rashness with which we purchased our lives."

> It began to snow on the way, and at one point the car got stuck. Members of the Hitler Youth were at the ready with shovels to dig us out. The driver nervously told us to put our heads down so that they wouldn't recognize his cargo. My heart was in my mouth until we got moving again.
>
> It was beginning to grow dark by the time we arrived at the frontier. Our driver recommended that I not be taken through the German border post because children were sometimes subjected to nasty body searches. Instead I was led to a nearby inn, settled in a corner with a cup of cocoa, and told to wait there until they came back to fetch me. How long did I wait? Twenty minutes? Half an hour? Longer? I have no idea. . . . Left to wait alone, I was absolutely terrified: what if they didn't come back for me? I had no passport or money, and what could a seven-year-old do alone anyway? The body search, I guess, might have been even more traumatic. (Furst and Furst 57)

These dramatic stories help the modern reader understand the desperation the Jews experienced while trying to elude the Nazis. They also show us the resiliency of those persecuted. But in the final result, only a few escaped. Frederic Zeller, who was one of the lucky ones, came from a large Jewish family whose members hailed from a variety of Eastern European countries — Poland, Hungary, Czechoslovakia. Families had to make appalling decisions to survive. Children were frequently sent out alone so that their parents could move more easily without them. At times fathers had to leave their families. Being released from prison or concentration camps frequently meant having to leave Germany or Austria within twenty-four hours. Sometimes marriage to a foreigner helped a spouse survive. Many escaped from Germany, only to be trapped and deported to a concentration camp in another country. At the end of his autobiography, Zeller documents what happened to his family members. His family's history of those who perished and those who survived indicates how much people were at the mercy of fate. The four cousins who had escaped through the "children's railroad" — Frederic, Lilian, Susi, and Norbert — survived. Susi and Norbert's father, who had been transported to the no-man's-land at the Polish border, escaped and made it to Chile, where his two children joined him.[6] Their mother, who tried to join her husband in Poland, disappeared when Poland was overrun. Frederic and his sister, Lilian, went to England; Frederic emigrated to the United States long after the war. His father fled to Antwerp and joined the flood of refugees going south through France. He was interned and deported to Auschwitz in 1943 and did not survive. His mother never left Berlin. She was picked up and transported to Maidanek and did not survive. An aunt and an uncle on his father's side both perished, but another uncle and his wife survived the war and the bombs by hiding in Berlin. On his mother's side, an aunt fled first to Belgium, then to the south of France, only to be interned and later disappear. Another aunt, her husband, and their daughter fled first to Prague and then to Denmark, were smuggled into Sweden by the Danes, and survived the war. Another of his mother's brothers survived by emigrating very early to Haifa. Most of the children of these aunts and uncles survived. Among his family's friends, the Papiermeisters escaped to the United States in 1938. In the de Wyze family (the family in Holland that helped him), the parents died, but one son survived Auschwitz and other camps. A daughter survived Theresienstadt, and another survived hidden in Holland. What happened to Zeller's family and friends was typical of the experiences of many Jewish families.

The autobiographical voices we have heard in these two chapters bring into sharp focus how quickly a person's security and comfort can be jeopardized by external events and changing political realities. The brief glimpses into their changing lives cause us to pause. As human beings we are inordinately vulnerable to social disruptions. But at the same time, while these passages convey terror and anxiety, we also hear the voice of the autobiographer. In the autobiographies of Arthur Koestler and Lion Feuchtwanger, for example, we hear the righteous indignation of these authors and their insistence on quickly bringing this indignation to the attention of the British and the Americans. From Döblin's account we recognize the disorientation of a broken man. From Yehuda Nir, Frederic Zeller, George Clare, and Lilian Furst we hear not only the fears of children and teenagers and the drama of escape but also resolute courage in the face of adversity. These autobiographers who tell us what it was like to be targeted by the Nazis and to escape their nets also remind us through the imagery and style of their voices of the limitations of autobiography. Renée Fersen-Osten is not the young child she was in 1942 but a middle-aged woman recalling herself as a young child. She recasts the memories of her child's responses to disruptive events in a poetic form which she published only in 1991. As readers we respond to its authenticity, but we can't forget that her rendering was completed fifty-one years after the events. In telling her story, she uses recognizable narrative and poetic strategies, as do all of these authors. As readers we can appreciate their personal versions of history, even if we recognize the artifice they use in telling their stories.

chapter four

After the War:
Coming to Terms with Exile

"You speak our language"
They say everywhere
With amazement.
I am the stranger
Who speaks their language.
    Hilda Domin, "Stranger"

Erik Erikson, the noted psychologist of identity formation, writes about his intellectual quest to document the development of psychological identity after he was exiled from Austria. As he says, "Migration means cruel survival in identity terms, . . . for the very cataclysms in which millions perish open up new forms of identity to the survivors" (Erikson 748). Those who chose exile had to deal with their changed lives. Those who survived the war and were now living in relatively comfortable circumstances still needed to come to terms with their exile.

In a letter to Hermann Hesse in 1941, Thomas Mann writes from the United States about his exile sojourn since 1933: "we have learned to recognize an interlude as an era. In spite of everything we have lived, worked, and made our way, but of course when I think of Switzerland I always wonder whether I shall ever see it and Europe again" (Simpson 227). For those who had reached a safe haven, the difficulties did not abate, but life went on. As the immediate crisis of abruptly having to leave their homelands receded, the exile experience still affected them. For Carl Zuck-mayer, Georg Grosz, and Oskar Kokoshka, well-known figures in the artistic world, the exile experience became a major focus in their autobiographies.

Memoirs of Integration

The community of German writers and artists who found refuge in California during World War II forms an interesting microcosm of the adjustment, assimilation, and/or return of exiles.[1] Lion Feuchtwanger quickly found his way into the culture and lifestyle of California, as did many composers such as Ernst Korngold and Arnold Schoenberg and movie directors such as Billy Wilder and Fred Zinnemann. Of course, it is not so difficult to continue working in a medium like music or film where the language barrier is not as significant. For writers as well as actors whose artistic medium is the written or spoken word, working in a new language and culture is irredeemably frustrating. Surprisingly, some writers like Feuchtwanger had great success in Hollywood. But other German writers — Carl Zuckmayer, Heinrich Mann, Franz Werfel come to mind — found it difficult to continue their careers in the United States.

Carl Zuckmayer, the noted German dramatist, described the initial reception of intellectual exiles in the United States in his memoir *A Part of Myself*, published in 1966. At that time he had returned to Germany after his sojourn in the United States during the war. Zuckmayer, whose dramatic career was at its height in the Weimar Republic, was seventy when he completed his memoir. Although he recounts his early years in Germany and his literary successes, he emphasizes his years as an exile in the United States and his resourceful actions in meeting the challenge of making a living for himself and his wife during the lean war years. Unlike some of his colleagues who became successful writers in Hollywood, Zuckmayer could not abide the California lifestyle. Instead, he lived out the war years as a farmer in Vermont.

Zuckmayer gives a particularly devastating portrait of a writer's life in Hollywood. Many refugee writers were offered positions with the large studios. Being a contracted writer with a Hollywood film studio meant a good paycheck for refugees who had been living with virtually no money and few opportunities for publication of their work. It also meant, however, that they had very little control over the subject matter or the style of their writing. When Zuckmayer first arrived in Hollywood, he obtained a seven-year contract at $750 per week, but he gave up all rights to his work and could be fired with one week's notice. Nevertheless, he enthusiastically took on a project that absorbed him, a screen treatment of Arnold Zweig's *The Case of Sargeant Grischa*, the story of a Russian soldier falsely accused of sabotage during World War I. In the middle of this project, Hal Wallis, the studio head, notified Zuckmayer that he was needed for another project. Wallis didn't think the time was ripe politically to put forward a favorable portrait of a Russian. Wallis asked Zuckmayer to write a treatment of Don Juan set in Renaissance Italy. When Zuckmayer pointed out that Don Juan came from Spain, Wallis responded that that made no difference. He wanted a story about Don Juan and the de Medicis. Zuckmayer explained that Wallis really meant the Borgias, because he kept talking about the climax being an affair between Don Juan and "the famous lovely poisoner" (Zuckmayer 351).

The director Fritz Lang counseled Zuckmayer to take the new offer and settle down in Hollywood with a good income and three months' vacation to do his own work. But Zuckmayer couldn't stomach the lifestyle. He didn't take the offer and was fired. Zuckmayer vividly describes the desolation he felt in Hollywood despite the income he had been offered:

> Never have I been so wrapped in the mists of depression as in this land of eternal spring, in whose irrigated gardens with their chlorinated swimming pools and dream castles perched on the slopes of canyons, short-lived pleasure is at home, while in the depths sprawls a dreary, murderous wasteland; the city of Los Angeles, one of the ugliest and most brutal metropolises in the world. (347)

For Heinrich Mann, Werfel, and Bruno Frank the outcome was worse. Picking up the threads of their writing careers in an alien culture may well have contributed to their deaths.

Like Zuckmayer and Döblin, many exiles in California assimilated the California lifestyle with difficulty, but they did continue their work abroad. Thomas Mann and Bertolt Brecht could not possibly obtain the spiritual nourishment they needed from the Hollywood scene. In general, the enclave of German intellectuals lived as a community unto itself, staying focused on German culture and the German language. The scholar Theodor Adorno endured this life apart with a growing, bruising pessimism which he recorded in his autobiography, *Minima Moralia*. California, with its climate so different and culture so removed from those of Germany, became home to Feuchtwanger, Schoenberg, Wilder, and many others. But for Thomas Mann, Brecht, Adorno, Zuckmayer, and Döblin, life in the United States turned out to be an interlude, if at times a pleasant one.

The success or failure of settling in a new culture and resuming one's occupation depends on many variables. Clearly, facility with foreign languages plays a major role, but other factors also contribute — education, political views, philosophical views, psychological resiliency, and economic viability. Hannah Arendt chose to remain in the United States, teaching at the New School of Social Research and writing her books on political philosophy in English. Her facility in learning English may well have been crucial for her, as her biographer Elizabeth Young-Breuhl points out, particularly since her husband, Henry Blücher, could not quickly adjust linguistically. Brecht's return to East Germany after the ludicrous episode of his testifying before the House Un-American Activities Committee in 1947 illustrates how out of tune his political views were with the dominant political atmosphere of America after the war. During this unpleasant political era, Thomas Mann also chose to return to Europe, but he settled in Switzerland, not Germany, reluctant to return to the country that had denied him citizenship. Many intellectuals did return to Europe (Remarque also to Switzerland) and some even to Germany. Max Horkheimer and Theodor Adorno returned to Frankfurt am Main to continue the work of the Frankfurt School. Like Brecht, however, their motivation to return may have been exacerbated by the political climate in the United States in the fifties, namely, the witch-hunting atmosphere influenced so much by Senator Joseph McCarthy. Hanns Eisler, the noted composer, was forced to return to Europe under threat of deportation because of his leftist views.[2] Thousands of others remained in the United States or in other new lands — Britain, Canada, Brazil, or Australia. In the United States, these exiles led productive lives as scholars, writers, or artists and melded into the culture of the United States.[3]

After the war, when the danger had passed, many European writers and artists summed up the events of their lives in traditional autobiographies, narratives chronicling the events of their lives. Zuckmayer, Döblin, Arthur Koestler, Georg Grosz, Alma Mahler-Werfel, and Oskar Kokoschka told their life stories, particularly highlighting their exile experiences. And while they may take a reflective stance of the events of their lives, their thoughts of exile help shape our understanding of this experience.

In his autobiography published in 1946, *A Little Yes and a Big No*, Georg Grosz highlights his newfound artistic style in the United States. In the turbulence of the German revolution after World War I and the wildly decadent life of the inflation period in the early Weimar Republic, Grosz found fame and fortune while capturing the excesses of the age in his characteristic drawings. Highly influenced by Nietzsche and the culturally pessimistic Oswald Spengler, Grosz portrayed the German soul as it dissolved. He described the eccentricity of the time. "Strange people entered my life: writers, scholars, vegetarian astronomers, sculpturors [*sic*] with persecution-complexes, a public benefactor with secret vices, a drunken translator, painters, philosophers and musicians" (Grosz 149). His politics of anarchy and nihilism led him to participate in the politically charged Dadaist confrontations in Berlin and elsewhere in Germany. Nothing was sacred; he and his cohorts mocked everything.

By the time the twenties had come to an end, Grosz was an independent artist, famous throughout Germany. But his keen focus on the Berlin types of the twenties helped him to anticipate the hatred brewing in Germany. He described his part in this dying circus life as a "minute part of the chaos; I was the splinter that was miraculously saved when the wood went up in the flames of the new barbarism" (Grosz 201).

Amused by *Time* magazine's view of him as the "Mild Monster" arriving in the United States (Grosz 237), he receded from stylish public life and retreated to his studio, where he took up oil painting again. Forty years old when he moved to the United States in 1932, he noted that a "great deal that had become frozen within me in Germany melted here in America" (Grosz 270).

In this autobiography written in 1946, the fifty-four-year-old Grosz rejects the glamour of his former role as chronicler of the grotesque and the bizarre. In the United States, Grosz led a more simple artistic existence of teaching and illustrating for American magazines and book publishers. He depicts the extremities of his lifestyle in Berlin and portrays for the reader some of the well-known figures as well as the lesser-known eccentrics of the period. The message of the autobiography, however, is the survival and new pragmatic life of a very lucky artist, one who escaped from Nazi Germany. He considers himself to be one of the very lucky ones. At war's end, he had already made the transition in his art and his life. Had he remained in Germany, he surely would have been imprisoned.

Oskar Kokoschka, a contemporary of Georg Grosz, wrote his autobiography, *My Life*, in 1971 when he was in his early eighties. Born in Vienna in 1886, he was the stereotype of the "genius bohemian" artist who lived from commissions and the largess of some patrons but mostly friends. Known primarily as a painter, he also wrote drama and fiction and later taught drawing and painting. Although he presents his life story as a narrative of events, his style and commentary clearly show his eccentricity, perversity, and exhibitionism. When he writes his autobiography he is also something of a curmudgeon, and his strong, authentic voice illumines his twentieth-century world in an interesting way. But Kokoschka resolutely recognizes what exile meant in his life. As he spent most of his life on the margins of society, he apparently did not suffer loss as much as some exiles, but at times he experienced the self-defeating paralysis of exile.

Kokoschka studied the great models of art to learn about himself and his society. Referencing Albrecht Dürer's copper engraving *Melencolia I*, he saw the central figure's staring into space not only as fear but also as hope. He saw her trying to know herself even though she was "trapped in space and time" (Kokoschka 212). For him the trick was to understand this but not to despair. The tribulations of his life, some trivial, others monumental, gave him little security, but he was an actor who met the challenges head on. He introduced the last chapter of his autobiography by summing up his "restless life" (Kokoschka 197). In truth, *My Restless Life* might have been a better title to his autobiography, for his restlessness and search to understand visual experience helped him to cope with the strong personal, economic, and political currents that battered him in life. In this last chapter, he recalled what Rembrandt's final self-portrait, painted in 1699, helped him as an exile to see. At the beginning of his exile in England, he viewed the painting in the National Gallery in London: "I saw it properly for the first time on one of those London winter days when, without the means to survive, I felt myself to be on the outer fringes of human existence. The picture gave me courage to take up my life again" (Kokoschka 210). Rembrandt painted this self-portrait when he was suffering from dropsy and his sight was failing. What gave Kokoschka hope was Rembrandt's power to paint the process of his own decaying body. For Kokoschka, painting meant the expression of life even if the subject himself was dying or, in his case, suffering as an exile with no prospects. The strength and resiliency of his dynamic personality allowed him to be who he was despite the ordeals of life.

Zuckmayer, Grosz, and Kokoschka were artists who had achieved fame and, in Grosz's and Kokoschka's cases, notoriety before they were displaced by the rising tide of fascism. Their audiences expected them to write autobiographies, reviewing their challenges and successes. And while these autobiographies detail their life's stages, the disruption of exile becomes one of the major themes in each of them. But in their narratives, they overcome exile. Nostalgia for a lost life or excessive psychic revelations do not become part of their narratives. They led successful artistic lives before exile, and although they had to weather severe changes, they insist that they resumed their artistic careers relatively easily.

But for many exiles, the dramatic changes in their lives were problematic. And in the later decades of this century, exiles continued to write about their experiences fleeing the menace of the Nazis and the upheavals of war. The topic still haunts those individuals who lived through these turbulent historical times. Furst notes that even today she has not let go of the terrors of being forced into exile.

> Even now, an American citizen, tenured in a major university, holder of an endowed chair, with savings, investments, disability insurance, a retirement pension, a beautiful house, a car, a long list of publications: still I am liable to agonies of anxiety and insomnia because, alone, at some level, I still feel so terribly vulnerable to the contingencies of an untrustworthy world. (Furst and Furst 23–24)

Although she enjoys the securities of our modern life, her childhood experience continually reminds her that she is still at risk. The scars of exile are permanent.

Exiles want to set down their experiences for a variety of reasons: to revisit the life they left behind, to become witnesses to major historical events, to philosophize about their disrupted identities, and, in many, many cases, to help heal these rifts of identity. Elias Canetti, for example, left Vienna in the late thirties for London. In the late seventies he began publishing a detailed autobiography of his birth and childhood in the Sephardic community of Bulgaria. He depicted his family's move to London, the death of his father early in his life, and his mother's influence on him as they lived in several places on the continent. His university years in Vienna sparked his writing career. The published three volumes of this copious autobiography concern only his life before exile. Yet facing the loss of his ancestral home in Bulgaria and the death of his father, his frequent moves during his youth, and finally achieving success in Vienna — all inform the autobiography, which I discuss in further detail in chapters 6 and 9. He was apparently completing a fourth volume when he died in 1994.

Mircea Eliade, the well-known writer and scholar, wrote a two-volume autobiography late in his career. As a life-long diarist,

Eliade also frequently spoke of his exile experience in his multi-volume diary, published in the seventies and eighties. His diary accounts of exile express more of his sorrow at being exiled from his homeland of Romania, while his autobiography gives the reader a summation of the effects of exile on his life and his prolific writing career, as I highlight in chapter 8.

In the second part of this study, I want to review exile autobiographies like Canetti's and Eliade's that explore such rich themes as nostalgia for childhood, the intellectual or spiritual response to exile, the role of language, and particularly the psychic devastation of exile. In this first part, "Disrupted Lives," I have dealt primarily with "focused memoirs" that set down selected versions of the events of the thirties and forties — the personally devastating events that disrupted the comfortable patterns of people's existence. Eye-witnesses to our century's defining horrors, some wrote their testimony in the immediate shadow of their experiences while others recollected it in the middle or last years of their lives. Taken together, their mosaic of experience gives their distant readers at least some understanding of their uprooting. They depicted the collapse of their European world. Koestler, who spent the thirties in Russia and Germany and as an exile in France and who finally joined the French foreign legion before escaping to England in 1940, ends his two-volume autobiography written in the fifties, *Arrow in the Blue*, with the following statement: "At this point ends this typical case-history of a central European member of the educated middle classes, born in the first years of our century" (423). His weary sentiment expresses the reality of this time; his story is only one among many of those disrupted. In the subsequent chapters, I want to concentrate on the cumulative effects of these experiences for the lives of exiles as they express them in a wide range of autobiographies. Frequently, the experience changed lives so significantly that many exiles established new identities. While losing one's homeland and lifestyle was overwhelmingly threatening, reestablishing a connected life in a new world provided the necessary healing, and, in many cases, the process of describing these changes added to their healing.

Surveying exiles' autobiographies shows the resiliency of the human being. Faced with the loss of homeland, native traditions, personal treasures, and even language, many adjusted to a new life and even flourished in it. While the experience proved so overwhelming that some could not continue, these psychologically damaging events do not defeat most. The long list of suicides, which includes well-known writers and artists such as Stefan Zweig, Walter Benjamin, Ernst Toller, and Ernst Weiss, does attest to the severity of the toll in human terms. The broad range of autobiographies shows the other side, the many decisions made to choose life and recovery.

A discussion of the theoretical dimensions of exile autobiography follows. It situates this type of writing in the current critical debates on the form of autobiography. The remaining chapters focus on the themes of exile examined in these autobiographies — the themes of loss, disruption, and reintegration, with an emphasis on the renewal and resurrection of personal identity.

part two

Reconstructions

chapter five

Crossing Boundaries: Theoretical Dimensions of Exile Autobiography

Going into exile is "The journey of no return." Anyone who sets out on it dreaming of coming home is lost. He may return — but the place he will find is no longer the one he left, and he himself is no longer the one who left. He may return to people he missed, to places he loved and did not forget, to the region where his own language is spoken. But he never returns home.

Carl Zuckmayer, *A Part of Myself*

For a man who no longer has a homeland, writing becomes a place to live.

Theodor Adorno, *Minima Moralia*

In her dissertation on thinking, *The Life of the Mind*, Hannah Arendt speaks of creating meaning. Her words can shed some light on the creative process involved in writing an autobiography: "The meaning of what actually happens and appears while it is happening is revealed when it has disappeared; remembrance, by which you make present to your mind what actually is absent and past, reveals the meaning in the form of a story" (Arendt 133). The autobiographer creates a life story from remembrances of the past. James Olney notes that the style of autobiography has altered through the ages. Earlier autobiographies stressed the *bios*, the life. More recent autobiographies have stressed the *autos*, the self ("Cultural Moment" 20–21). Modern thinkers such as Jacques Derrida and Michel Foucault insist that the act of writing causes the text to take on a life of its own. According to them, the self, which as Olney notes "was not really in existence in the beginning" ("Cultural Moment" 22), disappears into the text. The self, like Arendt's meaning, is a fiction, a story.

The range of exile autobiographies encompasses both the enumeration of experiences and the permutations of the self. In part I, I focused on autobiographers who suffered exile due to the rise of fascism in Germany and who depicted their flight, survival, and integration into new cultures. As "focused memoirs" these autobiographies fit Paul John Eakin's definition of memoir as an autobiographical narrative where "the individual is perceived, respectively, as the actor in or the witness to history" (*Touching the World* 142). In such personal narratives, the autobiographer's review of historic events, not his or her subjectivity, is the primary issue, although the autobiographer's subjectivity is affected by the uprooting events they experience (Eakin, *Touching the World* 139). For the modern reader, the autobiographers delineated in part I provide gripping narratives of authentic experiences of being displaced by disruptive social and political events in the thirties and forties. Part II focuses on autobiographers who explore more deeply their subjective response to displacement and integration. Thus their identities are of paramount importance because in traversing cultures, exiles must accommodate new cultural identities in order to survive. I will feature both those who successfully negotiate the transit to a new culture and those who do not.

The texts treated in the following chapters emphasize a "self-story," the ruptured identity of a displaced self serving as the motivation. As these self-stories are created in the present, the actual events and experiences connected with them have long since disappeared; these are self-stories of the mind. Olney calls them metaphors of the self. Where the process of telling the self-stories is psychologically necessary to rehabilitate the dislocated self, the impulse to reimagine the past is almost seductive. The exile's uprooted self is partially healed through the writing process.

Czesław Miłosz, the noted Polish exile writer, confirms that autobiography is a literary form suited to the exile writer. Certain literary genres, particularly the realistic novel, "cannot, by definition, be practiced in exile" because the writer, no longer in touch with his or her roots, cannot "preserve his postulated and imagined presence in the country he comes from" (Miłosz, "Notes" 282). But, as he notes, "On the other hand, the condition of exile, by enforcing upon a writer several perspectives, favors other genres and styles, especially those which are related to a symbolic transposition of reality" (Miłosz, "Notes" 282).

The exile autobiographer's task is precisely to transpose a (past) reality symbolically, creating a self-story that is a fiction, but a comforting and self-affirming fiction. These self-stories are therapeutic in that they reestablish continuity for the self that was disrupted when propelled into exile. Before examining the therapeutic aspects and the theoretical dimensions of exile autobiography, however, it is important to understand some general critical perspectives on autobiography.

The Autobiographical Subject

In the past two decades there has been an explosion of critical writing concerning the shape and form of autobiography, a form of life writing seen until recently as marginal literature. Numerous critical texts have defined it and treated the form's literary worth. Olney, who was instrumental in focusing critical attention on autobiography, suggests that this burgeoning critical activity in autobiographical studies has come about in part because emphasis has shifted from seeing autobiography as a record of the artist's life to perceiving it as a representation of the artist's self. For Olney, this "shift of attention from *bios* to *autos* — from the life to the self — was . . . largely responsible for opening things up and turning them in a philosophical, psychological, and literary direction" ("Cultural Moment" 19). In other words, recent critics have been more concerned with the autobiographer's literary representation of his or her philosophical, psychological, cultural, and additionally political or spiritual self rather than the truth value of the narrative of events in his or her life history.

This change in critical emphasis to the self rather than the life becomes problematic, however. The narrower definition of autobiography as a (truthful) account of the events of the autobiographer's life must, by implication, be expanded. A range of thought concerning the form of autobiography constructs a continuum with the narrow definition at one end and a broad definition at the other: an autobiographer conveys his or her (inner) experience in a literary form or other medium. The broad definition allows us to interpret as autobiographies creative or imaginative works like poetry, novels, or short stories. Even visual works — film and paintings — can, under this rubric, be seen primarily as fictional, creative self-stories.[1] Thus, setting the limits of the genre and selecting a canon of autobiographies become questionable tasks, as critics Paul Jay, Eugene Stelzig, Felicity Nussbaum, and Elizabeth Bruss have pointed out. At the same time, discussions of the genre and canon of autobiography also reflect changes in thinking about canons in general. Feminist and minority scholars of autobiography have asserted that autobiographies by women and minorities have been excluded from canon discussions. Moreover, postmodern critics have asked penetrating questions about the nature of the "self," "individual," or "author" as well as the nature of "subjectivity," all concepts important to the autobiographical project. This section looks critically at some of the ways exile autobiography fits and does not fit into the general critical discussion of autobiography. Thus, my discussion of the theoretical dimensions of exile autobiography begins with a brief review of some current issues in autobiographical criticism. I also examine how autobiographical critics have treated the concept of the self, both historically and in the postmodern era, during what might be termed the philosophical unraveling of the self.

In his book *Being in the Text: Self-Representations from Wordsworth to Roland Barthes*, Paul Jay cautions against trying to define the genre's limits or to establish an autobiographical canon. Rather than dwell on such frustrating endeavors, he emphasizes the changing structure of autobiography: "There will always be the temptation in defining autobiography as a genre either to create borders that are too exclusively narrow or ones that are so large as to be meaningless" (Jay 18). Stelzig, who also stresses the futility of defining the genre's limits, punctuates the argument with a pertinent slogan: "no genre of autobiography, no canon" (5). He does, however, suggest some advantages for continuing the discussion of formulating a canon (or canons). Such dialogues bring into relief the process of canon-making, for

> precisely because this dynamic area of literary and cultural study [autobiography] is still in the process of critically defining itself, its object, its procedures, and its limits, it is also an ideal setting in which to observe up close the very process by which canons come into being or begin to sort themselves out in an ideologically charged and exciting time in which old critical and cultural certainties have effectively been challenged and in which the boundaries between disciplines are being displaced or redrawn. (Stelzig 9)

In focusing on the structure of autobiography, rather than genre and canon definition, Jay highlights another more important and worrisome problem in studying autobiography. What problems do authors face when trying to make themselves the subjects of an autobiography? Jay determines that an author must face the challenge of "how to use one medium — language — to represent another medium — being" (21). Basing his argument on Paul de Man's remarks in his well-known essay, "Autobiography as De-facement," Jay refers to the problematic issue of referentiality when he says, "And if the border between autobiography and fiction is erected on a privileged notion of referentiality, then the study of autobiographical works will always be partly founded upon an illusion" (18). According to Jay, de Man questions the traditional autobiographical premise that the autobiographer's referentiality defines the author's self-story. Jay quotes the following passage from de Man:

> Are we so certain that autobiography depends on reference, as a photograph depends on its subject or a (realistic) picture on its model? We assume that life produces the autobiography as an act produces its consequences, but can we not suggest, with equal justice, that the autobiographical project may itself produce and determine the life and that whatever the writer does is in fact governed by the technical demands of self-portraiture

and thus determined, in all its aspects, by the resources of his medium? (76) [2]

De Man rejects the idea that an autobiographical work represents a "privileged form of referentiality." Instead, he views the "subject as a textual production" — that is, the autobiographical subject is not the person the events happened to in the past, but a construct or fiction created for the book itself (Jay 18). This brings us to issues in the ongoing debate in theoretical circles. Who is the "subject," and what is the "self"?

Traditionally, autobiography has been defined as a literary work in which the author is also the subject or protagonist of the work. But if the writing of the autobiography changes the author, as de Man and others suggest, then it is difficult to get a stable view of the self, which is being written as the autobiography is being written. On the other hand, once the autobiography is finished, the dynamic self, so to speak, no longer exists, and what remains is a textual self that can further change according to the reader's response.

Reviewing some historical definitions of self or individual can elucidate some of these problems. In his history of the humanities, *Education's Great Amnesia*, Robert Proctor notes that "a personal self came into being along with the humanities in the Renaissance" (48). Proctor discusses Petrarch at length as an example of this evolving awareness of self. Petrarch sought from his reading of the ancients such as Cicero examples of heroic men's deeds which would serve as models for his own behavior in the uncertain times he lived in. Such cataclysmic events as the Black Death had brought overwhelming changes into his life. In reading the ancients as he did, Petrarch had to experience his own being as a unique and autonomous self which he could objectify, act upon, and compare to other such autonomous selves. Proctor interprets Petrarch's reading as a general turning inward and a reaction to the knowledge that human beings were no longer one with the cosmos. But according to Proctor, Petrarch misread the ancients because he projected this view of human nature into their heroic exploits: "Petrarch had to presume, as most people still do today, that inner consciousness, individual uniqueness, and experiential autonomy are part of human nature" (49). This powerful view of human nature has endured in Western thought but is erroneous. Proctor points out that this Western definition of the self is invalid in a cross-cultural setting. Here he is quoting Clifford Geertz:

> The Western conception of the person as a bounded, unique, more or less integrated motivational and cognitive universe, a dynamic center of awareness, emotion, judgement, and action organized into a distinctive whole and set contrastively both against other such wholes and against its social and cultural background, is, however incorrigible it may seem to us, a rather peculiar idea within the context of the world's cultures. (Proctor 72–73)

Western writers who have studied Oriental religion and philosophy also argue that the autonomous, unified self is inadequate. Alan Watts, a writer known as an interpreter of Oriental religion and philosophy for the West, notes that the Western mind is imbued with this view of the self based on the Western concept of dualism.

> The *someone*, the unique and specific ego, who knows and feels, who responsibly causes actions, who dwells *in* the body but is not quite *of* the body, who confronts its experiences as something other, who is the inward controller of thinking and willing — *this* is assumed in every phase of our culture and in all the practical matters of everyday life. (Watts 9–10)

Watts sees this subjectivity "largely determined by [Judeo-Christian] theological and mythological images" and contrasts this view with other conceptions of the human individual: "Hindus and Buddhists . . . do not idealize the separateness of the individual, and have never felt that reality is severely divided into the spiritual and the material, the infinite and the finite, the Creator and the created." Moreover, he notes that the individual defined by science is more of a "pattern of behavior in a field" while the individual defined by ecology is an organism inseparable from its environment (Watts 9).

The concept of the unique, unified self has nevertheless persisted in the Western tradition and is a leading model in the literature and thought of major Western countries. Perhaps the most idealized models of the unique, self-willed self are the tragic heroes and heroines of Goethe's and Schiller's humanistic classicism. Iphigenia, the quintessential humane figure who selflessly heals the vision of her brother Orestes, embodies the heroine whose unselfish actions can right a distraught world.

This Western view of the individual has played an important role in the study of autobiography, because implied in many definitions of autobiography is a unique, integrated, transcultural, transhistorical, and gendered view. Georg Misch's large historical study of autobiography inherently illustrates this. Feminist critics such as Shari Benstock and Susan Stanford Friedman have challenged autobiography critics George Gusdorf and Olney as being proponents of such views, as chapter 8 shows. Thomas Couser notes that autobiography the "literary form, and democracy the political form, [are] most congruent with this idea of a unique and autonomous self" (13). For him, the "idea of individual autonomy in the texts that defined and constituted America implied the legitimacy of autobiographical discourse" (Couser 13). He further notes that when this view of the autonomous "self" comes under attack, the genre of autobiography comes under attack.

Felicity Nussbaum delineates the theoretical problems with the autobiographical subject, as the title of her book, *The Autobiographical Subject: Gender and Ideology in Eighteenth-Century England*, suggests. Nussbaum, a feminist materialist with a debt to new historicism, characterizes the narrow definition of autobiography: "the formal aspects of the genre have been frequently codified as narrative with a beginning, middle, and end which purports to be true, is told retrospectively, and whose author is the same historical being as the first-person narrator and protagonist" (*The Autobiographical Subject* 4). Her definition is based in part on Philippe Lejeune's well-known definition from *Le Pacte autobiographique*, "a retrospective prose narrative produced by a real person concerning his own existence, focusing on his individual life, in particular on the development of his personality" (Nussbaum, *The Autobiograph-*

ical Subject 4, quoting Lejeune). Yet Nussbaum quickly points out the inadequacies of Lejeune's historical assumptions about subjectivity, gender, individuality, essentialism, and a transcultural and transhistorical identity: "Implied within this definition are assumptions of an individuality that is distinct from collective humankind; of the existence of an essence, a personality, which unfolds in the narrative of the past; and of the irrelevance of women's life-writing" (*The Autobiographical Subject* 4).

Nussbaum reveals the inadequacy of definitions based on the Western unique model which fail to encompass autobiographies written by women and suggests that other models are appropriate. Jay, too, in his analyses of autobiographies by dominant men writers as varied as Wordsworth, Joyce, Proust, Carlyle, and Roland Barthes, shows the breakdown of the Western model of self. He details the fragmented and atomized structure of these works written during the nineteenth and twentieth centuries. In general, he postulates that autobiographers in tune with the major literary forms of their time reflect their awareness of the changing concept of subjectivity. The fragmented structures of their works mirror the erosion of the integrated, unified self.

Couser sums up the critical stance of recent autobiography studies by showing that the autobiographical subject has undergone a change from a unique, bounded self to a provisional one. He remarks that this trend has eroded "the distinction between fiction and nonfiction" and has deconstructed "the apparent relation between the self and its textual embodiment":

> Structuralism and post-structuralism . . . suggest that autonomy is found not in individuals but in the working of linguistic codes. Autobiography, then, is seen not as *produced by* a preexistent self but as *producing* a provisional and contingent one. Indeed, that self is seen as bound and (pre)determined by the constraints of the linguistic resources and narrative tropes available to the "author." (Couser 19)

In this view, autobiographers do not render historical selves but create ones shaped by culture.[3]

Many heralded this changing concept of the subject and subjectivity. Jay points to Nietzsche to show how the Western concept of self was transformed philosophically. Nietzsche's *Will to Power* is the "clearest and most relevant philosophical articulation" (Jay 28). Jay argues that Nietzsche's challenging of the theory of the subject has become an "axiom" in "contemporary literary theory":

> [Nietzsche's] central and most crucial assertion is that the psychological subject is not an ontological given that exists before we invent or project it; he holds that the Western tradition of the "self" is just that — a constructed tradition. This "self," recognized as an epistemological construction, clearly for Nietzsche refers not to a natural, privileged, and potentially unified psychological condition, but rather, to a historically constituted set of ideas and assumptions whose referents are complexly dispersed within the very language we must use to think the self into being. (28)

The self we think into being is a product of the language we use to think ourselves into being.

These debates about subjectivity and the philosophical and linguistic subject of autobiography have led critics Michael Sprinker and Elizabeth Bruss to speak of the demise of the genre of autobiography. The traditional subject, the "I," is no longer a self-contained entity but a construct, built from language. The ahistorical self does not really exist (Sprinker 342; Bruss, "Eye for I" 296).

Felicity Nussbaum's essay "Toward Conceptualizing Diary" defines this "human subject constituted by history, language, and culture." In this context the self is not a person or a memory or exactly a fiction but a place of intersecting discourses:

> The poststructuralist concept of the self redefines a self as a position, a *locus* where discourses intersect. We *believe* that the different positions make an autonomous whole, but that *feeling* that we are constant and consistent occurs because of memory. If human subjects attend to inconsistencies and contradictions, the self may seem less self-evident. (Nussbaum, "Conceptualizing" 131–132)

A person's memory provides the continuity which allows a sense of identity. In the poststructural definition, however, this identity is only a "network of symbolic relations," mostly semantic (Steiner 87, quoting Lacan) or an interweaving of discourses. Memory and illusion allow the individual to feel the self to be an "autonomous whole." For the exile, social discontinuity, particularly uprooting experiences and general upheaval, frequently breaks the thread of memory and consciousness and fragments the sense of self.

Olney provides a completely different perspective on the "fiction of the self," for he sees "structuralist, poststructuralist, and deconstructionist" critics still debating about the "self and consciousness":

> I think the direction taken in the performances of structuralist, poststructuralist, and deconstructionist critics is a revealing one, for, however much they talk about genre or linguistics or deeply-lying structures, what they are still troubling about is the self and consciousness or knowledge of it, even though in a kind of bravura way some of them may be denying rather than affirming its reality or its possibility. ("Cultural Moment" 23)

Olney sees the denial of consciousness as part of the task of understanding consciousness.

Eakin makes a good case for the middle ground between the two positions. His complex study, *Touching the World*, sets about the task of reclaiming referentiality for the autobiographical project. In it, drawing on thinkers from many disciplines, he emphasizes the paradoxes in writing autobiography. The self is as much construct as autobiography is, he argues and adds, "When it comes to self, then, autobiography is doubly structured, doubly mediated, a textual metaphor from what is already a metaphor for the subjective reality of consciousness" (Eakin, *Touching the World* 102). For Eakin, the self is both "subject and object":

> ontogenetically considered, the self is already constructed in interaction with the others of its culture before it begins self-consciously in maturity (and specifically in autobiography —

where it exists) to think in terms of models of identity. This is what I mean when I say that the self of an autobiographical text is the construct of a construct, and that culture has exerted a decisive part, through the instrumentality of models of identity, in the process of identity formation, whether literary or psychological. (*Touching the World* 102)

According to Eakin, the self in autobiography is neither absolutely autonomous nor absolutely culturally determined but draws on the tension of the interrelationship of individual and culture. Eakin also notes that memory is the factor which builds self-continuity (*Touching the World* 187–188).

Viewpoint, then, is critical. From the viewpoint of most modern critics, the self no longer exists as a unified, ahistorical being. From the viewpoint of the individual, the author, or the autobiographer, the illusion is mostly intact. Moreover, psychological health is more evident when the individual maintains a sense of psychological continuity, even if that sense of continuity is an illusion. Exiles whose self-continuity is disrupted have strong impulses to reestablish lost psychological continuity. The act of writing an autobiography helps to reestablish the thread of their identities.

Interpreting autobiography as a process that creates the self, then, facilitates understanding the exile's therapeutic motive in writing autobiography. For the autobiographer seeking some unity of consciousness, the act of writing becomes therapy. But for the critic, who readily sees through the autobiographer's illusions, the form becomes amorphous, and its rigid borders blur. In Jay's discussion of the psychological and philosophical problems inherent in the autobiographical project, he notes that the psychological and philosophical "analysis will unfold side by side." He suggests that "the problem of the subject as an ontological construct is always conflated with the problems that the autobiographical subject is seeking to both depict and resolve in his text" (Jay 22).[4] Jay differentiates between the critic concerned with the "changing textual forms for literary self-representation" and the autobiographer concerned with "personal needs that animate the subject who writes about himself" (22).

Autobiography as Therapy

For a better understanding of the therapeutic aspect of exile autobiographical writing, it is important to delve deeper into the psychological motivations for writing exile autobiography. Examining autobiography critics who interpret the process of writing autobiography as therapeutic will be as germane as looking at psychologists who offer theories on the psychology of displaced people.

Jay, who critiques the literary representation of the author's self, nevertheless recognizes the importance of the psychological motivations of the autobiographer. As he notes, "If all writing is a form of self-analysis, then autobiographical writing is probably the most *explicitly* self-analytical" (Jay 25). For him, the self-analysis in autobiographical writing further bears comparison with the "transforming power of [Freud's] talking cure" (Jay 25).[5] Whether writing or talking about the self, the subjects are creating their cures. "The subject's cure is bound up in the ability to participate in generating a creative story in which key recollections are linked to form a therapeutic autobiographical narrative" (Jay 25). He quickly notes, however, that as Freud established in his discussion of the "Wolf Man" case, these "past events recollected in such a process may not in fact be 'events' at all, but, rather, imagined moments in a 'history' being created in and by the act of analysis itself" (Jay 25). What becomes important for autobiographers, particularly those in psychological distress as most exile autobiographers are, is creating the story, not the reality of the story. Creation is a part of their cure. And in this regard we have moved even farther away from the earlier autobiography critics for whom truth was a major criterion for an autobiography.

In "A Healing Art: Therapeutic Dimensions of Autobiography," Marilyn R. Chandler delineates how and why much modern autobiography, particularly twentieth-century autobiography, can be seen as therapeutic. Her reading of autobiographical accounts of the Holocaust in particular led her to this conclusion. She noted how important it was for these autobiographers to tell their stories, to find language to describe the "unspeakable" that they had experienced. Like Jay, she notes that an aim of autobiography "is to effect some kind of healing from past wounds or chronic distress" (Chandler 1). In suggesting how writing autobiography can heal the author's past hurts, she discusses how the medical community uses metaphor in its thinking about diagnosis and cure:

> The terms disease, disorder or breakdown, for instance, each imply slightly different notions of illness. And as any diagnostic metaphor implies a particular notion of disease, so it also implies a particular therapeutic approach — one that will complete the metaphor. So, for instance, if we describe a problem as atrophy, the healing act will be to reconstitute; if imbalance, it will be to restore balance; if deficiency, it will be to supplement; if fragmentation, it will be to reintegrate. (Chandler 6)

Having set up this framework for healing, she illustrates how the writing of autobiography aids this therapeutic process. Chandler suggests that autobiographical strategies "imply particular images of the healing process, i.e., purging, restoring, realigning" (Chandler 6). Basic narrative strategies perform the healing function: "Designing and telling a life story is purgative, reconstructive, integrative, transformative activity. The basic requirements of narrative — pattern, structure, closure, coherence, balance — all engage a writer in crafting a whole out of fragments of experience" (Chandler 6).

For exiles, whose lives become fragmented by the experience of exile, writing an autobiography can begin the healing process. In a sense, the self-story that the exile autobiographer completes may return the sense of wholeness. Chandler asserts that wholeness is "a fundamental principle in organic medicine and a ruling metaphor in psychotherapy" as well as "a formative notion in the construction of personal narratives" (10). The autobiographical writing heals someone in chronic distress by providing generative metaphors and a story that helps establish continuity and wholeness. It is well to remember, however, that this constructed wholeness — the self-story based on fragments of experience — is still an illusion. In this sense, it is more of a therapeutic tool than a reality, as Eakin suggests in his earlier work, *Fictions in Autobiography*.

Eakin describes the autobiographical act as a process in which the author furthers his or her self-definition. Noting his debt to Erik Erikson, Eakin suggests that writing autobiography is an act of "self-creation" and identity formation. Thus he sees writing autobiography as a developmental activity:

> [T]he autobiographical act is revealed as a mode of self-invention that is always practiced first in living and only eventually — sometimes — formalized in writing. I view the rhythms of the autobiographical act as recapitulating the fundamental rhythms of identity formation: in this sense the writing of autobiography emerges as a second acquisition of language, a second coming into being of self, a self-conscious self-consciousness. (Eakin, *Fictions* 8–9)

For Eakin, the act of writing an autobiography continues the developmental process of identity formation: "I would like to propose a more comprehensive conception of the autobiographical act as both a re-enactment and an extension of earlier phases of identity formation" (*Fictions* 226). The writing of an autobiography, then, is "not merely . . . the passive, transparent record of an already completed self but rather . . . an integral and often decisive phase of the drama of self-definition" (Eakin, *Fictions* 226).[6]

Eakin's view acknowledges the psychological benefit of writing autobiography for those who seek integration of self. In delineating the autobiography of exile Saul Friedländer, *When Memory Comes*, Eakin illustrates how pertinent autobiographical writing is for displaced people who have experienced memory gaps, name changes, and loss of cultural identity (*Fictions* 235–255). Redefining the self, or reconstructing the self, as in Friedländer's case, brings the writer closer to a "united consciousness" (Eakin, *Fictions* 238). Psychological integration is paramount to those who have experienced displacement.

Psychological theorists Erik Erikson and Robert J. Lifton further illuminate the psychological dynamic underlying the exile's penchant for writing autobiography. Erikson, himself an exile, sums up the connections of his life history with his theoretical views on the life cycle and identity formation crises in an autobio-

graphical essay "Autobiographic Notes on the Identity Crisis."
For Erikson, who was trained by Freudians (in particular, Anna
Freud), his own life history was important for his evolving psychological theories. First, he had an identity crisis when he learned
that he had been adopted. His parents were Danish, and he had
been adopted by a German-Jewish couple, Dr. and Mrs. Theodore
Homburger. He changed his name to Erikson when he came
to the United States. In addition, his background as a children's
teacher helped him focus on the developmental psychology of
adolescents. Finally, because he had experienced the trauma of
exile himself, including the trauma of learning to write and communicate in a new language, the concept of identity and continuity of self became central to his thinking. In fact, Erikson, in a de-
parture from Freud's emphasis on sexuality, believed that identity
and the crisis of identity, particularly compounded by the upheaval of world events in the thirties and forties, was the most
significant factor of psychology during his era, and thus he felt
that the "study of identity . . . becomes as strategic in our time as
the study of sexuality in Freud's time" (747). As early as 1950 he
wrote, "We began to conceptualize matters of identity at the very
time in history when they became a problem. For we do so in a
country which attempts to make a super-identity out of all the
identities imported by its constituent immigrants" (Erikson 747).
Erikson defines the identity crisis as both psychological and sociological. "It is partially conscious and partially unconscious . . . a
sense of personal continuity and sameness. . . . Throughout life
the establishment and maintenance of that strength which can
reconcile discontinuities and ambiguities depends on the support
first of parental and then of communal models" (Erikson 732). The
psychological development of the individual needs both psychological health and a supportive environment.

In addition to understanding that identity formation has psychosocial implications, Erikson also sees identity formation as historically oriented, which has important ramifications for autobiography. "Life histories," he notes, "are inextricably interwoven
with history" (Erikson 732). Given his own life history as an exile,
this last concept explains why he says of the exile experience that

"[e]migration can be a hard and heartless matter, in terms of what is abandoned in the old country and what is usurped in the new. Migration means cruel survival in identity terms" (Erikson 748).

Robert J. Lifton, a psychological theorist influenced by Erikson, studied the meaning of the term "cruel survival." Lifton writes about the psychology of the survivor in extreme situations, specifically studying the psychology of holocaust and transformation. Like Erikson, much of his theory derives from his clinical training, and like Erikson he focuses on identity and identity conflict. He too sees identity as a psychosocial and a psychohistorical phenomenon. His ideas differ from Erikson in important ways, however, for he not only sees change and continuity as important factors in the psychology of modern life but also believes that the trauma of extreme — life and death — situations is the most salient feature for individual psychology in the modern world. Whereas Erikson saw problems of identity as the major psychological force in his time, Lifton sees the individual's response to death and holocaust as the major force in our time.

Lifton bases his ideas on interviews with survivors of traumatic but transformative events. He has written psychological perspectives about Chinese thought reform, the Chinese Cultural Revolution, Hiroshima survivors, and Vietnam veterans. In interviewing survivors of these holocaust situations, he saw consistent patterns of response and transformation. These boundary situations challenge personal identity, and survivors can have many types of response. A major response important for exiles is a phenomenon Lifton terms "psychic numbing," a form of desensitization, an incapacity to feel or to confront certain kinds of experience. Psychic numbing causes the cessation of what Lifton terms the "formative process." It causes the "impairment of man's essential mental function of symbol formation or symbolization" (Lifton, *The Life* 27). Although Lifton first formulated this concept of psychic numbing during his interviews with survivors of Hiroshima, "[his] assumption is that psychic numbing is central in everyday experience as well, and may be identified whenever there is interference in the 'formative' mental function, the process of creating viable inner forms" (*The Life* 27). Lifton notes that during these periods when the individual feels "one's inner forms and images become inadequate representations of the self-world relationship and inadequate bases for action," then "one comes to feel the self disintegrating" (*The Life* 38). What Lifton identifies here is a phenomenon many exiles have expressed in autobiographical form, as we have seen from Alfred Döblin, Arthur Koestler, and Lion Feuchtwanger. The autobiographical act, cataloging this disintegrating self and creating new strategies for reformulating it, becomes a healing process.

Erikson's concern with problems of identity and Lifton's concern with identity formation and internal symbolization in the face of extremely uprooting situations are crucial to an understanding of the psychology of exiles. Another psychologist, William F. Brewer, lists four attributes that contribute to an individual's "sense of self." "The self is composed of an experiencing ego, a self-schema, and an associated set of personal memories and autobiographical facts" (Brewer 27). Writers and thinkers and, in particular, autobiographers project such a "self." Olney notes, for example, that the "thread of consciousness" connects "the various transformations of self, creating the individual's sense of self" (*Metaphors* 27–28). For exile autobiographers, the self-schema or self-story undergoes cataclysmic transformations, and the ego experiences severe shocks. Sometimes, as in the case of Saul Friedländer, even Olney's "thread of consciousness" is broken. Olney also points out that we, like Heraclitis, cannot step twice into the same stream. Yet there is still "a oneness of self, an integrity or internal harmony that holds together the multiplicity and continual transformations of being" (Olney, *Metaphors* 6). Most exiles seek to recover this feeling of "oneness of self." The autobiographical act speeds that recovery.

Memories of life experiences contribute significantly to the sense of continuity and sameness that constitutes the "sense of self." Interestingly, psychologists in a new field of inquiry, "autobiographical memory," have delineated what autobiographical memory is or is not. They define "personal memory" as a "recollection of a particular episode from an individual's past" (Brewer 34). These are memories that add to the person's self-schema or self-story. These researchers caution that trauma can prevent identification with such autobiographical memories. For example, one researcher explains that a recalled autobiographical memory will not be added "to the person's theory of self or sense of continuity . . . if that recalled memory is not recognized as the person's own" (Rubin 6). Another notes that in recalling memories for the purpose of autobiographical projects, "the person's current self-knowledge and feelings about self [may] mediate the reconstructive process" (Barclay 84). As most autobiography critics have noted, "In this sense, autobiography is an artifact, not based on precise recollections but manufactured to best represent one's contemporary view of self" (Barclay 84). For exile autobiographers, these ideas are important because reconstructing the self-schema or self-story is an overriding motivation for writing. Autobiographical memories are important, but the disrupted context of the events of their memories plays a significant role in how the self is recollected. Certainly Erikson's and Lifton's theories concerning self and identity as well as the insights of psychologists specializing in autobiographical memory show affinities with the patterns of recuperative or transformative selves revealed in exile autobiographies. Many autobiographies such as Friedländer's seem to have been written to demonstrate the reassembling of the self in a new cultural context. Writing an autobiography becomes a way to reconstitute the self. For many exiles, this means trying to reconstitute the self they perceived themselves to be before their exile. In such autobiographies, nostalgic pictures of childhood become powerfully consoling word pictures which allow the authors to reconnect to the past, in a sense to reconnect the memory thread. Nabokov and Canetti, among others, have written such depictions.

For some, however, reconstructing the self before exile becomes problematic because the pre-exilic self may encompass a belief system or worldview no longer valid for the postexilic self. In *Memoirs of an Anti-Semite* and *The Snows of Yesterday*, Gregor von Rezzori writes idyllically of the fading Balkan aristocracy at the end of the Austrian empire, but his depiction of an overriding, destructive anti-Semitism intrudes on his nostalgic tone. Similarly, authors confront problems when remembering and writing about childhood and adolescence from the distance of their modern adult lives. In *Patterns of Childhood*, Christa Wolf conjures up a nostalgic portrait of her youth during the Nazi period yet is hard put to justify her adolescent infatuations with the symbols of Nazism.

The psychological appeal for exiles in looking back to the past, even though it may bring bittersweet pain, is rooted in a feeling of rupture in the present. The exile looks to the past to reconnect to the network of psychological supports — homeland, cultural identity, worldview, native tongue — that he or she knew in a different time. Lifton speaks of "psychohistorical dislocation, and of the breakdown of symbolizations around family, religion, authority in general, and the *rites of passage* of the life cycle" (*The Broken Connection* 296). When "psychohistorical dislocation" occurs, as in the uprooting experiences of exiles, the "problem of formulation" emerges. People in these holocaust situations lose the "capacity to construct the kinds of immediate and ultimate image-feelings that give form to experience" (Lifton, *The Broken Connection* 295–296).

While psychologists like Erikson and Lifton suggest that connections to external cultural supports are necessary for the preservation and continuity of the self, postmodern thinkers such as Foucault and Lacan insist that it is precisely these cultural layers which are the social and political discourses that shape the traditional concept of the self. When these cultural layers are deconstructed in the present, the firm contours of the traditional "I" dissolve. For exiles, however, historical and cultural layers still exert a powerful reality in the mind. Even though exiles may recognize that the past is an illusion, their urge to re-create it does not abate. Joseph Wittlin, a Polish exile writer, comments on the vitality of the past for exiles: "[T]he exile lives in two different times simultaneously, in the present and in the past. This life in the past is sometimes more intense than his life in the present and tyranizes [*sic*] his entire psychology" (105). For the reader, however, the encultured self becomes transparent in exiles' autobiographies, precisely because the reality of the enculturation no longer exists.

Studying exile autobiographies reveals how identity is bound up with culture by demonstrating what happens when a person is compelled to negotiate a new culture. I contend that the autobiographical act plays a significant role in making the transformation necessary to pick up life again. In the following chapters, I will show what strategies exile autobiographers adopt to cope with the catastrophic events in their lives. For most, the autobiographical act helps to heal the disruption in identity that they experience. The strategies they develop, however, can differ radically. The nostalgia for childhood provides solace for Nabokov, Hoffman, Wolf, and Rezzori. Miłosz, Wittold Gombrowicz, Stefan Zweig, and Thomas Mann approach the experience from an intellectual aspect. Mircea Eliade constructs a personal mythology to surmount the experience. For Arthur Koestler, Eliade, and Elias Canetti, the ability to establish identity in a new language structures their response to exile. And finally, Hoffman and Wolf find that the inner language of their historical selves complicates their integration into a new culture. These exile autobiographers cross unanticipated boundaries of identity which cause them to reflect on the meaning and continuity of their lives. Writing down their life stories helps them overcome the injuries of exile.

In *Fictions of the Self*, Eakin points to the profound effect of language when he says that the "power of language to fashion selfhood is . . . life-sustaining, necessary to the conduct of human life as we know it" (191). I would assert that exile autobiography, with its focus on reconstructing the discontinuous self through the written word, is an example of this "life-sustaining" power of language. The self may be illusory, but the illusion is vital psychologically. In the critical debate, then, exile autobiography becomes a form that clarifies, because of its unique nature, the self/language relationship. The exiles sought to reconstruct cultural supports which the modern reader perceives as historically outworn discourses. Yet for exile autobiographers, the illusory selves they create become affirming, life-sustaining metaphors.

chapter six

Childhood and the
Mystery of Origins

[T]he richness of childhood may only be the result of the constant
rethinking we devote to it.
    Christa Wolf, *Patterns of Childhood*

Autobiographical critics have pointed out that childhood
memories and the earliest years of life fascinate autobiographers.
Georges Gusdorf stresses that autobiographers who write about
their childhoods are "exploring an enchanted realm that belongs
to [them] alone" (37). Richard N. Coe argues persuasively that
the autobiography of childhood forms a major division of autobiographical writing. In his study of approximately four hundred
childhood autobiographies, *When the Grass was Taller: Autobiography and the Experience of Childhood*, Coe shows that the mysterious realm of childhood attracts mature writers, particularly
poets, for the "self-as-child is as alien to the adult writer as to the
adult reader"(1). The autobiographer explores the dimensions of
his or her childhood world: "Childhood constitutes an alternative
dimension, which cannot be conveyed by the utilitarian logic of
the responsible adult" (Coe 2). Trying to understand and re-create
that alternative consciousness that was once the author's own becomes a compelling reason to write about it. In addition, trying to
fathom the mysteries of one's origins, family, ancestry, and culture
that made up the backdrop against which childhood was played
out compounds the motivation. Coe found that autobiographies
of childhood increased in those centuries — the eighteenth, nineteenth, and twentieth — in which the concept of childhood and
its importance to society developed. For autobiographers, the
meaning of childhood as a special period of the life cycle became
increasingly important after Rousseau. Coe also argues that the
genre best suits democratic societies. This type of autobiography

"has to be accomplished in a democratic social and cultural climate — whether in the spiritual democracy which constitutes the vision of Christ, or in the sociopolitical democracies whose cornerstones were laid by Rousseau and the French Revolution" (Coe 15). Thus, the genre has become particularly popular in twentieth-century Western literature.

For many exile autobiographers, childhood becomes an important subject, for inevitably the roots of their childhood experiences have been lost to them. For some, nostalgia for this lost anchor overwhelms them, and re-creating their childhood in an autobiography acts as a salve for their wounds. For others, their sincere longing for their lost childhoods causes intense inner scrutiny. Their nostalgia for places now inaccessible or destroyed can also be imbued with feelings of revulsion now that, as adults, they face up to the unpleasant political views that underlay the comforting lifestyle of their early lives. This chapter examines exile autobiographers who have cataloged their childhood memories and who lament the passing of the cultural location of these memories. At the same time, it also examines those autobiographers who wrestle with their nostalgia for a way of life that they now find distressing.

According to Coe, "mere nostalgia" is rarely the motivation for writing childhood autobiography (62). He notes that autobiographers are generally not motivated to recapture their childhood from a sense of paradise lost: "[I]n many cases the urgent need to exorcise a childhood which was *not* paradise, but rather uninterrupted hell, constitutes the overriding motivation" (Coe 67). Nevertheless, those who do feel the world has changed may indeed write to recapture a lost world: "The vision of paradise lost, then, only becomes truly powerful as a motivation when it is given life and intensity by some other force, when it is something more positive than mere regret or homesickness for the unattainable" (Coe 62). Overwhelmingly, exile autobiographers who talk about their childhoods do so with a sense of irretrievable loss even if they recognize their loss as problematic. As Coe suggests, their longing evolves from their sense of disrupted identity in the present. Thus it is a motivation beyond a "mere nostalgia" for the past.

Even so, nostalgia can play a role for childhood autobiographers in general. Coe sees it as providing some authors with inspiration:

> There is, however, . . . one special context in which mere nostalgia can intensify to the point of being a genuine source of inspiration; it is not so much that the child itself, now an adult, has forever outgrown the splendors of the past, but rather that civilization and "progress" have annihilated perhaps totally and irretrievably, an ancient way of life and replaced it with something crude, rootless, and modern. (64)

Exile autobiographers are more readily motivated by this sense of loss, although it is rarely their sole motivation. They exhibit a regret for a way of life that has been obliterated. For some, even the name of their hometown has been changed or the political face of their homeland totally reconfigured. The autobiographer's longing for this lost place allows him or her to create vivid portraits of that early life, now forever past. Michael Seidel has defined an exile as "someone who inhabits one place and remembers or projects the reality of another" (ix). Joseph Wittlin emphasized that psychologically an exile may be living in the past more than in the present. It is as if exile autobiographers need to record those happy childhood experiences; otherwise they, like their childhood homes, will disappear. Indeed, they idealize their childhood memories so completely that the reader can identify this theme as a trope of the lost paradise for exiles.

Vladimir Nabokov demonstrates this trope brilliantly. Known in later decades of the twentieth century as a powerful American novelist, Nabokov was exiled in 1919 with his family from their estate in Russia. Although his autobiography states that his father belonged to the great classless intelligentsia of Russia by choice, in truth he belonged to a very well off, well-educated family who owned numerous estates and houses in St. Petersburg and traveled extensively in Europe and England. In 1919, the privileged Nabokov began his exile when he was eighteen years old. Although his family had to flee their homeland, he and his brother were able to complete their schooling at Cambridge before beginning their odyssey of exile. This novelist who began his career in

Russian, publishing his first works in his native language, later mastered English as the medium of his writing. The course of his exile took him from Russia to England, Germany, France, and finally the United States.

Referring to Nabokov's autobiography, *Speak, Memory*, Eva Hoffman, a later exile, characterizes this "unhoused" poet as the "least marred by rage, or inferiority, or aspiration" and notes that "of all the responses to the condition of exile, his is surely the most triumphant" (198). Indeed, his autobiography may easily be characterized as celebratory. Hoffman speculates that perhaps his "aristocratic freedom" (198) allowed him to concentrate so completely on the sensibilities of his writing subjects, himself as well as the other figures in his autobiography (197). The reader is treated to glimpses of the young Nabokov ensconced in the country estate in Vyra or the townhouse in St. Petersburg, the son of high-born, moneyed people, one of two sons of an estate that took fifty servants to run. According to Nabokov, however, the nostalgic tone of the portrayal of his youth is not the embittered loss of such wealth and privilege but rather the loss of connections to warm childhood memories. "The nostalgia I have been cherishing all these years is a hypertrophied sense of lost childhood, not sorrow for lost banknotes" (73). Like many other émigrés, this aching nostalgia causes Nabokov to paint glistening descriptions of his youth in Russia, that "enchanted realm." In thinking of Vyra, Nabokov wrote: "a sense of security, of well-being, of summer warmth pervades my memory. That robust reality makes a ghost of the present. The mirror brims with brightness; a bumblebee has entered the room and bumps against the ceiling. Everything is as it should be, nothing will ever change, nobody will ever die" (77).

Meditating on Nabokov's *Speak, Memory*, Hoffman considers how nostalgia encapsulates the past for the exile:

> Loss is a magical preservative. Time stops at the point of severance, and no subsequent impressions muddy the picture you have in mind. The house, the garden, the country you have lost remain forever as you remember them. Nostalgia — that most lyrical of feelings — crystallizes around these images like amber.

Arrested within it, the house, the past, is clear, vivid, made more beautiful by the medium in which it is held and by its stillness. (115)

Hoffman aptly describes the way nostalgia motivates many exiles and conditions their tendency to portray scenes of their childhood so expressively. The childhood haunts are not only vivid but also dynamic, sometimes even perfect, but they are frozen moments of time, like a loop of film that plays over and over again for the exile. It doesn't change, it only happens.

These arrested and arresting pictures, however, introduce the reader to an array of comfortable scenes of European family life in the early part of this century. Nabokov portrays Russia, Hoffman Kraków. Saul Friedländer gives us a child's-eye view of Prague in *When Memory Comes* and Susan Groag Bell in *Between Two Worlds* the smaller Czech town of Troppau. Elias Canetti focuses his child's eye on the Sephardic community in Bulgaria, and the Mann brothers, Klaus and Golo, picture the family vacation home at Bad Tölz. In all of these portrayals and more as well, the nostalgic pull of family security, hearth and home, causes these exiles to idealize their childhood memories.

The following passage from *Speak, Memory* illustrates Nabokov's evocative style of writing about memories of his early life.

How utterly foreign to the troubles of the night were those exciting St. Petersburg mornings when the fierce and tender, damp and dazzling arctic spring bundled away broken ice down the sea-bright Neva! It made the roofs shine. It painted the slush in the streets a rich purplish-blue shade which I have never seen anywhere since. On those glorious days *on allait se promener équipage* — the old-world expression current in our set. . . . We drift past the show windows of Fabergé whose mineral monstrosities, jeweled troykas poised on marble ostrich eggs, and the like, highly appreciated by the imperial family, were emblems of grotesque garishness to ours. . . . [A]s I look up I can see, strung on ropes from housefront to housefront high above the street, great tensely smooth, semitransparent banners billowing, the three wide bands — pale red, pale blue, and merely pale — deprived by the sun and the flying cloud-shadows of any too blunt connection with a national holiday, but undoubtedly celebrating now, in the city of memory, the essence of that spring day, the swish of the mud, the beginning of mumps, the ruffled exotic bird with one bloodshot eye on Mademoiselle's hat. (Nabokov 111)

This passage of Vladimir riding through St. Petersburg with his brother and governess, the beloved Mademoiselle, fairly sparkles with light. It is almost as if he sees through crystal, for everything shines brightly in the crisp air of winter. The picture is both lush and dynamic. There is a rush of movement, the plushness of luxury, the bright, crystal-like winter morning, and the winter pale but shining colors. It is a picture that carries the authority of wealth and prestige.

This shining picture contrasts significantly with his later description of life as an exile in Berlin.

As I look back at those years of exile, I see myself, and thousands of other Russians, leading an odd but by no means unpleasant existence, in material indigence and intellectual luxury, among perfectly unimportant strangers, spectral Germans and Frenchmen in whose more or less illusory cities we, émigrés, happened to dwell. These aborigines were to the mind's eye as flat and transparent as figures cut out of cellophane, and although we used their gadgets, applauded their clowns, picked their roadside plums and apples, no real communication, of the rich human sort so widespread in our own midst, existed between us and them. It seemed at the time that we ignored them the way an arrogant or very stupid invader ignores a formless and faceless mass of natives; but occasionally, quite often in fact, the spectral world through which we serenely paraded our sores and our arts would produce a kind of awful convulsion and show us who was the discarnate captive and who the true lord. Our utter physical dependence on this or that nation, which had coldly granted us political refuge, became painfully evident when some trashy "visa," some diabolical "identity card" had to be obtained or prolonged. (Nabokov 276)

In addition to describing one of the banes of exile life, the dreaded bureaucracies of "host" countries, this passage pales beside the previous, light-drenched description. Using imagery that calls to mind the arrogance of colonialism, Nabokov conveys a life where the "host" country's peoples simply did not exist for the exile Russians. They were only background for the lively community of the exiles. In contrast to the brilliance of the previous passage, this passage is drained of color. The spirited life of the exile community exists offstage. Nabokov does not portray it as he had done above; rather, he portrays the tight-knit community of exiles existing in a shadow world of unreality until the real world breaks through their self-deceiving facade.

Hoffman, too, exhibits such a contrast between her native city, Kraków, and her new city in exile, Vancouver, Canada.

> Cracow to me is a city of shimmering light and shadow, with the shadow only adding more brilliance to the patches of wind and sun. I walk its streets in a state of musing, anticipatory pleasure. Its narrow byways, its echoing courtyards, its jewel-like interiors are there for my delectation; they are there for me to get to know. The quiet street that takes me to my music teacher's is nearly always empty and almost strange in its placidity. It's as if no one lived here, as if time stopped serenely and without fuss; but then, a breeze blows, making the sky clear, and the street is enveloped in warmth. In the park where I play with my friends, there are winding paths that let us out onto the wider, more lucid avenues, and a weeping willow by the pond that is just about the most graceful thing I know: it's so melancholy, and melancholy is synonymous with beautiful. My friends and I play near that tree, jumping rope or drawing in the sand. (38–39)

For Hoffman, Kraków is still the present where she plays, runs, and discovers the city. The city shimmers, jewel-like, but is also tinged with shadows. It is full of secrets and intrigues the child Eva, but it also gives up these mysteries. Interestingly enough, the city also responds to her emotional makeup. Melancholy, a positive emotion for her, is symbolized by the beautiful willow tree that weeps over the pond in the park.

In contrast to her description of Kraków, where she is a little girl at home in its twists and turns, Hoffman responds to the houses of Vancouver with an emotional flatness: "To me, these interiors seem oddly flat, devoid of imagination, ingenuous. The spaces are so plain, low-ceilinged, obvious; there are no curves, niches, odd angles, nooks or crannies — nothing that gathers a house into itself, giving it a sense of privacy, or of depth — of interiority" (102). This passage makes it even clearer that she found the city of Kraków and its interesting old homes synonymous with her own interiority. She is now undergoing a psychic numbing as Lifton has defined; the different style of city and houses plays into this flattening of experience for her.

What is most interesting in the juxtaposition of these two exile autobiographers is the similarity of emotion and feeling that they expressed despite the vast difference between their experiences. Nabokov's primary exilic experience arose following the Russian Revolution. He was born in 1899 and began his exile in 1917 when he was eighteen. He was accompanied into exile by his family, and although his family suffered financial setbacks, the exile did not disrupt his schooling in England. Hoffman, in contrast, was born in Poland during World War II, the daughter of two lower-middle-class Jews who survived the war by hiding and still later emigrated from Poland in 1959. Hoffman was thirteen years old when she sailed to Canada. The similarity of the two exiles' emotional experience overcomes the diversity of their backgrounds.

Nor does age dim these early pristine images. Nabokov published the first version of his autobiography in 1951 at the age of fifty-two and revised it in 1960 at sixty-one. Hoffman published *Lost in Translation* in 1989, in her forties. Canetti, who started publishing his detailed, three-volume autobiography in the 1980s during his seventies, began the first volume, *The Tongue Set Free*, with a vivid portrayal of his earliest memories in the family compound in Ruschuk, Bulgaria. Klaus Mann, Thomas Mann's oldest son, published his major exile autobiography, *The Turning Point*, in

1942, when he was thirty-five. Golo, his younger brother by two years, published the German version of his autobiography, *Reminiscences and Reflections* (1990), in 1986, when he was seventy-seven. Despite their different ages when they conceived their autobiographies, both brothers drew poignant word pictures of some of their happiest childhood episodes. Klaus Mann idealized the family retreat in Bad Tölz:

> We have a house in Tölz and a spacious garden where many games can be played that couldn't be played elsewhere. The days of immutable brightness are long. . . . Tölz is the heart and kernel of the childhood myth, but its reality has become rather flimsy. I have not entered the house since the day we left it. Of course I still remember the arrangements of the rooms, the shape and color of the furniture, the magnificent view from the terrace. But all details are blurred and transfigured, too intensely imbued with nostalgia and dread. (17–18)

And yet, not all was blurred. The following vivid description of this childhood paradise suggests Mann's intense emotional investment in that former life:

> Paradise is imbued with the bitter-sweet fragrance of conifer, tonic herbs, and raspberries, fused with the scent of moss that has become warm in the sun — the vast, powerful sun of a summer day in Tölz. The clearing where we spend the morning picking berries lies in the midst of a stately forest, the beautiful wood of fir trees which commences right behind our house. This is by no means a forest among others of a similar kind, but *the forest — matchless, mythic*, representative, with its solemn twilight, its smells and noises, the perfect formations of its mushrooms, and shrubs, its squirrels, rocks, rivulets, and unassuming flowers. (23–24)

Here Klaus Mann uses many motifs which can be seen as clichés of exilic nostalgia for childhood — the lost paradise, the recollections of physical surroundings imbued with an exaggerated sense of light, smells, and textures. Even if he consciously mythologizes the image, connecting it as he does to the trope of the German

Romantic forest, the intensity of his yearning for this petrified picture strikes the reader as real.

Because of World War I and the ensuing food and money shortages, the Manns gave up this vacation house in 1917. Golo Mann describes their last day there:

> On the last day Klaus and I strolled through the garden one more time, bidding farewell to all those familiar things — the "hut," a shed for garden implements and such, where we had often played, our wading pool, and the four chestnuts under which we had breakfast in the summertime. It was our first farewell; Klaus was ten, I eight. (31–32)

While Golo Mann's reminiscence is certainly not as effusive as his brother's, it is nevertheless clear that his yearning for this place in their childhood is just as strong.

Elias Canetti, too, cherishes his earliest memories. The first section of Canetti's *The Tongue Set Free* plays out his early adventures and terrors, typical childhood autobiographical themes, against the exotic backdrop of his hometown of Ruschuk, Bulgaria. His memories of the different ethnic groups allow him to paint an interesting and diverse locale. In this town teeming with the languages and mores of people from a variety of ethnic backgrounds, Canetti begins to sort out the community meaning of the different groups. He distinguishes the assumed superiority of the Sephardic Jews to other Jews. The Sephardic Jews had immigrated to this area centuries before but preserved their Spanish heritage in their attitudes and their language, Ladino. "With naive arrogance, the Sephardim looked down on other Jews; a word always charged with scorn was *Todesco*, meaning a German or Ashkenazi Jew" (Canetti, *Tongue* 5). He points out that he was only six when his grandfather warned him against marrying such a Jew. He writes, too, about the Gypsies coming every Friday to the family compound for food and wood. These people who moved in a group, "huddling so close together" and wearing colorful rags as clothing, fascinated young Canetti even though he feared them (Canetti, *Tongue* 13). He learned the ways of the Bulgarian peasant girls from the ones who babysat him. There was also the Turkish influence in the region and even in his family. He gives a memorable picture of his Grandmother Canetti, who "remained most Turkish": "She never got up from her divan, I don't even know how she ever got there, for I never saw her walking, and she would sigh from time to time and drink another cup of coffee and smoke. She would greet me with a lamenting tone and, having said nothing to me, she let me go, lamenting" (Canetti, *Tongue* 16, 17).

Canetti was six when his family moved to England and from there to Austria and Switzerland after his father's early death. He returned to his birthplace, Ruschuk, only for brief visits in the ensuing years. But even though he spent only a few years as a young child in this setting, the scenes of the Arditti and Canetti families in Ruschuk stand out in his long autobiography.

Saul Friedländer and Susan Groag Bell both write of their early childhood in assimilated, middle-class Jewish families in Czechoslovakia. For both, recognition of their Jewishness dawned when Hitler's policies began to encroach on their comfortable childhood worlds. Friedländer, only five when his parents fled to France, was astonished as an adult to realize that images of the Prague he left behind still reverberated powerfully for him:

> Whether I consciously remember it or not, I caught all the signs of this city: the most insignificant baroque town still immediately arouses in me a powerful echo that can only come from these childhood impressions. Isolated images, but precious ones, nonetheless: of streets and shop windows lighted up for the year-end festivities, the feast of Saint Nicholas, Christmas of course, and New Year's. (17)

He writes of days on walks in the city and in the parks with his nursemaid and other excursions with his parents. Later, after he moves to Israel with its exotic landscape, he recognizes that the landscape of his early childhood, "hedgerows and fields, coulds, dead leaves — and crows as well," is the one most to his liking (Friedländer 99). In speaking of childhood landscapes, Hoffman echoes Friedländer's sentiments:

It [her Polish childhood] has fed me language, perceptions, sounds, the human kind. It has given me the colors and the furrows of reality, my first loves. The absoluteness of those loves can never be recaptured: no geometry of the landscape, no haze in the air, will live in us as intensely as the landscapes that we saw as the first, and to which we gave ourselves wholly, without reservations. (74–75)

Susan Groag Bell left Troppau (Opava), her small, provincial hometown in Czechoslovakia, when she was twelve years old. She left with her mother for England in 1938. Her father, an attorney, planned also to emigrate but waited too late and was sent to a concentration camp, where he died. Bell remembers a leisured, cultured lifestyle of comfortable and sometimes luxurious apartments. She recounts years of a contented life with her mother of shopping, going to the dressmaker's, having afternoon tea frequently with her mother's friends, enjoying elegant meals, or looking forward to various sojourns with her mother to area spas and even trips to the capital of culture, Vienna. Perhaps the following passage best gives the rhythm of her family's lifestyle in Troppau: "While my father and I used to sit at the small table in the bay in front of the drawing room balcony, he drinking his breakfast coffee and I my chocolate, my mother breakfasted in bed. Afterwards, when he had left for his law office in the Wagnergasse, my mother consulted the cook about the meals for the next two days" (Bell 13–14). This bourgeois pattern of life abruptly ended for her family when Hitler invaded the Sudetenland. In England, her mother at first entered domestic service but later became a tax auditor, making her own living for over thirty years.

Others write with equal fondness and affection for their early childhood homes. Georg Grosz in *A Little Yes and a Big No* catalogs his early years in Pomerania, where his parents ran a hotel. Jacov Lind in *Counting My Steps* recounts his childhood years in his parents' lower-class home in Vienna. Frederic Zeller in *When Time Ran Out: Coming of Age in the Third Reich* describes his painful years as the son of lower-class Jewish parents in Berlin in the thirties. Friedländer suggests that these cherished memories shine a light beyond the darkness of exile:

> For each of us who lived through the events of this period as children there is an impassable line of cleavage somewhere in our memories: what is on this side, close to our time, remains dark, and what is on the other side has the intense brightness of a happy dawn — even if our powers of reason and our knowledge point to obvious links between the two periods. When one looks back to the other side of the line an irrepressible nostalgia remains. (33–34)

The nostalgic yearning for these precious, crystallized moments demands the attention of the adult childhood autobiographer. These encapsulated moments of childhood must be immortalized through writing. Friedländer, as we shall see in chapter 10, used such memories of treasured moments to recapture an identity he had all but lost: "I must write, then. Writing retraces the contours of the past with a possible less ephemeral stroke than the others, it does at least preserve a presence, and it enables one to tell about a child who saw one world founder and another reborn" (135).

For these autobiographers, the world of childhood preserves a magical world where light shone at its brightest. Reconstructing this world through words is a comforting and healing process for writers who have undergone psychological distress. For Friedländer, Nabokov, Bell, Hoffman, the Mann brothers, and others, the childhood world remains the essence of paradise for the adult writer. Those autobiographers for whom the pull of nostalgia is as strong and the pictures of childhood as vivid recognize that the individual world these isolated childhood pictures describe is part of a larger world undesirable to them as adults. Gregor von Rezzori and Christa Wolf are two excellent examples of autobiographers whose happy childhoods were part of lifeways that ideologically are less appealing to them in their later lives.

Gregor von Rezzori, seventy-seven when he published his autobiography, *The Snows of Yesteryear*, describes his birthplace and childhood home in an ironic passage in which he catalogs the vicissitudes of Czernowitz, almost a city in exile, in a region known as the Bukovina:

> Czernowitz, where I was born, was the former capital of the former duchy of Bukovina, an easterly region of Carpathian forestland in the foothills of the Tatra Mountains, in 1775 ceded by the former Ottoman Empire to the former Imperial and Royal Austro-Hungarian realm as compensation for the latter's mediation in the Russo-Turkish War; the Bukovina was at first allocated to the former kingdom of Galicia, but after 1848 it became one of the autonomous former crown lands of the House of Habsburg. (275)

Indeed, the above quote only tells part of the story of this city and region. After the fall of the Austrian Empire at the end of World War I, Czernowitz and the Bukovina became part of Romania until the end of the Second World War, when they became part of the Ukraine, a period Rezzori refers to as the "Rumanian interlude . . . hardly more than a fresh costume change in a setting worthy of operetta" (*Snows* 276). The city's name was changed from Czernowitz to Cernauti to Chernovtsy. After the breakup of the Soviet Russia, it underwent further changes.

Rezzori's Austrian parents were in the Bukovina as colonials of the Austrian Empire and chose to remain there when it became the possession of the Romanian monarchy. Growing up on an estate outside of Czernowitz, Rezzori thought of himself as an Austrian, even though the Austrian Empire had already been dissolved by the time he was four: "That the Austro-Hungarian monarchy has not existed since 1918 is well enough known, yet in Czernowitz-Cernauti, people acted as if they didn't quite believe it. German remained the everyday language of most people, Vienna was the closest metropolis, and no one thought of denying it the rank of capital" (*Snows* 275–276). His family returned to the estate in 1918 at the end of World War I, having fled to Austria to escape the war. They remained as the elite in the region even though their political power base, the Austrian Empire, had disappeared after the end of World War I. Rezzori suggests that his family deluded themselves by staying in the Bukovina merely because of their reputation in the area:

> My family's fictions were only too transparent: we lived the years 1919–1939 in the illusion of having a pseudo-feudal position in the world; this was based neither on prestige enjoyed in an existing society nor on wealth, but merely on the position my parents and particularly my grandparents had held before the First World War. (*Snows* 35)

Furthermore, his family, like others in this region, never faced up to their loss. "Today [people] speak of the Bukovina as if it were still a political entity even though it disappeared as such in 1940" (Rezzori, *Snows* 276). Nevertheless, for Rezzori this place that no longer exists and didn't exist, even while he was there, as his family believed it to is still the treasured world of his childhood. Rezzori admits that now he is reluctant to divulge his place of origin, primarily because of "three score and fifteen years of [his] earthly existence" only the first ten years of his life were spent in the Bukovina. He also regrets that Czernowitz had a reputation for certain types of behavior, specifically as the setting of most Galician-Jewish jokes and as the breeding ground of an unmistakable type of individual, the "Slavienese" rapscallions (Rezzori, *Snows* 277). In time, the reality of his younger life receded because it was only accessible in memory. The "erstwhileness" and "irreality" of his origins began to alienate him. "It began to sound to me as if I had invented Czernowitz — and with it, myself" (Rezzori, *Snows* 277).

Rezzori tells the story of his childhood through five people who helped to shape it — his nursemaid, Cassandra; his mother; his father; his sister; and his governess and teacher, Bunchy. Some autobiographers tell the stories of their lives through portraits of others. This is particularly true of women, as Mary G. Mason delineates in "The Other Voice: Autobiographies of Women Writers." Rezzori's use of the form, however, seems to be a way of distancing himself from his early memories. He characterizes himself as a detached person without a strong inner emotional life: "There were few emotions, however stormy their inception, that did not quickly perish in the cool climate of my inner self" (Rezzori, *Snows* 249). He sees himself as standing apart, commenting on his rather eccentric family. This form of autobiography, where the principal is only incidentally displayed in the portraits of others, suits his iconoclastic persona in the autobiography.

In some respects, *The Snows of Yesteryear* more clearly represents the childhood autobiographies that Coe describes. Childhood autobiographers more consistently depict painful childhoods in dysfunctional families instead of idyllic childhoods. Although Rezzori, like other exile autobiographers, introduces the theme of paradisiacal childhood, he describes these moments as only a brief and welcome interlude in the otherwise rancorous interactions of his family. Rezzori was born in 1914, the eve of the First World War. Fleeing from possible Russian interference in the Bukovina, the family found refuge in a region near Trieste and later in southern Austria. When the war ended and they returned to Czernowitz, the real idyll of his childhood began. But this childhood idyll is overshadowed by his estranged family. At age ten he was sent to boarding school when his mismatched parents finally separated. They subsequently divorced. For Rezzori, the breakup and dissolution of his family presaged the breakup of the European world: "By 1925 we were already what later hundreds of thousands of Europeans were to become: refugees, exiles, leaves tossed by the storms of history" (*Snows* 16).

This feeling of exile that he experienced as a child was intensified by the status of the family within a changing political scene:

[W]e did not belong to Romania, which had surrendered to its Balkanization and was therefore part of the East. It was the year 1922; Europe was not yet divided, as it was to be after 1945, yet even then we felt definitely and consciously that we were "occidentals." That this would make us doubly homeless we were to experience later on, when we moved to the West and in many respects felt like Easterners there, felt this even more acutely at a later date, when our homeland irrevocably became part of an East that was fundamentally and ideologically separated from our own world. The disintegration of our parental home preceded by two decades the disintegration of Europe. (Rezzori, *Snows* 49)

In this confused and confusing shadowland of family rift and tension and uncertain *patria*, the young boy found a comforting world of home and landscape. He describes "the melancholy spaces of a landscape peopled with peasants and shepherds through which the silver band of a river meanders lazily, edged by hills and mountains shaded by forests" (Rezzori, *Snows* 42). Once again the mirror of memory captures the sunlit childhood refuge in the ensuing pictures: "My memory places the house in a garden where beeches, birches and ash trees convey great airiness and luminosity" (Rezzori, *Snows* 79). Returning home after being at boarding school, he quickly realizes a "shrinking of dimensions attendant upon any comparison between mythicized and factual past" concerning his family home. "During my childhood these rooms had embodied all the spaciousness and glamour of the entire world" (Rezzori, *Snows* 79). His nostalgia for this childhood paradise "transposes this house into the perennial sunshine of a Bonnard painting" (Rezzori, *Snows* 80). Likewise, his memories of the nursery fill him "with a sensation of freshness and luminosity, a fastidious cleanliness and restful quiet, broken only occasionally by happy or belligerent noise, a combined sensation which even today represents for me the incarnation of all desirable well-being" (Rezzori, *Snows* 95).

These nostalgic pictures of a contented childhood are only islands within his world of a maddeningly dysfunctional family. He characterizes his mother as pathological and states that she directed much of her pathology onto her children. Thus he and his sister, already being raised in a convoluted political situation, were isolated and not allowed to interact with local Romanian children. At the same time, they were at the mercy of their mother's pathological directives. The limits of Rezzori's world stopped at the boundaries of the family estate. In retrospect, too, his life was further complicated by his father, a rather detached observer who spent much of his life away from the family. His father, a man who liked to destroy the illusions of others, played many scenes for the sake of the grotesque and was among other things intensely anti-Semitic. For the adult Rezzori, this anti-Semitism throws a distressing veil of concern over these favorite childhood scenes. He refers to his father's overriding anti-Semitism as "outright pathological" and articulates his mortification from his father's anti-Semitic words and actions (Rezzori, *Snows* 165–167). He also conveys the insidiousness of anti-Semitic beliefs and actions and their internalization in the society of the German community in the Bukovina in his autobiographical novel *Memoirs of an Anti-Semite*, as the title alone suggests.

In his very early years, Rezzori spent his time under the care of his nursemaid, a bizarre but affecting character whose mixed ethnic background expanded his horizons. His only playmate was his sister. Like Friedländer, the landscape became engraved on his memory, as did the petrified visions of some of his childhood memories. But the tensions of his family life and the politics of his family's lifestyle alienated him. After his parents' separation when he was ten, he attended boarding school, a singularly depressing experience for him. Very early, he recognized that his own feeling of being an Austrian was not the view of his Austrian schoolmates. They saw him as an "occidental" oddity, characterizing him as a "Balkanic gypsy from the remotest southeastern backwoods" (Rezzori, *Snows* 220).

Rezzori's alienation made him an exile long before his mother and her second husband physically had to leave the Bukovina as "repatriated Germans" under Hitler. Recognizing the class distinctions his family harbored, he sees in their disintegrating way of life a reflection of European catastrophes. In the retrospective view of the autobiographer, he dissects the consequences of these changes:

For the class to which my parents belonged, this meant a fall into chaos, into impotence and deprivation, hopelessness and squalor. What today is designated by the collective noun *bourgeoisie* lived with an imperturbable faith in what Robert Musil's Count Leinsdorff called "property and learning." All the trust in life that these two pillars had supported collapsed together with them. The resulting changes in reality were so sudden, unpredicted and incomprehensible that at first they seemed more like a monstrous nightmare. The desire to wake from the bad dream gave rise to the utopia of the 1920s, one of the worst byproducts of which was to be the Third Reich. But most people remained stunned and paralyzed: sleepwalkers in an alienated present. (Rezzori, *Snows* 64)

Showing great sympathy for the changes brought to his family as members of the bourgeoisie, he also recognizes the false class consciousness of his parents. He marks the end of his childhood with an incident during which he began to see his nursemaid, Cassandra, his "brood-warm" protector, the same way his "bourgeois" parents did:

We still lived in a time in which an almost unbridgeable gulf gaped between the so-called educated classes and the so-called common people. My family's situation, based on the abstract image of a once privileged position — mainly the myth of former wealth, which encouraged us to live beyond our true means and to indulge in expensive habits we could no longer afford — placed us absurdly far above the "common people," who, for the most part, lived in abject poverty, a poverty borne humbly and with eyes raised in admiration to their "masters." For the first time I thought of Cassandra as belonging not to my own lineage but to that other race of the poor, the know-nothing and the lowly. At the same time, there awoke in me a sense of the social pecking order. (Rezzori, *Snows* 40–41)

Categorizing his family as the "flotsam of the European class struggle, which is what the two great wars really were," Rezzori tries to put into perspective his "childhood . . . spent among slightly mad and dislocated personalities in a period that also was mad and dislocated" (*Snows* 200).

In her impressive autobiographical novel, *Patterns of Childhood*, Christa Wolf, like Rezzori, strives to reconcile her childhood during the Third Reich with her modern sensibilities. Wolf is generally not considered an exile writer since she remained in East

Germany and became one of Germany's late-twentieth-century representative writers. I am including her in this study because as a young girl she experienced the same alienation and uprooting brought on by social upheaval as all other exiles. While *Patterns of Childhood* addresses her guilt in regard to her childhood under Nazism, a common theme among postwar German writers, it also addresses the psychic ramifications of losing a belief system and a geographic homeland, bringing about "psychic numbing," which I explore further in chapter 10. Written in 1972, when Wolf was forty-three, this complex autobiographical novel delineates Wolf's crises of consciousness following her childhood and refugee experiences.[1] In the voice of the narrator/autobiographer, she carefully reveals her childhood self — a self she has for the most part relegated to the deep recesses of her mind, for the treasured memories and the comforting associations of the child within her carry overtones of ideological beliefs inimical to her in the present.

In an early short story by Wolf entitled "Change of Perspective" the young heroine, a girl of about sixteen, is moving with her family on their trek from their abandoned homeland to the promise of a better life in the West at the end of World War II. Enduring the deprivations that this trek brought for millions of refugees from the East, this young girl, along with her family, is "liberated" by American soldiers, portrayed stereotypically as naive and ingenuous. She doesn't want to be liberated, however, and can't understand why the American soldiers want her to be so happy. She is not happy losing her identity, an identity formed in Hitler-dominated Germany.

Patterns of Childhood, its title first translated as *A Model Childhood*, dissects Wolf's childhood and teen years, which are inextricably bound up with the ideology of the Third Reich. When the war ended, the heroine of this work, Nelly, like Wolf, does not want to be liberated by any of the Allied troops that she ends up living under — American, British, or Russian. The narrator of this intricate autobiographical novel speaks in the second as well as the third person, making it her task to become acquainted with this young girl, Nelly. In denial, she has closed off the memories of herself as the child Nelly. The narrator/autobiographer now disapproves of many of the events in her childhood which are a part of Nelly's fond memories. Allowing Nelly to drag them out becomes a painful yet bittersweet experience.

Because Nelly's nostalgia is filtered through the censoring mind of the narrator, her portrayal of childhood memories is more muted than some I have already discussed. Wolf as the autobiographer generally does not describe Nelly's memories with the exaggerated luminosity of Nabokov, Hoffman, and even Rezzori. But as the narrator notes defensively to her teenage daughter Lenka, Nelly's childhood was a "normal and happy" one. Nelly grew up in Landsberg an der Warthe (Gorzów Wielkopolski, Poland) during the years of the Third Reich. Her ordinary youthful experiences — childhood fears, school, after-school activities, and a teenage crush on her teacher — are irrevocably intertwined with the events and attitudes of those years. What was pleasing and normal for Nelly, however, sometimes causes the narrator to shudder. Nelly idolized one of her early teachers, Herr Warsinski, and her memories of him and thus the memories of the narrator are intact:

> Nelly loves Herr Warsinski. Undamaged, he rests in her memory in different poses. He enters on command. His face and chest. A wart on the left side of his chin, full, not to say flabby, cheeks: a strand of ash-blond hair sweeps over his right eye, which is watery-colorless. Or his entire figure: in that case usually walking, with a slightly dragging left leg. Speaking: May we have silence, please! And I mean right now! Where do you think you are, in a Jew school! With or without his brown uniform, with or without his belt support across a slight paunch. Anyone who lets me down when we salute the flag is really going to get it. Our Führer works day and night for us and you can't even keep your traps shut for ten minutes. (Wolf, *Patterns* 98)

Ordinary, everyday events — a teacher calling an elementary class to order — included the propaganda of the period and cause the adult narrator, who now lives with the recognition of that reality, to reconsider such scenes. Part of the motivation for writing this work for the narrator, then, as we shall see more completely in chapter 10, is to try and place this "happy, normal" childhood of the Nazi period into some kind of perspective. Like so many Germans, her past is now very painful for her, but it is her past, and she must reconcile the good with the bad.

Nelly grew up in a petit bourgeois family who kept a store in Landsberg an der Warthe, Germany — an ordinary German city in the eastern part of the Reich. Now, however, this city has become Gorzów Wielkopolski, a Polish city. When Nelly and her family were forced to flee their home, Nelly began to succumb to the slowly dawning recognition that her belief in the Führer and her faith in the Hitler Youth were misplaced. As she grew older, some of her most attractive memories of childhood and her teenage years become tainted with the demeaning policies of the period.

Nelly, for example, adored the Führer, even if those around her, her mother in particular, occasionally disparaged him openly.[2] She gladly participated in the widespread celebrations on the Führer's birthday or on other festive occasions. At fifteen, she was a vibrant part of the Hitler Youth and vividly remembers their marches and gatherings. Interestingly, the narrator remembers the crowd images but can't remember the faces of her friends in the movement:

> Only group or crowd images seem to have been remarkable. Marching columns. Rhythmic mass exercises in the stadium. Halls filled with people singing: Sacred Fatherland, when dangers abound / your sons surround / you, sacred fatherland . . . A circle around a campfire. Another song: Rise, O flames; again no faces. A giant rectangle in the market square, made up of Hitler Youth, boys and girls; they stand in formation, an assassination attempt has been made on the Führer. Not a single face. (Wolf, *Patterns* 229)

Nelly never saw the Führer in person, but when she was five she joined her family and neighbors waiting to see him in Landsberg an der Warthe. He ended up not coming, because "fellow Germans in other towns and villages had been altogether too enthusiastic over him":

> It would be interesting to find out how the five-year-old Nelly did not only know, but felt what the Führer was. The Führer

was a sweet pressure in the stomach areas and a sweet lump in the throat, which she had to clear to call out for him, the Führer, in a loud voice in unison with all the others, according to the urgings of a patrolling sound truck. The same truck which would also broadcast where the Führer's automobile would arrive. The people bought beer and lemonade at the corner saloon, shouted, sang, and obeyed the orders of the restraining police and SA cordons. They stopped and stood patiently. Nelly could neither understand nor remember what was being talked about, but she took in the melody of the mighty chorus, whose many single shouts were building up toward the gigantic roar into which they were meant to break, finally, in a display of powerful unity. Although it frightened her a little, she was at the same time longing to hear the roar, to be a part of it. She longed to know how it felt to be at one with all, to see the Führer. (Wolf, *Patterns* 45)

One of her most enchanting memories as a young girl was the Hitler Youth garrison's celebration of the summer solstice. In this passage the narrator separates her memories from the research she has done preparing for the book:

Nelly stood on that July night, leaning against her mother, when the Hitler Youth garrison celebrated the summer solstice. Strings of torches along the edges of all the hills, a woodpile suddenly blazing up, and the cry from many throats: "Germany, thou holy word / Full of infinity." (The information about the sequence of events was obtained from the 1936 volume of the *General-Anzeiger* [town newspaper] in the State Library; the images — "Strings of torches," "blazing woodpile — " come from memory.) The motto of the festive hour was: "We want to glow, so that by our deeds we may give warmth to future generations." . . . When Nelly got cold, her mother wrapped her in her own warm jacket. At the end she cried with exhaustion because "it was just too much for her." Otherwise she rarely cried. A German girl does not cry. (Wolf, *Patterns* 130)

The impressionable young Nelly always took to heart the admonitions of the Nazis.

Most of the time, Nelly's childhood flowed normally. She fought with her brother, played with dolls, went through the collection mania — photograph or autograph albums. The narrator tells her daughter, we wrote the same things in autograph albums as you do. "Steel and iron will rust and bend, but our friendship will never end!" her daughter retorts (Wolf, *Patterns* 180). But the narrator notes that they also put quotations from the Führer in their books as well. "Whoever wants to live must fight. Anyone who refuses to fight in this world of never-ending struggle does not deserve to live!" (Wolf, *Patterns* 181).

At times, the ordinary events of Nelly's life became extraordinary. As she grew older, she got a crush on her teacher, as teenage girls frequently do. Her idol, Dr. Juliane Strauch, extolled the "ideal German woman" to Nelly and her friends, encouraging them to support the Führer and his policies without reservation. Juliane herself, however, had "black hair and markedly Slavic features, which the biology books defined as 'flat,'" the narrator notes (Wolf, *Patterns* 220–221). And Nelly, like other Germans who lived through this period, learned to cope with the injured soldiers whom she visited in the hospital and the Ukrainian women workers to whom she took presents for Christmas. She collected tin foil and participated in the dreaded herb collections, picking yarrow, St. John's bread, and chamomile to dry in the attic. She tried to understand her aunt's concern about her aunt's retarded twin sister, Aunt Dottie, who disappeared, a victim of Hitler's "*euthanasia program*," of those "unfit for life" (Wolf, *Patterns* 196–197, italics mine). She learned early that she didn't want to be Jewish. But to Nelly, her life was normal.

Nelly's life did change, of course, when the family had to leave their home in Landsberg an der Warthe. At the end of January 1945, they became refugees and trekked westward for almost a year. Nelly succumbed to tuberculosis and was sent to a sanatorium in the north of Germany. She finally left the sanatorium in 1946.

Nelly's childhood memories force the narrator to confront her past and her adult guilt. As a child and teenager, Nelly stubbornly held to her beliefs. The narrator's childhood memories, however, are a reminder to the reader of how pervasive ideological precepts spread within a society.

Frederic Zeller, writing about his own childhood as a Jew in Berlin, notes that brand new games arose after the rise of Nazism:

> A complete change from Cowboys and Indians, or Hide and Seek. We played Communists, Nazis, and Social Democrats. We addressed "mass meetings" through funnel-shaped, rolled-up newspaper, resembling the mechanical megaphones used by agitators in those pre-electronic days. We strutted up and down and gave fist or raised-arm Nazi salutes. The Social Democrats were out of luck, nobody volunteered to play those, they had no salute. We yelled party slogans at each other, staged street battles complete with "police" who rushed in with water hoses. (15)

He also describes the day a truckload of SA storm troopers made it snow in summer. The uniformed men "threw lumps into the air that burst apart and snow came down" (Zeller 14). Running behind the truck like the rest of the kids, "squealing in the white blizzard," he found that they were made up of "thousands of white swastikas, stamped out of very thin paper, each half a finger long" (Zeller 14). He was very disgruntled when his mother made him get rid of his "neat white swastikas" (Zeller 15).

In the beginning chapter of *Patterns of Childhood*, Wolf lets the reader know that she considers herself to be on trial:

> It is interesting that we either fictionalize or become tongue-tied when it comes to personal matters. We may have good reason to hide from ourselves (at least to hide certain aspects — which amounts to the same). But even if there is little hope of an eventual self-acquittal, it would be enough to withstand the lure of silence, of concealment. (8)

Her excavation of the past to become acquainted with the child she "abandoned" leads her to confront submerged memories of her childhood and the present implications of her "happy and normal" childhood. Throughout the novel, the narrator's questioning voice dramatizes the pain of bringing the child Nelly into the sunlight. The four-year process of writing this work for the narrator and thus for Wolf only brings her an uneasy truce with herself. "The child who was hidden in me — has she come forth? Or has she been scared into looking for a deeper, more inaccessible hiding place? Has memory done its duty? Or has it proven — by the act of misleading — that it's impossible to escape the mortal sin of our time: the desire not to come to grips with oneself?" (Wolf, *Patterns* 406). For Wolf, like Rezzori, the rupture of self may be too broad to heal over. The autobiographical writing process, however, helps to bridge this fissure. In her guise as narrator/autobiographer, Wolf found delineating the contours of the past in words to be a painful necessity. Rezzori and Wolf are both survivors, but being a survivor means living with who they were as well as who they are. Both use defensive strategies to protect their assaulted identities. Rezzori uses his ironic vision to distance himself from his roots in his sardonic account. He focuses a strong beam of light on an interlude of happy childhood within the dissolution of a family within the dissolution of an era.

In contrast, Wolf meets head on the implications of her "happy and normal" childhood. During the long period as a refugee, the young girl Nelly recognized that she wanted to "live for a long time" (Wolf, *Patterns* 335). The narrator/autobiographer realizes that she (you in the text) is a survivor. For her, "[t]o be inconsiderate — without looking back" is "a basic requirement for survival; one of the prerequisites that separate the living from the survivors" (Wolf, *Patterns* 334). During one of Wolf's public appearances, during which she read part of the manuscript, questions arose from the audience about the efficacy of her self-appointed task:

> Question from the audience: And do you believe it's possible to come to grips with the events that you write about?
> Answer: No. (The deaths of six million Jews, twenty million Russians, six million Poles.)
> In that case — follow-up question — what's the use of bringing it up again and again? (*Patterns* 334)

In parentheses in the text, the narrator shows the reader the thoughts that obsess her mind. And, drawing on readings that she has made concerning those who have lived through the catastrophe of the Third Reich, she also shows the reader why she must continue her project:

> (Survival syndrome: the psychosomatic pathology of persons who were exposed to extreme stress. As studied in patients who had to spend years of their lives in concentration camps or under other conditions of persecution. Main symptoms: severe, lasting depression, with increasing difficulty in relating to others, states of fear and anxiety, nightmares, survivor's guilt, disturbances of memory and recall, increasing fear of persecution.
>
> A doctor's remark on the results of his research: The world of the living and the world of the survivors are infinitely far removed from each other, they are light-years, or rather, shadow-years apart.) (Wolf, *Patterns* 334–335)

Wolf has to confront the meaning of her childhood. In the face of what others suffered under Hitler, denial would definitely be easier. But for her, denial is over, despite the pain.

Wolf's autobiographical journey brings her shadow-years into relief. She, too, is a survivor, but she thrived on the other side during her childhood. What is more, she wanted that other side to continue. Now, in the present, decades beyond the end of the Third Reich, its atrocities still obsess her. "For all eternity, an insurmountable barrier separates the sufferers from those who went free" (Wolf, *Patterns* 235). Her sin is not to have known the criminal face of those twelve years during her "happy and normal" childhood.

Exile autobiographers look to the comforts of childhood as a place of refuge, a time resting whole in the memory banks of their minds, where the trauma of later transformations does not exist. They recreate images of another time and place where they were protected children in an effort to heal their altered identities in the present. For most, these intense pictures connect them reassuringly to a time of emotional wholeness. The "intense brightness" of the "other side" reminds the exile of a happier time. Sustaining the shocks of this side makes the "irrepressible nostalgia" for the luminous "paradise" of the other side hard to ignore (Friedländer 33–34). Only those for whom these treasured memories float in a wider emotional sea of conflicting memories find the recovery of childhood experiences painful. For the rest, the pull of nostalgia is irresistible. For those whose daunting experience of exile severed their physical and emotional ties to their childhood, detailing their memories of that other, brighter side in words may be a psychic lifeline in the present.

chapter seven

The Intellectual Response

Moreover the question arises whether from now on there will be any room at all in Germany for the likes of me, whether I will be able to breathe that air at all. I am much too good a German, far too closely linked with the cultural traditions and the language of my country, for the thought of an exile lasting years, if not a lifetime, not to have a grave, a fateful significance to me.

Thomas Mann, 13 March 1933

A country or a state should endure longer than an individual. At least this seems to be in keeping with the order of things. Today, however, one is constantly running across survivors of various Atlantises. Their lands in the course of time are transformed in memory and take on outlines that are no longer verifiable.

Czesław Miłosz, *Native Realm*

The four authors considered in this chapter, Czesław Miłosz, Witold Gombrowicz, Stefan Zweig, and Thomas Mann, responded strongly to exile but chose not to dwell on their personal experiences. Acknowledging the extensive changes exile created in their lives, they were most concerned with placing their personal experience in a larger context. Their autobiographical writings resulted from their reflective and philosophical views of their experiences. They sought to envelop the exile experience in works that explain or illuminate why such a devastating experience has happened in this modern world and what they and their audiences can learn from it. Their autobiographical works are vastly different in tenor, form, and style, and yet these authors asked the same pressing question. What sense can be made from this overwhelming experience?

Both Miłosz and Gombrowicz were relatively young men when they went into exile. For both, exile changed their writing and thinking. But as young men, they were able to continue their literary careers by incorporating the experience into their intellectual development. Both responded by writing autobiographical works delineating their changed intellectual perspectives. They wanted to establish meanings for this uprooting experience. Stefan Zweig and Thomas Mann were much older men when they experienced exile and had already achieved international fame. For Zweig, who was in his fifties at the time, exile was devastating. His response in the form of his autobiography, *The World of Yesterday*, attempted to re-create the secure world of his youth. In a world that had become chaos for him, he sought to reintroduce order. In the end, exile defeated him; he committed suicide in South America in 1942. Thomas Mann, the most eminent German exile writer, responded to his exile in the United States by trying to understand and explain how the Germany of Goethe could end in such catastrophe.

Czesław Miłosz: *Native Realm*

The Polish writers Czesław Miłosz and Witold Gombrowicz were active in literary circles in Poland in the thirties. The war and their subsequent exiles, however, put them on divergent professional paths. For Miłosz, exiled at twenty-eight, and Gombrowicz, exiled at thirty-five, separation from their Polish roots became a crucial and imperative theme.

Miłosz, winner of the Nobel Prize for literature in 1980, spent the war years in Warsaw and outlying districts. After the war he was sent to the United States as second secretary of the Embassy of the People's Poland. He broke with the Communists in the fifties, exposing the devastating influence the Communists had on writers in *The Captive Mind*. In 1961 he took a teaching position at Berkeley and became one of the most respected exiled Polish writers as well as an illuminating interpreter of Polish literature for Western readers.

Primarily known as a poet, Miłosz also wrote essays, novels, and his autobiography, *Native Realm: A Search for Self-Definition* (1968).[1] In this intellectual retelling of his life story, Miłosz eschews "probing into the subconscious" but tries to "evaluate" his "inner experience, as it is preserved in memory" in the changes of the landscapes of his past. He sees this endeavor as "looking upon himself as a sociological phenomenon" (*NR* 4–5). By seeking to define himself by the unique geography of his past, he can elucidate his background and exile as an Eastern European. He uses the personal events of his own life to illustrate the intellectual, religious, and political influences of life in Eastern Europe at that time.

Miłosz was raised in Wilno (historically known as the capital of Lithuania), a city that has been influenced by the Lithuanians, the Poles, and the Russians, depending on the prevailing political winds. He recognized that "hereditary encumbrances . . . endure, not in the blood, but in words, in gestures, and in the unconscious reactions of . . . people" (*NR* 18). Nevertheless, he was well aware of the difficulty of ordering "contradictory traditions, norms, and an overabundance of impressions" (*NR* 67). He consequently documents "scenes" of his life within a series of reflective, essayistic chapters focusing on the intellectual environment of his life. With chapter headings such as "Place of Birth," "Ancestry," "Journey into Asia," "City of My Youth," "Catholic Education," "Nationalities," "Russia," "Journey to the West," and "The G.G.,"[2] he tells the reader about his various journeys, both physical and intellectual. Beginning with a far-ranging description of his family's roots, he moves on to depict a nomadic early childhood. His family followed his father's career as a road and bridge builder for the Russian army, so young Miłosz was introduced early to war and to Russian as well as German soldiers. When he finally returned to Wilno to start school, its more evenly paced everyday life replaced the jumble of fast-moving impressions and landscapes.

His boyhood experiences were typical for the area. He went to Catholic schools, chafing somewhat from their strictness but learning from their rigor. With three school friends he sought a wider arena, traveling on his first trip to Paris in 1931 and returning as a student in 1934–35. He began to study Marxism at the university, which led him to more radical thinking. In the late thirties he pursued writing poetry while working as a "publican" for the Polish Radio. He first worked in Wilno, but because he was seen as a radical he was fired. The more liberal radio organization in Warsaw then hired him. He saw his life as a civil servant as dishonest, but it gave him the opportunity to continue his writing. He became a leader among a group of leftist poets known as the Catastrophists, a group which broke completely with past Polish poets and became harbingers of an apocalyptic future.

By 1940, when the Red Army occupied Wilno and all of Poland's eastern provinces, he describes himself as leading a fairly dissipated life of drinking and feasting at the salon of his friend Felix. When the Germans suddenly occupied Wilno, however, he tortuously made his way through the countryside by foot, evading the Nazis at every turn, to reach Warsaw. He felt he would be better off there during the remaining years of the war. Some of the best passages of the book describe life in the GG, where the Poles "erected an underground state — with underground financing, administration, school system, army, and press" in response to the Nazis' liquidation of all Polish institutions — businesses, schools, universities, presses, radio, and so on (*NR* 230).[3] During this period, he published underground works and supported himself mostly by working as a porter for the libraries of Warsaw, transporting books around the city. His German boss had decided to redo the library system, a monumental task which Miłosz hoped would prevent him from being sent to more dangerous zones for Germans, such as the Russian front. Miłosz found his unlimited access to Polish and foreign books during the war astonishing. The freedom to read gave him consolation other Poles in the GG did not have. Trapped on the outskirts of the city when the uprising in Warsaw began in August 1944, he hid with friends in warehouses and a granary. The Germans caught him and placed him in a makeshift "camp," but a nun he had never met before rescued him. By the fall he had survived by helping a farmer dig potatoes in an outlying village for food.

Miłosz was not a part of the Polish Home Army. As a leftist, he did not succumb to the conservative "political fantasy of prewar Warsaw" (*NR* 242). But he also notes that he "differed sharply . . . from the Communists" (*NR* 257). He berates himself for his lack of heroism during the war. In his thirties by this time, he had been drifting, and with the advent of the war he spent his time surviving. He did not join the resistance to fight against the Germans. Nevertheless, this period led to a breakthrough in his thinking. With life as he had known it collapsing, he discovered "new and vital patterns" of poetry: "From the stress of daily tragedy for millions of human beings, the word had burst and fallen into pieces. All previous forms had become meaningless" (*NR* 238). He breaks his reflective narrative off at the end of the war. He omits the story of the Red Army's occupation of Poland and how the Communists chose a "nonparty poet" to be sent abroad. He added two chapters which presented an overview of his five years in America as a cultural attaché and his subsequent rejection of the People's Poland. He reflects on this episode of his life through the history of his friend and mentor, "Tiger." Just when Miłosz exiled himself to Paris, his friend, who had been living there, committed to the "new" Poland.

After periods of severe deprivation as a refugee in Paris, he finally "stopped worrying about the whole mythology of exile." For him, Poland and France "fused together": "My native Europe, all of it, dwelled inside me, with its mountains, forests, and capitals" (*NR* 294). He found a way to live in the present yet retain his native realm.

Miłosz tells his story within the intellectual geography of his background. Placing episodes of his personal history within the history of the myriad changes of his native soil and his subsequent dwelling places, he constructs a meditative autobiography which gives as much insight into Poland's recent history and politics as it does into his own experiences. His prose, enhanced by his poetic vision and punctuated by his occasional pointed aphorisms, unravels his tangled history of places, languages, and images. In the beginning, Miłosz notes that he does not see the images of his life "in chronological order as if a strip of film, but in parallel, colliding with one another, overlapping" (*NR* 3). In this captivating autobiography, he does not seek the chronological truth of who he is. Instead, he peels back the layers of his Eastern European world.

Witold Gombrowicz: Stranded in the Argentine

Whereas Miłosz sees himself as a product of Eastern European influences, Gombrowicz wants above all to reject such effects of the past. Gombrowicz focuses on the individual in the present. Thus, unlike the themes of reminiscence and loss prevalent in most exiles' stories, the theme of Gombrowicz's exile is the struggle against the grip of his past. He revisits his past in order to destroy it. Casting himself as "something dying in a desert, a cripple cast onto an alien shore, without a homeland, etc. . . . . an exile, astray, lost," he responds by seeking authenticity. "I have to mobilize all the strong points of my situation thereby showing that I can live better and more authentically."[4]

Gombrowicz grew up in an upper-class Polish family. Well educated, he pursued a career in law until the thirties, when he began publishing his first works, a group of short stories followed by his most famous novel, *Ferdydurke*. Like Miłosz, he had participated in the literary milieu in Warsaw and had attained some critical acclaim as a writer before war broke out. In 1939, he was given a chance to sail on the maiden voyage of the Polish liner *Boleslaw Chrobry* as one of two writers invited on the trip. After he arrived in Buenos Aires, Hitler invaded Poland, trapping him on the other side of the world. He had one opportunity to return to England to fight in the Home Army exiled there, but he chose to remain in Buenos Aires, thus beginning a twenty-four-year voluntary exile from Europe.

Gombrowicz's first years in the Argentine were desperate. Just acquiring enough money to buy food consumed all his energy. He did not speak Spanish, and after his money ran out he lived from hand to mouth. Eventually, he began to meet members of the Polish community and Spanish literary circles, who gave him support. Toward the end of the war he even began to write again, working on the novel *Trans-Atlantik*. His life took on some stability when he obtained a job at a bank in Argentina. Working as a bank secretary during the day, he wrote at night and on weekends. After the publication of *Trans-Atlantik* in 1952, he gained recognition as a Polish exile writer. He published a series of what he termed "aggressive notes" in the Polish exile journal *Kultura*, published in Paris. In 1963, he received a Ford Foundation grant which allowed him to spend a year in Berlin. From there he went to France, where he spent his remaining years. He died of a heart attack in 1969.

Gombrowicz's primary autobiographical writings are in a three-volume collection, published as *Diary*, and a book, *A Kind of Testament*, edited by Dominique de Roux. *A Kind of Testament* establishes the facts and chronology of Gombrowicz's life and career, but *Diary* is the more provocative work. Its three volumes contain the collected pieces he published in *Kultura* during his years in the Argentine. In *Diary* he directs his considerable intellectual anger at his readers. Although he recounts some mundane events such as having dinner or meeting someone at a café, he seems to include these events for effect. *Diary* is, for the most part, a defiant polemic against his past, against Poland, and against the reigning exile writers' community. While there are intense moments of intimacy in the book, it is primarily an intellectual confession, emphatically registering his complaints against the Western intellectual world. At the end of volume 1, he systematically outlines his disgust with what he terms the three great moralities of his time — Catholicism, Marxism, and existentialism. His blasts against these intellectual currents, however, are consistently bound up with his very real and painful life. Ruthless with his critics, he is just as ruthless with himself. He relentlessly strips away all pretensions. His biographer, Ewa Thompson, praises his honesty: "Nowhere in the *Journal* can one find a passage where the speaker tries in all seriousness to present himself to best advantage" (103).

Few writers reveal their own, very human transgressions with such passion and intimacy. Gombrowicz confesses to writing nasty graffiti in the bathroom of a bar or indulging in myriad degradations he contrives even if he doesn't reveal all their sordid details. When he brings some of the more shocking particulars of his thinking into his writing (his flirtation with the homosexual community, for example, or his diatribe against women), he does it to analyze his emotional and intellectual reactions to these subjects. Moreover, he does not shy away from revealing his own fears and frustrations. In volume 1, he provides an account of his travels to the beach Mar del Plata for a writer's retreat. Alone in this remote setting, he dwells on his own isolation and loneliness: "I do not want loneliness crawling all over me senselessly, I need people, a reader" (D 172). One night in the midst of a violent storm, he stretches out his hand, and the storm stops suddenly. When he withdraws his hand, it starts up again. Rationally assured that he is not controlling the storm, he fears moving his hand again just in case. In this passage, he carefully delineates his tenuous grip on sanity. Very few writers are so deliberate in their depictions of such scenes.

Having been devastated by the depression of the several-day retreat, he tries to disentangle his emotions within the intellectual framework of existentialism. Much of his writing based on his seeking the authentic life redounds with the vocabulary of existentialism. In arguing with himself about existentialism, however, he pointedly disavows this philosophical view current in Europe at the time. He has been described as the "recognized creator of Polish existentialism" (Kraszewsk 611), but in the *Diary* he claims that existentialism, along with Marxism, is a bankrupt ideology. Acknowledging his debt to existentialism in his first novel, *Ferdydurke*, he insists that when he sat down and actually studied Kierkegaard's, Heidigger's, and Jasper's existentialist writings, he found tenets he could no longer accept. He allows that trying to live authentically on the terms espoused by these writers can't be done. For him, it is "impossible to meet the demands of *Dasein*, and simultaneously have coffee and croissants for an evening snack. To fear nothingness, but to fear the dentist more" (D 184). For Gombrowicz, when life intervenes, the lofty weight of abstract speculations collapses against its absurdity.

Gombrowicz revels in destroying widely held ideas, yet in *Testament* he classifies the topics of his diary to help his readers know who he is. He writes in order to "throw myself into relief, to explain myself" (D 115). He comments on his work and his polemic with the critics. He sustains his war with literature and art, with philosophy, with Poland, and records his observations on "man, creature and creator of Form" (D 116). He concludes with the eccentric games he plays with the reader. *Diary* is a work guaranteed to irritate and provoke.

The published *Diary* is divided by years, but there are no specific dates, only designations of Monday, Tuesday, and so on. When Gombrowicz collected the serialized pieces for publication, he noted that instead of a preface, he introduced the work with the following "foreword":

> Monday: myself
> Tuesday: myself
> Wednesday: myself
> Thursday: myself. (*D* 112)[5]

Indeed, this is a fitting introduction, for the work is, most of all, about his conflict of Me — the individual — with the prevailing intellectual modalities. His polemic against the "post-war tendencies which condemned the word 'myself' — the Church or Marxism" batters the reader. With insolence, egotism, and stubbornness, he again and again forcefully reminds his readers that the individual's formidable struggle with life matters more than anything.

In direct contrast to most exile autobiographers, Gombrowicz revels in his exile. Even though he frequently comments on his great loneliness and alienation in the Argentine, he categorically insists that the true homeland must be the individual. "Has man ever lived anywhere else other than in himself? You are at home even if you were to find yourself in Argentina or Canada, because a homeland is not a blot on a map but the living essence of man" (*D* 59). Positing the authenticity of the individual, he dissects with great relish the stereotypes of the prewar Polish intelligentsia, the maudlin exile community, and the weak and ineffectual new Polish literary community under Communism. Gombrowicz's ruthless diatribe against Poland, its history, and those who deplore its loss is indicative of his insistence on breaking with the past. Defining his identity is uppermost in his thinking. He needed to deny his cultural roots to shape his new identity.

Because Gombrowicz lived on the other side of the world as an exile, he maintains he wrote this unusual diary as a way to "become famous." Noting that most people buy diaries because the author is famous, he hoped that by reading his diary, people would help enhance his reputation as a writer (*D* 110). His strategy worked. He shaped his audience at the same time he shaped his identity. His serialized diary became "infuriating" to his Polish public (*D* 114). His insistent voice from the distant land of Argentina enraged his critics. He became what he wanted, a writer to reckon with.

This peculiar blend of intellectual jousting coupled with a very gritty depiction of his own frequently indefensible behavior jars at the same time it fascinates. It is easy to understand how his audacious assaults angered those he attacked. But his brash approach engrosses as well, for he reveals himself in all his scheming imperfections. He never lets go of the alien or outsider stance that exile has providentially provided him. Stopping in Goya, a small provincial town he came across in his travels, he sees himself as an "exotic foreigner." He becomes a "stranger to himself." He leads himself around the city as a "person unknown to myself. I sit him down on a chair" (*D* 203). His alienation helps him fling off his cultural accoutrements. He sums up his task: "My method consists of this: to show the battle I wage with people for my own personality and to exploit all the personal sore spots that arise between them and me, for a more and more distinct delineation of my own I" (*D* 92). His exile experiences provided him with the impetus to engage in this intellectual battle for his self.

Stefan Zweig: *The World of Yesterday*

At the time of his suicide in 1942 in Brazil, Stefan Zweig was one of the best-known writers of the German language. Born in Austria in 1881, he grew up in the last great years of the Austrian Empire and began his major writings after World War I. His autobiography, *The World of Yesterday* (1943), with the German subtitle *Memoirs of a European*, is a fascinating account of the span of his lifetime, for it covers the last decades of the Austrian Empire, the First World War, the chaotic period between the wars, and finally his exile, first to England, then to the United States, and ultimately Brazil. His thoughtful account of his life set against these frequently disruptive and devastating events conveys brilliant word pictures of the events he witnessed. His accounts of inflation in Germany and Austria in the twenties or of his first glimpses of the Brownshirts in the rather provincial town of Salzburg in the early thirties are startling descriptions of these events. When he published *The World of Yesterday*, he was nearly sixty and renowned as one of the most intellectual and respected exiles to have left Europe. His prolific works had been translated into more languages than any other living German writer, and he held a worldwide reputation as a leading proponent against the rising nationalism in Europe. He defined himself first as a European, not an Austrian. He was above all known as a humanist who abhorred war. When forced into exile, he was also one of the wealthiest writers in Europe because he had been so frequently translated abroad. Curiously, though, this once best-selling author is hardly read today, as a 1984 literary conference on Zweig has shown. Of all his works, *The World of Yesterday* may be the most frequently read because it gives a panoramic view of a former time.

Yet, for all of its cultural and historical value, *The World of Yesterday*, as George Iggers notes, is fragmentary and uneven. Zweig's perspective is limited to the immediate literary and artistic circles in which he moved. He does not acknowledge the political or social ramifications of the world he described. Nor is his work a personal document in the ordinary sense of modern psychological autobiography. While the narrator's voice moves through historical events, drawing portraits of famous and some infamous people as well as providing testimony of some of the more important events in the early part of the century, the reader is not introduced to Zweig the son, the husband, the stepfather, or even the man. In this regard it is more a self-serving memoir than an autobiography. Unlike Miłosz and Gombrowicz, Zweig simply fails to report the revealing scenes of his life. Instead, Zweig creates a historical persona that dovetails with his reputation as a leading writer and thinker of his day but does not capture the flesh-and-blood man. To see more of who Zweig was, the reader must turn to other documents of the era — autobiographies by friends and his ex-wife, Friderike Zweig, his letters to Friderike, and his biographers' accounts, particularly the definitive study of his life, *European of Yesterday: Stefan Zweig* by Donald Prater. Juxtaposing the views expressed in *The World of Yesterday* against these other documents helps explain why he was compelled to take his own life, an event that profoundly shocked his readers, who could not equate his suicide with his authorial persona.

The World of Yesterday as a document of exile shows how Zweig, the sophisticated, worldly writer, could not understand or accept what was happening to his world. In *The World of Yesterday*, Zweig returned to a bygone era that made rational sense to him. His carefully crafted persona is reprised in the autobiography, but the real Zweig is not. The real Zweig could not cope with what to him was the end of his view of Western European intellectual life. He re-created yesterday's world before he chose to leave his present world — in exile in Brazil in 1942 as the war raged in Europe. As a matter of fact, a close study of *The World of Yesterday* and the other personal documents mentioned above reveals not the urbane, elegant, famous defender of rationality, a writer deserving of accolades, but a defensive, cautious, vain, and sometimes petty and abusive man who, when faced with changes that interfered with his freedom to pursue his lifestyle, chose an easier way out. Certainly clues about his relationship with his first wife, Friderike, and, to a certain extent, with his second young wife, Lotte, exhibit one-sided relationships which sometimes were emotionally abusive. Unlike his friend Zuckmayer, who had the resiliency to survive exile by becoming a farmer (an undertaking very removed from his previous life), Zweig succumbed to despair and suicide. His frustrations of living as an exile and his fear of aging caused him to surrender to depression.

The portrait I am painting of Stefan Zweig is harsh but, I believe, valid. It is pertinent to understand how the despair and frustration of exile became a catalyst for renewal and unexpected strength for some people, while for others the experience caused only an abiding grief. Clearly exile overwhelmed Zweig. He had led a privileged life in Europe as a popular writer who always had sufficient economic support to pursue his gentlemanly literary life. He also had a controlling personality that allowed him to be selfish of himself and his time and to devote his energy to his writing. He practiced his cultured literary life amid comfort. His possessions included a ten-thousand-volume library, a well-run household on the Kapuzinerberg in Salzburg overseen by his supportive wife, Friderike, and a very valuable collection of first drafts of important music and literature. His ability to travel at will to the capitals of Europe and to associate with leading intellectual figures on his own terms was also part of his well-defined existence. When this world collapsed, when he could not travel from country to country without frustration and time-consuming journeys to bureaucrats for visas, when he was inundated with requests to speak out against fascism and categorically could not bring himself to comply, when he was burdened by fellow exiles seeking monetary help, and when he no longer had ready access to the world's libraries, he collapsed. I do not mean to suggest that Zweig was unsympathetic to his friends' needs. As one of the few writers who did not lose his wealth, he helped many less fortunate artists, but he deeply resented spending time dealing with such endeavors. He relentlessly rejected exile communities and exile politics. When he settled in England, he escaped the exile community by removing himself to Bath. Moreover, he ultimately traveled to Brazil during the early part of the war to escape the exile community in the New York area. Zweig was a famous man who could not face losing his privileged life, for if he lost it, he lost his ability to maintain his persona. Was he vain and shallow? Yes, I think a case can be made for that portrayal. At the same time, he was also genuinely troubled by what was happening to his friends and to the Europe that he knew. His defense against this catastrophe was to turn backward, to re-create "the world of security," as he phrased it in his autobiography. He pursued the illusion of a rational world where intelligent and educated men could speak and write of high-minded ideals. When this illusion was crushed with the ascent of Hitler, he could not persevere. As many critics have observed, it is hard to sympathize with Zweig's refusal to speak out against Nazism given his Jewishness and his stature.[6] A more realistic appraisal of his psychology will help make his behavior more understandable.

In his biography of Joseph Fouche, published in 1928, Zweig

writes what the critic Wilma Iggers has termed his "ode to exile" (12). In praising the effect of exile on such religious figures as Moses, Christ, Mohammed, and Buddha and interpreting widely such experiences as blindness (Milton), deafness (Beethoven), isolation (Luther), and prison (Cervantes) as personal exile, Zweig recognizes the role of exile in increasing the strength and contributions of such individuals. But like so much in Zweig's writings, this was an abstract idea, one he could distill from the writings and contributions of others. When faced with the real fact of exile, he began to define it differently.

Wilma Iggers maintains that Zweig's sustained traveling before his exile was an attempt to create the isolation and the idea of exile to enhance his creativity. But these travels were generally to the busy capitals of Europe where he had contact with many well-known and important literary figures. The real grind of exile was different. Even though Zweig did not share many of his fellow exiles' deprivations such as lack of funds and internment, he began to chafe under the severe inconveniences to his lifestyle — traveling without a passport, always seeking permissions from officials, and being at the mercy of border guards. Even though he turned his back on Austria, after he finally allowed Friderike to sell the house on the Kapuzinerberg, he began to reminisce and become nostalgic about his native country. Prater notes that he never ceased to question whether he would ever see his books, papers, and household goods again after they were stored in England. Zweig became severely depressed about the loss of his vision of Europe (his abstract view of a united and cultivated Europe), but he also complained bitterly about the minor inconveniences of having his baggage searched like that of a common criminal or of the British officials not knowing who he was. George Iggers contends that Zweig remained impervious to the destructive political trends of his time and points out that during the period between the wars he returned to his lettered world as quickly as possible. Zweig wrote in part because of his apolitical stance. As George Iggers argues, "political conditions bother him relatively little as long as he can continue to enjoy the freedom as an individual to communicate with his peers" (6). He even closed out personal distress. Prater observes that it is "incredible" that Zweig could finish a four-hundred-page novel, *Beware of Pity*, "with such a deeply troubled spirit" during the divorce and breakup with Friderike and the beginning of his new life with Lotte (*European* 271). But Zweig had always demanded first his freedom and time to concentrate on his work. His relationships with his wives, particularly Friderike, show how demanding and self-centered he was.

Wilma Iggers explains that Zweig's view of marriage "reinforced in him the attitude of a gentleman of the old school: First Friderike, who freed him of all practical concerns of daily life and who worshiped him even after he deserted her for a young woman and then Lotte, who joined him in suicide while he, evidently oblivious of her, in his farewell letter to the world stated that he was leaving the world alone" (17). During their nineteen years of married life, Zweig depended upon Friderike to cope with the trials of living. He wanted the trappings of a gentleman such as a beautiful house to display his possessions, but he did not want to cope with the myriad details that such an existence entailed. He wanted his life free of entanglements so that he could travel and work when, where, and how he pleased. According to Prater, Friderike first made the century-old house in Salzburg livable and then acted as mediator between Zweig and the large number of guests that came to visit them there. His real disposition becomes apparent during the final four years of their marriage. After Zweig began his relationship with Lotte, the evidence suggests that he was torn between the glamour of a new relationship with a young woman and the pull of his relationship to Friderike. His indecisiveness, however, does not excuse his continuing demands and expectations of Friderike, for she, after all, was watching her life tear apart at the seams.

Zweig's egocentrism dominated all aspects of his life. Wilma Iggers describes his household in Salzburg: "the house on the hill with huge collections and files, a workshop, a wife, a staff of servants, many guests and Zweig, the master, as its center" (12). Friderike took care of all household details as well as cataloging Zweig's collections of manuscripts and books and acting as a screen for much of his correspondence. If he didn't want to see someone or reply to some query, he generally asked her to handle it. As their relationship deteriorated and he actively began to avoid Salzburg under the guise of the pain Austria now brought him, he still expected her to have everything ready for him when he returned. He wanted to dispatch the important items quickly in order to leave again as quickly as possible.

Many who have written about Zweig, including Prater, who has had the most extensive access to his correspondence and to personal descriptions of him, speak of his shyness, his sensitivity to noise, his fear of conflict, his concern for his freedom. But I wonder what these descriptions mean. Zweig did not appear to be shy when as a young man he approached famous writers or sent his work to the most famous people of the day. In his letters to Friderike, he sounds weary of large gatherings and of people who want to see him or want something from him but whom he doesn't want to see. He nevertheless made time for those he did want to see.

Does freedom mean being free of those who don't interest you or abusing those who love you because you can? According to Prater, during the divorce from Friderike, it was agreed that mental cruelty would be the grounds, and Alix, his stepdaughter, would attest to "Stefan's habit of locking himself away in his room and refusing to speak to the family" (271). Prater relates numerous times that Friderike was placed in difficult positions vis-à-vis Stefan's friends. When he didn't want to see them, she would have to tell them he wasn't in the house, only to have him suddenly appear. These episodes indicate a controlling personality who is more concerned with personal conveniences than with the feelings and desires of others, especially his loved ones. Certainly the self-effacing writer of *The World of Yesterday*, who again and again talks about how lucky he was to have known such worldly writers as Rilke and Thomas Mann or to have been able to travel to such exotic countries as India, is hard to reconcile with the whining voice in his letters to Friderike.[7]

Nowhere is his uncaring and tyrannical behavior clearer, however, than during the breakup of the Salzburg house. In Prater's view and in Friderike's biography, *Stefan Zweig*, and in many of Zweig's letters, especially those quoted in Prater, Zweig made relentless demands on Friderike at the same time he blamed her for many aspects of his life which brought him discomfort.[8] He frequently showed a selfish face to Friderike and her daughters which he carefully hid from the glittering world of letters he inhabited. To those outside the family circle, he continued to show his persona of the sophisticated, world-renowned writer. Zweig found it more and more difficult, however, to project this persona as the realities of the thirties and the early forties encroached on his life.

Portraits by Zweig's friends during these years note his physical and mental disintegration.[9] By now only tangentially involved with Zweig, Friderike nevertheless remained loyal, as she did following his death. In New York she always tried to find ways to alleviate his depression. Others who talked of his transformations were less sanguine. Zweig's determination to remain aloof from the politics of exile disturbed many people, as it disturbs critics today. Certainly in light of the harassing events concerning the Jews in Europe, his avowed silence in regard to Hitler and his lack of sympathy toward the exile community are hard to fathom.[10]

In his article "Stefan Zweig and the Illusion of the Jewish European," Leon Botstein, one of Zweig's harshest critics, discusses the bankruptcy of Zweig's insistence on what Botstein terms the radical individualism of the (cultivated) intellectual with regard to politics or history. Botstein portrays Zweig as an idealistic intellectual who mediates between cultures but ignores the historical details of those cultures. Zweig prefers the rarefied world of the spirit and the word to the dirty reality of politics. Botstein observes that in his lectures on Vienna, Zweig concentrated on a nostalgic view of it as a cultural center, omitting the "immense social conflict, poverty, overcrowding, anti-Semitism, ethnic and religious segregation that existed in Vienna" (91). Indeed, Zweig's position is ultimately that of an intellectual isolationist:

> Zweig, as an assimilated urban Jew, used the traditions of European learning and the self-consciously artistic idealized sense

of history and intellectual as routes to a legitimate rejection of politics and to finding solution to his own place as a Jew. Zweig concluded his career with a pessimistic glorification of the possibility of freedom for the isolated individual, no matter how desperate the external world. (Botstein 105)

Botstein asks the question which I underscore: "Was Zweig too wedded to his fame and success in the largely Gentile German-speaking world?" (96).

Zweig's legacy turns on how we answer this question. By all accounts, the critical acclaim and wide distribution of his works that he enjoyed when he was alive did not continue when he died. Zweig's historical works, as Botstein asserts, can no longer be taken seriously. Although his bibliographer notes that his fiction continues to be published with some frequency, Zweig is not considered an important part of the German canon (Klawiter 326–327). And what of his autobiography? Harry Zohn calls it the "mirror of an age rather than a life" (vi) and attributes Zweig's lack of personal detail to his being a far "too shy and modest a man to want to write the story of his life" (vi). Like many, Zohn becomes an apologist for Zweig's actions. Prater concedes that even if it is not entirely accurate in places, Zweig "succeeds as few others have done in conveying the reality and the atmosphere of a period" (*European* 307). Prater does, however, stress that Zweig slights Friderike by not acknowledging her considerable part in creating the autobiography. Zweig moved to Ossining, New York, where she had settled, when he was finishing the book to be close to her. He needed her help remembering details as he did not have many of his papers with him. Botstein questions whether the work will later even be valuable as a document of the times:

Ironically, perhaps only his autobiography, *the World of Yesterday*, continues to be read, cited and used. Because of its curious lack of personal detail, the distortion of what detail was included, and its constant effort to be general, incisive and wise, *The World of Yesterday*, too, may fade as useful, and as revealing a source document on the early twentieth century as it now appears. (83)

Zweig's polished style helps to make *The World of Yesterday* very readable, and his word portraits do capture the atmosphere of the periods he knew. It is important to remember, however, that the narrator writes about the "world of security" or the events he has witnessed through the eyes of one who has been divested of his security. Although the truth quotient of autobiography may not be as important as it once was, the psychological authenticity, such as is found in Miłosz or Gombrowicz, is paramount. Zweig created in *The World of Yesterday* a sham persona. Unable to cope with the realities of his life in exile, he tried to re-create the world he believed in. Ernst Lothar, a fellow Austrian, notes, "Emigration is for a young man with no memories" (Zweig xi). Nowhere is that clearer than with Zweig. As is evident from the many personal glimpses of Zweig's disintegration in exile, he could no longer sustain his famous and familiar persona. His supports for this persona — his consuming literary life or his well-maintained Kapuzinerberg existence — no longer existed. To him, suicide seemed like a natural consequence of his disintegrating world.

Thomas Mann: Germany's Autobiographer

When Zweig died, Thomas Mann was living in California. Unlike Zweig, who had disdained the role of exile spokesman, Mann always complied when called upon to articulate the exiles' concerns. In fact, he felt it was his duty to convey his disbelief and disgust over Hitler's actions. Deeply affronted by what was happening in his country, he frequently commented publicly on political events as he had done earlier in the Weimar era. It was even more natural for him to continue this role in exile. He had also spent much time trying to understand how Hitler and the Nazis had been able to achieve their power. As always, the clues for him were bound up with Germany's cultural history.

In May 1943, after Thomas Mann, sixty-eight, had finished work on the *Joseph* tetralogy, he turned his attention to a subject which had already preoccupied him as a possible novel, the Faust legend. Mann called the resulting novel *Doctor Faustus: The Life of a German Composer, Adrian Leverkühn, as Told by a Friend*, the "novel of his epoch." Michael Beddow described it as the work that comes "as close as Mann ever came to a comprehensive autobiography" (16). Like most of Mann's fiction, the work draws heavily on autobiographical elements, but it is more. As the "novel of his epoch," it was not only the autobiography/biography of what it meant to be an artist in his epoch but also the autobiography of Germany, of at least "his Germany," the philosophical and cultural traditions of his milieu, which provide the significant ambience in all his works. At issue for him when he wrote *Doctor Faustus* was the burning question in his and many another educated German's mind: how could this enlightened tradition have resulted in the barbarism of Nazi Germany? The resulting complex and multilayered novel is his answer.

In 1933, Mann went into exile at the age of fifty-eight. He had already achieved international recognition for his works *Buddenbrooks, The Magic Mountain*, and a series of critically acclaimed short novellas including "Death in Venice" and "Tonio Kröger." In 1929 he received the Nobel Prize and was highly sought after as a lecturer and artistic celebrity. The story of his exile is very familiar. He and his wife were on a lecture tour of the European capitals of Amsterdam, Brussels, and Paris and then planned a vacation in Arosa, Switzerland, when the Reichstag in Berlin was burned to the ground. Hitler's response, the purging of most of his enemies, made it very dangerous for outspoken critics of his regime. Meanwhile, a group of Munich officials and artists signed a petition protesting Mann's current lecture on Richard Wagner, "Sufferings and Greatness of Richard Wagner." On the recommendation of his daughter Erika and his sons Klaus and Golo, he remained abroad, a decision that assured that his home and personal possessions would fall into Nazi hands. Although Mann's home on Poschingerstrasse in Munich was being watched, Erika did successfully retrieve some manuscripts; most important, the manuscript Mann was working on, the first novel of the *Joseph* tetralogy. Mann and his family briefly took refuge in the French coastal town of Sanary sur Mer, where his friend René Schickele had a home and where later exiles, the Werfels and the Feuchtwangers, established homes. After a short period of time, however, he moved to Switzerland so that his two youngest children, Michael and Elizabeth, could continue their schooling in German. As he so poignantly stresses in his diaries of this period, the work on the *Joseph* novels provided the ordering principle in the midst of this uprooting and personal loss (Mann, *The Story* 18).

In 1938, when events in Nazi Germany made Hitler's true intentions more apparent and more dangerous for émigrés in Europe, Mann accepted a short-term teaching post at Princeton. Two years later he moved to Pacific Palisades, California, a significant refuge for him. He and his wife became U.S. citizens, and he remained in California until 1950, when he once again made his home in Switzerland. Upon choosing exile in 1933, Mann chose not to condemn his Germany. But he could not remain silent for long. In 1936, amid some controversy, he began his long tenure as a spokesman for German émigré authors.[11] In the United States he was called upon again and again to speak out against events in Nazi Germany. He recorded over fifty broadcasts which the BBC transmitted to the citizens of Germany, and he frequently lectured in the United States commenting on the events in his homeland. Toward the end of the war, a group of German émigrés wanted him to head their movement to "Free Germany" by setting up a democratic government to take over after fascist Germany's fall. On behalf of this group, he met with representatives of the U.S. State Department to broach the subject. The negative reaction of the American officials caused him to choose not to align himself with this group. His refusal embroiled him in a feud with other well-known exiles, among them Bertolt Brecht. Mann grew to love his adopted country and moved in well-connected political and educational circles. He became friends with President Roosevelt, whom he greatly respected as a leader fighting against Hitler.

Mann's reputation as Germany's leading intellectual writer and the most eminent spokesman for those in exile accorded him privileges but also brought him concerns. As Germany's preeminent exile artist, he needed to address the causes of Germany's cultural and political downfall. He did this not only in fictional works, particularly *Doctor Faustus*, but also in his numerous lectures, broadcasts, and essays written and published during his exile. He did not permit himself to lead the life of a reclusive artist, as Leverkühn does, but daily kept in mind national and international events. In his writings, he always approached these events from a historical, cultural point of view. As he shows in *Doctor Faustus*, the blame for the tragedy that befalls his homeland has its roots in Germany's cultural history. His perspective as an exile, cut off from the language of his art and the physical surroundings of his German world, gives him the distance, as does his ironic aesthetic stance, to be ruthless in his assessment of Germany's downfall. His exile views as well as his artistic stature as Germany's representative author allow him to confront the tragedy of Germany. One can say that he assumes the role of Germany's autobiographer. As T. J. Reed observes in *Thomas Mann: The Uses of Tradition*, Mann had to attempt this project, he had "to encompass and explain the German catastrophe. . . . He had put too much of his substance into the fight against Hitler, brooded too much over what made Hitler possible, suffered too much from the distortion of his country and its culture to be able to leave the account artistically unsettled" (360).

Although Mann wrote several autobiographical essays about his life (*A Sketch of My Life* [1930], *The Story of a Novel* [1961], written to highlight the creative process of *Doctor Faustus*, and *The Years of My Life* [1950], along with the earlier polemical and controversial work *Reflections of a Nonpolitical Man*), he never wrote an autobiography in the traditional sense. Mann was more interested in the era in which he lived and worked than in publishing the personal details of his life, like Stefan Zweig in *The World of Yesterday* and his own brother Heinrich in *Ein Zeitalter wird besichtigt* (An age is examined). But if he cannot be considered a traditional autobiographer, his work is imbued with his intellectual autobiographical details as well as thinly disguised personal events of his life. His wartime essays and *The Story of a Novel* in particular shed light on *Doctor Faustus* as the summing up of early-twentieth-century German artistic and intellectual life — the period of his own development as an artist.

Mann preferred to create novels which encompassed the broad dynamics of historical events. Reed offers that Mann "had spent a

lifetime evolving means . . . learning to say the general — by alle-
gory, symbol, myth — through the particular" (360). In *The Magic
Mountain*, for example, "he had embodied complex truths about
an earlier phase of German history and society in the fate of a
single individual" (Reed 360). In *Doctor Faustus* he personifies the
fates of German artists and intellectuals through the protago-
nists, Serenus Zeitblom and Adrian Leverkühn, and a host of well-
drawn minor figures. In this complex novel, he not only re-creates
the cultural and intellectual atmosphere of early-twentieth-century
Germany but also ladens the material with echoes of Luther's Germany as well as medieval and Romantic Germany by using the
Faust myth. While some critics have called the book a failure precisely because of the burdensome cultural and historical weight he
places on the plot and action, it is nevertheless a tour de force that
only Mann could have written.

In *The Story of a Novel*, Mann notes that he wants to "tell the
story of *Faustus*, embedded as it is in the pressure and tumult of
outward events," for himself and his friends (7). In letters where
he mentions the inception of this autobiographical book, he indicates that he also wrote it in the face of negative criticism of *Doctor
Faustus*. In *The Story of a Novel* he intended to explain the sources
he used to help readers understand his use of the montage techniques.[12] The memoir shows how important *Doctor Faustus* was to
him and how much it cost him to write it. Quoting frequently
from his daily notes and his diary, he discloses how difficult the
writing was and how much of his own life he put in the book:
"[h]ow much *Faustus* contains the atmosphere of my life! A radical confession, at bottom. From the very beginning that has been
the shattering thing about the book" (Mann, *The Story* 154).

Richard Exner has called *Doctor Faustus* "Thomas Mann's great
and generous gift to Germanists and literary critics," noting that
"it will last us until the end of Germanistic time" ("Response" 113).
Studies tracing the literary and cultural influences on this novel
have already become legion, in part because of the many autobiographical techniques Mann employed as well as his copious allu-
sions to the *Stoff* of the novel, which can be readily found in his

diaries, essays, and letters. *The Story of a Novel* even presents a blue-print for the models, literary works, and autobiographical references he employs, although as Gunilla Bergsten cautions, the critic must be watchful of Mann's irony in using this book to trace the sources of *Doctor Faustus* (14). In many respects, the novel's strengths are the autobiographical and realistic techniques Mann used to enhance his depiction of the fate of the modern German artist and thus Germany.

First of all, Mann unrelentingly portrayed actual traits of members of his family, friends, and acquaintances and actual events which happened to these real people. Second, his conscious use of montage — incorporating people in the public eye as well as events and places into the storyline — grounds the novel in the real past. Third, his complex use of literary and philosophical influences on his own thinking as well as that of any educated German gives the novel its cultural depth.

As many of his biographers and critics point out, Mann has always used personal experiences in his works. This inclination has caused a storm of protest on many occasions. Nigel Hamilton notes that the publication of *Buddenbrooks* scandalized the citizens of Lübeck because the characters transparently represented the townspeople. Outraged by his portrayal of them, they passed out a key to the book among themselves. Much of Katia Mann's *Unwritten Memories* is her view of what was real in her husband's works and what was not. Her words become almost a litany of experiences — the Polish family in Venice was real, cholera was widespread in the city, we did take a ride with an unlicensed gondolier, and so on. *Doctor Faustus* was no exception. But in this book, Mann resolutely exploited some of his more personal and painful experiences. To point out how clearly Mann borrowed from reality, Bergsten lists passages taken almost word for word from diaries, letters, and other writings.

Both of the Mann sisters who died by their own hands, Julia and Carla, became models for the Rhodde sisters, Ines and Clarissa, in the book. Clarissa's painful suicide after the rejection of a suitor parallels Carla's real suicide. Both drank cyanide. The fictional

Mrs. Rhodde was in the adjoining room and heard her young daughter as she tried to sooth her burning throat by gargling, shortly before collapsing on the sofa. In *A Sketch of My Life*, Mann describes the exact circumstances when his sister Carla took her life at their mother's home in Polling: "the unhappy creature hurried past her mother, locked herself into her room, and the last that was heard from her was the sound of the gargling with which she tried to cool the burning of her corroded throat" (Bergsten 20; Mann, *A Sketch* 39–40).

In another example of Mann's use of personal material, he based the idealized portrait of the young child, Echo, on one of his favorite grandchildren, Frido. Leverkühn's nephew Echo is one of the few people who breaks through the composer's cool and aloof exterior. Since in the novel Echo is taken from Leverkühn as part of the devil's pact, Mann has Echo die a very painful death from meningitis. After hearing Mann read the Echo passages, Golo and Mann's brother-in-law Klaus Pringsheim found the portrayal so realistic that they insisted that Mann's depiction of the child's death be kept from Frido's mother as long as possible. They feared she would be unnecessarily upset by it (Mann, *The Story* 220).

Mann began writing *Doctor Faustus* on May 23, 1943, in California. The narrator, Zeitblom, who tells the fateful history of the composer Leverkühn began his biography on the same day. Zeitblom provides a frame for the ongoing events of the war in Germany and is the voice of Germany's condemnation. The main time frame of the novel, however, revolves around Leverkühn's artistic career and goes back to the turn of the century, ending with Leverkühn's breakdown in 1930. Zeitblom, the conservative intellectual, provides a foil for Leverkühn, the arrogant artist who tempts fate in order to pursue the radical forms of his art. The composer consciously sought periods of euphoric creativity brought about by sickness. Leverkühn's Faustian pact with the devil is realized through his consciously exposing himself to syphilis through the prostitute Esmerelda. In the story of the composer's hubristic downfall, Mann drew heavily on the details of Nietzsche's biography.

But if Leverkühn and Zeitblom are the novel's principals, the voices of the minor characters are just as important for Mann's intentions. Like Georg Grosz's gallery of German types of the teens and twenties, Mann presents a gallery of intellectual and artistic types who demonstrate the cultural and intellectual currents of Adrian's (Mann's) time. Bergsten argues that in Leverkühn there is a chorus of voices. In fact, all voices in the novel add to the story of Germany's cultural history, and this history is seductive and dark. The intellectual and artistic elite, portrayed and many times caricatured in the novel, creates the ambience in which the likes of Hitler can begin to hold sway. Leverkühn, the quintessential German artist, flirts with this dark side of the German spirit to his detriment. As Leverkühn gave up his life to the devil, for Mann, modern-day Germany is literally being taken by the devil incarnate, Hitler (Mann, "Deutschland" 165).

To understand better how *Doctor Faustus* can be interpreted as the "novel of his epoch" and how much it contains the "atmosphere" of his life, it is important to look more closely at Mann's wartime essays. Two in particular shed light on Mann's view of Germany's cultural history which allowed National Socialism to take root: "What Is German?" published in 1943 in the *Atlantic Monthly* and, more important, "Germany and the Germans," the speech first given in June 1945 in Washington, D.C., and published in German as "Deutschland und die Deutschen."

In both essays, Mann speculates about the German mentality, meaning, of course, the educated German's mentality. As an émigré writer in "What Is German?" Mann sees the devastating events in Germany as a "historic curse, a dark destiny and aberration, rather than of crime and guilt" (80). He argues that the "German mentality" is essentially indifferent to social and political questions, and he sees National Socialism as a "mythical substitution" for the genuinely social: "Translated from political into the psychological, National Socialism means: 'I do not want the social at all. I want the folk fairy-tale.'" But he is quick to point out that "in the political realm, the fairy-tale becomes a murderous lie" (Mann, "What Is German?" 81).

While he reiterates Germany's apolitical stance in "Germany and the Germans," the essay broaches a more important idea, "German inwardness," a poor translation for the German concept *Innerlichkeit*. Bergsten explains that "inwardness" in Mann's sense "embraces depth of feeling, otherworldly speculation, a sense of the mysterious, demonic side of existence; inwardness finds its best expression in music" (128). According to Mann, the Germans' propensity to dwell on speculative thinking is both their strength and their weakness. German inwardness resulted in German metaphysical speculations, German music, particularly the German *Lied*, and Luther's Reformation as well as German Romanticism. This predilection for German inwardness, however, was also apolitical and led them into their current tragedy. Other nations internalized concepts of democratic freedom through revolutions. The Germans never learned to associate the concept of freedom with nation. "The German idea of freedom is folkish and anti-European, always very close to barbarism" (Mann, "Deutschland" 170).[13] Unlike other German émigrés, Mann doesn't see a good and bad Germany: "The bad Germany, that is the good one led astray, the good one in misfortune, in guilt, and ruin" ("Deutschland" 176).

At the end of "Germany and the Germans," Mann explains that he has presented a "piece of German self-criticism" ("Deutschland" 177). He elaborates further: "The inclination to self-criticism, which often leads to self-loathing, to self-condemnation, is German to the core" (Mann, "Deutschland" 177). Here Mann speaks in his role as Germany's autobiographer. His intent is to offer the self-criticism necessary not to condemn Germany's acts in the political arena but to understand how this sinking into barbarity could occur in a nation where cultural accomplishments had formerly reached such an apex. *Doctor Faustus* is the artistic novel that self-critically lays bare the intrinsic cultural patterns which led to the barbarism fostered on the world by the Nazis.

At the center of this disintegrating world, Adrian Leverkühn portrays the representative artist who gives in to the alluring dark side of German spirituality. In his remote world of artistic excellence, he creates fantastic, modernist music, but he ultimately pays as he succumbs to his devastating illness. He is the Faustian figure more closely allied to the Faust in the chapbook than to Goethe's Faust. He is not saved, and, like Nietzsche, he lives his last years in trembling insanity. Leverkühn's disintegration into madness is the strongest symbol of the ruin of Germany, but his musical voice is only one voice in the *Faustus* chorus. Leverkühn's biographer, Serenus Zeitblom, the schoolteacher, forced into retirement in the face of the rise of the Nazis, also speaks. The story of Leverkühn's meteoric musical career and his eccentric lifestyle is revealed through the sometimes halting and pedantic voice of his friend, Zeitblom. Using Zeitblom's voice as the narrator, Mann enriches the detailed cultural background of the novel. Zeitblom's self-effacing narration surrounds Leverkühn's brilliant executions and provides a needed balance to them. Zeitblom's narration is also the artifice that allows Mann to critique current events in Germany, including the revelations about the Nazis' most heinous crimes, the concentration and death camps.

Leverkühn's biography is situated within several subplots, each calculated to illustrate cultural trends evident in German society during his lifetime. In this way, Mann saturates the novel with German history and culture. Mann, the rational humanist, created characters he felt embodied the cultural icons that seduced the Germans into dangerous inward thinking. The Luther period is one such era. To infuse the work with the flavor of the Luther period, Mann incorporated archaic language from that period into the devil's dialogue. He also used characters' names based on people mentioned in Luther's *Table Talks* which sound odd to the modern German ear. The lusty Professor Kumpf reenacts legendary events from Luther's life. Kumpf hurls a roll at the devil in the corner, as Luther supposedly had thrown an inkwell at the devil cowering in his writing chamber. Always written with an ironic touch, these medieval references call to mind an epic but irrational period.

During their student years, Zeitblom and Leverkühn become tangentially involved with a student group known as the Winifred Society. This group of theological students suggests the German youth movement of the first part of the century, hiking through the mountains or lustily drinking beer at a local establishment. Their youthful philosophical discussions embrace ideas and thoughts which, as Bergsten notes, subtly show a connection with ideas later associated with National Socialism (34–41). The Kridwiss Circle, the group of sophisticated artists and scholars Leverkühn later visits in Munich, is based on real artists and intellectuals Mann met in his early years in Munich. These intellectuals seem to be drawn to radical artistic and elitist ideas that foreshadow the ideas of the educated groups who later supported Hitler.[14]

Mann also uses real people and real events to sharpen the focus on Germany's spiritual decline. In *The Story of a Novel*, Mann describes the montage technique: "The smuggling of living persons, named flatly by name, among the characters of the novel, with whom they take their place, equally real or unreal, is only a minor example of the montage principle" (32). Bergsten, who, along with Lieselotte Voss, has given the most complete references for Mann's *Doctor Faustus*, comments on the intricate development of Leverkühn's character, observing that "almost every detail can be found somewhere in real life or in literature; what is original is the new whole that Mann has constructed" (45). Bergsten further shows that Mann drew on real events and people from his own circle, literature, scholarly works, pamphlets, and almost anything that provided a core of an idea that could be interwoven into the text.

Mann also included incidents which characterized the petty behavior of the society's elite. The Ines Rhodde Institoris and Rudi Schwerdtfeger subplot becomes for Mann a "blend of tragedy and grotesquerie" (*The Story* 131). After marrying Institoris, Ines, now addicted to morphine, finally shoots Schwerdtfeger, her former lover, on a Munich streetcar. Mann observes that "these chapters attempt to paint the final stage of a society when it lies open to ridicule, totally at the mercy of intellectuals' picayune conspiracies" (*The Story* 131). The novel's complexity resides in the detailed background Mann created through distinctive language and places in his main and peripheral characters and plots and in the skill he showed in interweaving these details to create a unified story. The overall ambience achieves his desire — to create a historical panorama which forewarns of danger at the same time it indicts Germany.

For Mann, only a composer could be seen as the representative German artist. But making the protagonist of his work a composer presented his greatest problem: how to have the composer's musical works, written only in words, reflect the brilliance of a modern musical genius. Mann sought specific musical theory advice to carry out his plan. His advisor became the young émigré musician and philosopher Theodor Adorno, who lived nearby in California. Adorno, who had a firm grasp of the history and current developments of music, schooled Mann in verbal musical compositions. He talked at length with Mann about Leverkühn's music and provided critique for the manuscript. Leverkühn's music is integral to Mann's theme. At the beginning of his career, Leverkühn can only write musical parodies because real creative musical expression is no longer possible. He nevertheless yearns for a creative breakthrough to originality which he seeks through his pact with the devil. The composer achieves his creative breakthrough with two works — *Apocalipsis cum figuris* and *The Lamentation of Doctor Faustus*. The oratorio *Apocalipsis cum figuris*, according to Patrick Carnegy, is an "exploration in chaos" (108). Although rigidly constructed using the twelve-tone scale, the work symbolizes the barbarity Mann sees arising in Germany. Irrationality is brewing just below the surface of a sophisticated but spiritually decadent and stratified society. The cantata, *The Lamentation of Doctor Faustus*, Leverkühn's last and boldest work, is constructed to negate Beethoven's *Ninth Symphony*. Where Beethoven's symphony, based on Schiller's poem *Ode to Joy*, displays the confidence of a world centered on humanitarian ideals, *The Lamentation of Doctor Faustus* suggests only nihilism. Again using very rigorous construction based on the twelve syllables (in German) of Faust's statement from the chapbook, "I die as a good and as a bad Christian," the spirituality of the work disappears as each group of instruments fades, finally leaving only the lingering note of a high G played by a cello. Silence follows. Fulfilling the pact, Leverkühn succumbs to insanity.

Mann's indictment of Germany caused controversy almost immediately in his homeland. Even before the book was published there, he came into conflict with members of the so-called inner immigration who complained that the novel "expresses comprehensive and impious hatred of all things German, past, present and to come" (Beddow 100). More nuanced critical judgments of the novel came much later and have been mixed. I have emphasized Mann's artistry in bringing together his diverse sources into a creative whole. But his virtuosity is the reader's difficulty. Hermann Kurzke suggests that the reader's cultural sophistication is critical in making sense of Mann's montage techniques (283). Certainly today for German as well as foreign readers, many subtle references are lost without Bergsten's listing of sources. Many of the essays in the collection *Thomas Mann's Doctor Faustus: A Novel on the Margin of Modernism*, edited by Herbert Lehnert and Peter C. Pfeiffer, express ambivalence about the work.[15] Donna K. Reed, who has deep reservations about the novel's ultimate success, questions its narrow vision: "Critics have also argued that an artist's fate is something much too individual to symbolize a nation's destiny" (135). Reed also points out how narrowly defined Germany is — Mann sees only an elite Germany, never the broader social or political Germany (96). Beddow also charges that the techniques of this work had little influence on creative writers who followed Mann — Christa Wolf and Günther Grass, for example. These writers turned to other forms and structures in coming to terms with National Socialism.

Despite some fundamental criticisms, T. J. Reed nevertheless calls it a successful failure: "If *Doctor Faustus* is a failure, it is more impressive and more moving than most literary successes. . . . Faults and all, it is the greatest of Thomas Mann's works" (402). It remains to be seen how this work eventually will compare with Mann's other works, but it is definitely one of his most personal works along with *Buddenbrooks* and *Tonio Kröger*. Heinrich Mann records that his brother Thomas in exile believed, "Wherever I am is German culture" (150). As Germany's autobiographer, Thomas Mann completes in *Doctor Faustus* a devastating "piece of self-criticism" ("Deutschland" 177). But if he indicts Germany, he also indicts himself. At the very end of the book, Mann asks, "[W]ill the light of hope dawn?" (*Doctor Faustus: The Life* 510). Bergsten points out that Mann plays off his own name in the last line in the German edition: "A lonely man folds his hands and speaks: 'God be merciful to thy poor soul, my friends, my Fatherland!'" (*Doctor Faustus: The Life* 510).[16] In *Doctor Faustus* the twelve-year exile cast a ruthless eye on himself and on his homeland.

chapter eight

A Personal Mythology

To be able to live integrally, without letting yourself live in time, to live only in the instant and not let yourself be poisoned or crushed by the past, by history.

Mircea Eliade, *No Souvenirs*

In his autobiography, *My Life*, Oscar Kokoschka says, "When people write their memoirs they often claim that their actions followed from some sort of mystical intuition, but I tend to think that such things are tricks played by the imagination" (151). For Kokoschka, an artist who frequently lived by his wits and developed a rather practical approach to the vicissitudes of life, writing an autobiography meant cataloging the events and actions of his life. But what about those autobiographers who create a mythology of self? For them, the events and actions of their lives become the basis for mythological patterns of existence and their autobiographical writings the natural environment for the development of their personal mythologies.

Mircea Eliade, the Romanian scholar of comparative religions, creates a mythology of self in his copious autobiographical writings. This writer of scholarly treatises, journalistic essays, and fiction is also an inveterate autobiographer. Four volumes of his lifelong diary and two volumes of his autobiography have been published in English, although he died before completing the second volume. He spent much of his adult working life studying myth and contemplating the modern context of mythical symbols. Influenced by Jung, it is only natural that he would interpret the events of his life through the lens of myth. For him, his imagination is not playing tricks on him, but, rather, his imagination through the power of metaphor helps him to understand the events of his personal reality. Czesław Miłosz, Witold Gombrowicz, Stefan Zweig, and Thomas Mann expressed their autobiographical reactions to exile intellectually; Eliade reacted spiritually, utilizing the metaphor of myth to find meaning in personal trauma. Before turning to a detailed delineation of his response to exile, however, I would like to examine some critical views of autobiographies that may be classified as mythological.

In his survey of autobiographical theorists, Avrom Fleishman notes that myth is one of their major focuses and Jung's integrative psychology one of their major influences: "For Jung, life is a process of integrating the several parts of the mind, the conscious and unconscious aspects of living; and his followers see autobiography as the creation of a 'personal myth' — a unification of the disparate elements and latent impulses of the autobiographer's life" (22). Fleishman views James Olney as the critic who has produced in *Metaphors of Self* the "fullest application of Jungian psychology to autobiography," but he doesn't believe that Olney has translated "the process by which psychological integration is brought about" into literary terms (22–23). Rather, for Fleishman, it is Charles Mauron in his survey of French autobiographers who has accomplished the task of creating a "poetics of personal myth" (26). Mauron's poetics encompass four stylistic practices pertinent to autobiographical writing: memory traces produced in images, repetition, constellation of patterns, and dramatic scene and action. For Fleishman, Olney's emphasis on the autobiographer's creation of metaphors expressing the self roughly corresponds to Mauron's first three stylistic practices. Mauron's last practice — dramatic scene and action — is, however, "noticeable by its absence" from Olney's approach (Fleishman 26). Fleishman considers this dramatic action of the metaphors — discussed by Northrup Frye — to be the essence of autobiography: "It is the tale told by these metaphors — the drama of the metaphors themselves — that is the mythos of autobiography for the *way* in which metaphors dynamically become myths is the general model for the way in which autobiographical narrative generates a self or personal myth" (26).

Fleishman continues that it is pertinent to distinguish at least three senses of *myth* associated with autobiography: "the traditional body of tales that may serve as resources of metaphoric identification, the mythos or narrative that the autobiographer may construct of his metaphors in sequence, and the created identity or new self that he forms in the process of writing" (26–27). Fleishman's admonitions concerning the mythic approach to autobiography pertain to Eliade, who exhibits the above patterning in his autobiographical writings. Before discussing the personal mythology of Eliade, however, I would like to return to Olney.

In the introductory chapter to *Metaphors of Self*, Olney begins his discussion of the theory of autobiography by reminding the reader that "[t]heory is knowledge with meaning, and meaning everywhere depends upon a mind that means; such mind as we know only immediately and subjectively. Knowledge, then, must start there, with the mind and the self, and so also must theory" (16). The task of the mind, then, is to shape external reality. As Olney puts it, the mind of the human being becomes "a great shape-maker impelled forever to find order in himself and to give it to the universe" (*Metaphors* 17). For Olney, myths become "an attempt at explaining something about human nature and the human condition" (*Metaphors* 18). Writing autobiography becomes the autobiographer's myth of a personal universe: "The myth of an earthly paradise that each of us makes tells in all ways more about us than about a material universe" (Olney, *Metaphors* 18). At the same time, however, Olney acknowledges that this process of writing an autobiography changes the self or creates a new self: "It [the myth of an earthly paradise] expresses us in our selfhood as it creates us" (*Metaphors* 18). The metaphors of self create the organizing patterns from within, that is, from within the consciousness of the autobiographer.

The myths the organizing mind creates tell more about the mind creating them than about the material universe. This assertion helps to explain the objections leveled against the autobiographical critics who organize autobiography in this way. The autobiographer is likely to have blind spots that prevent him or her from seeing the world from the same perspective as the distanced critic. Feminists such as Shari Benstock and Susan Stanford Friedman have criticized Olney for theorizing autobiography with such blind spots. Benstock rejects Olney's view that the autobiographer's authority arises from the depth of his or her consciousness to create a unified and integrated identity, newly formed in the process of writing. Benstock sees Olney's view as well as that of Georges Gusdorf as deceptive: "Man enforces a 'unity and identity across time' by 'reconstituting' the ego as a bulwark against disintegration; that is, man denies the very effects of having internalized the alienating world order" (15). In her essay "Authorizing the Autobiographical," in which she uses Virginia Woolf's autobiographical writings as her context, Benstock criticizes Olney's view as ahistorical and not aligned with the precepts of language and the development of identity. Drawing on Lacan and Ragland-Sullivan, she posits that "the social constructs the personal . . . there is no original or instinctual unconscious. Everything in the unconscious gets there from the outside world via symbolization and its effects" (Ragland-Sullivan 99, quoted in Benstock 32). In the following passage, Benstock argues against Olney's claims, denying the validity of his basic ideas about the creation of consciousness (the inside quotes are from Olney):

> Language, which operates according to a principle of division and separation, is the medium by which and through which the "self" is constructed. "Writing the self" is therefore a process of simultaneous sealing and splitting that can only trace fissures of discontinuity. This process may take place through "the individual's special, peculiar psychic configuration," but it is never an act of "consciousness, pure and simple"; it always refers to "objects outside itself, to . . . events, and to . . . other lives"; it always participates in "the shifting, changing unrealities of mundane life"; it is never "atemporal." (Benstock 29; Olney, *Metaphors* 239)

Benstock expands Gusdorf's and Olney's definitions of autobiography. "[D]iaries, journals and letters," encompassing "random reflections on self and society," become valid genres for autobiography—a category seen by Gusdorf as "prior to" or "sources for" "the self-conscious autobiography" (Benstock 15). Likewise, Olney's view of unified identity shaped by the universal patterns of deep consciousness is displaced by the discontinuous self created in the historical moment through language. Both of these expanded views of autobiography more closely reflect the discontinuous self of the woman which has more often been created in such discontinuous texts as diaries, journals, and letters, private versus public forms.

In Susan Stanford Friedman's article "Women's Autobiographical Selves: Theory and Practice," the writing self of the woman is defined in terms of feminist theory of women's identity. Drawing on the theories of Nancy Chodorow and Sheila Rowbotham, among others, Friedman defines woman's self as relational to others and as a part of the group "other," that is, not a member of the dominant culture. Her definition of women's self and women's autobiography contrasts Gusdorf's "isolated being" of Western tradition and Olney's "[n]eoplatonic concept of the teleological self" that is "distinct from all others" (Benstock 36). Friedman sees the relational and collective identity of women to be "a source of strength and transformation" (Benstock 39), for it allows women autobiographers (and others on the margin) to seek a "new consciousness," that is, not a negative and thus alienating consciousness of the dominant culture but an alternative that encompasses their own experience.

Although Benstock and Friedman specifically are interested in theorizing women's autobiography, their views as well as Olney's illuminate interesting perspectives on the autobiographical writings of exiles in general and Eliade specifically. This prolific autobiographer's interest in myth and thus ahistorical patterns, his predilection for using the diary as a workshop for life patterns, and his inclination to interpret the symbol of the labyrinth as an individual symbol for his identity demonstrate aspects of both types of autobiography. The experience of exile, an experience that disrupts the illusory unified sense of identity and therefore marginalizes, plays a role here. Defining the patterns of his existence in meaningful metaphors helps him stabilize his life while coping with social changes, even though they may not acknowledge those social changes.

Mircea Eliade: Journey to the Center

Mircea Eliade was born in Romania in 1907, growing up mostly in Bucharest. A curious child, he spent most of his time reading and studying, although he was an extrovert and always had a large group of friends. He began his writing career as a young man in high school and never ceased writing until his death, amassing a large body of disparate works. He held wide-ranging interests, pursuing scholarly interests scientifically as well as allowing his creative side to flourish in novels and short stories. As a young *lycée* student, he saw the political independence of Romania at the end of World War I as the dawning era of Romanian culture. He came to see himself as one of the major interpreters of this new Romanian culture. A few years later as one of the smart young intellectuals of his country, he began to feel that his generation would only have a short period of time — it turned out to be about twenty years — to shape Romanian culture.

His translator and biographer, Mac Linscott Ricketts, notes that Eliade viewed time as his greatest enemy (Eliade, *Journal, Vol. IV* vii). Always conscious of the relentless push of time, he worked to overcome its restraints. Even in his teens he fought his need for sleep so he could gain extra time for learning and writing (Eliade, *Journey* 63). His battle with time only intensified as he grew older. After he began his writing career and later his scholarly career, he was ambitious enough to see himself as the creator of an oeuvre, not unlike Goethe, one of his idols. When he and many of his friends were forced into exile, he was deeply disappointed that his generation was cut off from continuing their mission of defining culture in Romania. In Paris, living in almost abject poverty in the fifties, he determinedly pursued his scholarly work on comparative religions as well as writing fiction. Eliade's concern about time prevented him from squandering it by seeking a teaching job, which would have relieved his poverty:

That which keeps me from living as I should like is the consciousness that I have to do something which no one else could do as well as I . . . I am not thinking necessarily of the time spent in the preparation and redaction of "the oeuvre." Time is "lost" whatever I do: it is preferable that it be lost in meditation and writing than at the cafe. No, it is not about the time devoted to "the oeuvre" that I lament but about my lost life. How many other freedoms would I not allow myself, if I didn't feel bound by the books I haven't written! (*Journal, Vol. I* 62)

Who is this man driven by such ambition? His autobiographical works provide some answers. The first volume of his autobiography, *Autobiography, Vol. I: 1907–1937: Journey East, Journey West*, which covers the period of his childhood and his adult years in Bucharest, shows a strong-willed person. He is thirsty for knowledge, fairly arrogant, impulsive, passionate, romantic in the sense of seeing his life writ large and charged with meaning, and most of all consumed by writing and thinking. He is not afraid to challenge the establishment around him or to live out the meaning of his life, particularly its spiritual meaning.

As a youth he was an inveterate student of literature as well as natural history. Later at the university he focused on the development of religions and, in particular, Oriental philosophy and religion. He learned languages — French, Italian, Sanskrit, Russian — in order to be able to read writers and scholars important for him and his work, although he confesses that he generally failed languages in school (Eliade, *Journey* 40). At the university he began to see himself as an Orientalist. His ambition to become a first-rate Orientalist led him to India at the age of twenty-three to study with one of his idols, the noted historian of India, Surendranath Dasgupta. He was able to make this trip because he had the courage to write to the Maharaja Manindra Chandra Nandry of Kassimbazar, Dasgupta's patron, whose address he found in the introduction to Dasgupta's major work, *A History of Indian Philosophy*. The maharaja agreed to support him in India, and the Romanian government gave him free passage on one of their ships.

Eliade had a romantic view of the Orient:

I felt that the Orient meant, for me, much more than a fairy-tale landscape or an object for study, that it was a part of the world that deserves to be known for its secret history or for the grandeur of its spiritual creations. It held a strange attraction for me, in which I seemed to read my fate: a mysterious enchantment sprung from unknown sources. (*Journey* 147)

Unlike the Europeans who held themselves aloof from "the natives" in insulated enclaves like the boardinghouse he first lived in on Rippon Street in Calcutta, Eliade immersed himself in Indian culture, finally being asked to live in the home of his mentor, Dasgupta, on the other side of Calcutta. His youthful passion, however, caused his life to take a different turn, for he began a passionate love affair with Dasgupta's daughter, Maitreyi. When her parents discovered their liaison, he was immediately dismissed from the home. He found refuge in a community of pilgrims and hermits in the Svarga Ashram in the Himalayas. Here he began what he characterizes as an "inner transformation" that brought him closer to understanding Indian spirituality:

> If "historical" India were forbidden to me, the road now was opened to "eternal" India. I realized also that I had to know passion, drama, and suffering before renouncing the "historical" dimension of my existence and making my way toward a trans-historical, atemporal, paradigmatic dimension in which tensions and conflicts would disappear of themselves. (Eliade, *Journey* 189)

Through the techniques of yoga, he could overcome the adversity of his failings. Looking back to this period, he recalls that "[t]he last events in Bhawanipore now seemed to me like a long wandering in a labyrinth. I felt that I should not be able to get out of that labyrinth until I should have returned to the 'center'" (Eliade, *Journey* 189).

It is here that the seventy-year-old autobiographer reveals patterns of behavior that Eliade repeated throughout his life.[1] It is also here that his critics and detractors take him to task. Continually on his path of life, Eliade gives meaning to adversity in spiritualist terms, whereas his critics see an egocentric, arrogant person who self-consciously dramatizes his mistakes and reversals. Nevertheless, for him this spiritual dimension creates meaning for the events of his life, and certain themes and metaphors become part of the self-mythology he develops in his autobiographies, diaries, fiction, and even scholarly works.[2] His transhistorical and atemporal approach to reality is at the base of his development of the discipline of humanistic study, the history of religions. He continually sees symbols in everyday reality and uses this perception for restoration.

The twenty-three-year-old Eliade did not, however, succumb to "historical" or "transhistorical" India, for that matter. Instead, a second sexual affair, this time with a young American woman, Jenny, at the ashram meant that he had to leave this refuge immediately. Eliade dramatically states that he would have awakened from his "Indian existence" at any rate.

> What I tried to do — renounce my Western culture and seek a "home" or a "world" in an exotic spiritual universe — was equivalent in a sense to a premature renunciation of all my creative potentialities. I could not have been creative except by remaining in *my* world — which in the first place was the world of Romanian language and culture. And I had no right to renounce it until I had done my duty to it: . . . I should have the right to withdraw permanently to the Himalayas at the *end* of my cultural activities. (Eliade, *Journey* 199–200)

In 1931, Eliade returned to Bucharest to serve in the army and began a productive ten-year period in his home country. Early in this period he finished his dissertation on Tantric yoga in India. At the same time, he was very much involved in writing novels that spoke to his generation. One of a group of young intellectuals called Criterion whose spiritual leader was Nae Ionescu, he became an inspiring lecturer. His charisma was only enhanced by his published fiction. An early novel, *Maitreyi*, recounted his love affair with Dasgupta's daughter in India. This autobiographical novel, in which he "of course . . . bathed that faraway world in a pale golden light, radiated from memory and melancholia," caused a sensation (Eliade, *Journey* 240). His friends were "baffled by his indiscretions," but his young followers, particularly young women, signed up for his courses at the university (Eliade, *Journey* 245).[3] He also wrote successful novels about his generation, particularly one called *The Hooligans*. His infamy was further bolstered by his personal relationships. In 1933 he found himself involved with two women. Already engaged in a volatile love affair with an actress, Sorana, he began a love affair with a friend, Nina, the divorced wife of an army captain. Eliade resolved this conflict by marrying Nina, an action some friends saw as a mundane solution:

> It would have pleased them to have seen me prolonging in Bucharest the adventure begun five years before when I departed for India: to see me, for instance, frequenting sophisticated circles, appearing at our meetings with exotic or extravagant mistresses, continuing to be what they had known me to be since adolescence — an original, a bizarre man. (*Journey* 272–273)

His ambition, however, to create an oeuvre helped him to take the less sensational course. Always conscious of the lack of time, his burning writing ambitions caused him to devote most of his time to his work.

The fear he had always harbored, however, that his generation could not continue to shape Romanian culture, took on a frightening reality in the reflection of transforming events in Germany. His mentor, religion professor Nae Ionescu, became embroiled with the nationalist Legionary movement, the Iron Guard. Eliade maintained that Ionescu's ideological stance was not meant to be political, but it affected Eliade nonetheless. Ionescu was detained along with most of his followers, including Eliade.[4] Eliade, however, had the good fortune to be released and was granted a government post in England. In 1940 he went on to Portugal, where he spent the remaining war years. His wife, Nina, died of cancer. Recognizing after the war that he dared not return to Communist Romania if he wanted to pursue his studies in comparative religions, he moved to France. When Ionescu died in 1940, Eliade felt released from the pressure of being his follower. He knew, however, that his career as an academic in Romania was over:

I was barely thirty-one . . . I did not view exile as a cleavage from Romanian culture, but only as a change of perspective, or more precisely as a displacement in diaspora. I thought of exile with no bitterness or notion of revenge. In a few years' time I had had, in Romania, everything but wealth: fame, notoriety, prestige. I had been, and perhaps still was, the head of the young generation. I saw the destiny of our generation; ten years of freedom . . . and then again to be conditioned by the historical moment. (Eliade, *Exile's Odyssey* 13–14)

Although Eliade can speak of his exile with philosophical resignation late in his life, the diarist frequently chronicled a longing for his lost Romanian "paradise." Nevertheless, drawing on the mythic metaphors that sustained his consciousness, Eliade directed his ambition and his work to a new arena.

For him the labyrinth came to symbolize regeneration. In Paris right after the war in 1946 and perhaps at the lowest ebb of his life, he was living in severe poverty cut off from his homeland, just beginning to be able to write well in French, and recovering from having lost his wife to cancer. Nevertheless, Eliade sustained himself through his transformative imagination:

I don't believe I'm the only one who can transcend repeated failures and melancholic, hopeless sufferings when, by an effort of lucidity and willpower, I understand that they represent, in the immediate, concrete sense of the word, a *descensus ad infernum*. Once you "wake up" *realizing* that you are wandering in an infernal labyrinth, you feel anew, tenfold those spiritual powers you considered long since lost. In that moment, any suffering becomes an "initiatory ordeal." (*Journal, Vol. I* 23)

The labyrinth with its associative myths becomes the touchstone for him in adversity.

In Paris he began his long ascent as a scholar of the history of religions that ultimately brought him to the University of Chicago. In 1948, he met and married Christenel Cottescu, another Romanian exile. Supported by her and his friends among the Romanian exiles, including the playwright Ionesco, and by the large network of international Orientalist scholars he had cultivated since he was a very young man, he began to make a name for himself. He did not accept a teaching position in Europe but published and read papers at conferences, and his reputation spread. In 1950 he received his first invitation to Eranos, a yearly gathering sponsored by Frau Olga Froebe and held every summer in Ascona, Switzerland. Here Karl Keyréni, Jung, and other important scholars of myth, religion, psychology, and other fields came together for provocative discussion. That year the Bollingen Foundation awarded him a three-year scholarship that ended his money worries.

As far back as 1947, Ananda Coomraswamy had written Eliade asking him to come to the United States. It seemed a likely place for him to settle. But he didn't find his way there until 1956, when he was invited to give the Haskell Lectures at the University of Chicago. University officials asked him to stay as a visiting professor in 1956–57 and hired him permanently in 1957. Established at last, he and his wife began the rhythm of existence they continued until close to his death. They spent the academic year in Chicago, returning to Europe every summer. He achieved wide academic fame at the University of Chicago, teaching seminars with such notable figures as Richard Rorty and Paul Tillich. He helped to found the American Society for the Study of Religions and retired in 1983, when he was honored with an endowed chair named for him.

Although as his translator notes, most of the works which established his fame as a scholar of religions were already published during his years in Romania and in Paris, he continued to publish scholarly works and fiction (Eliade, *Exile's Odyssey* xv). He wrote creative works — fiction, autobiography, his diary — in Romanian and his other works for the most part in French. When he died in 1986, he left a large body of work, his oeuvre.

The thief of time still snatched the recognition of this oeuvre from Eliade. While he had the ambition and fortitude to create divergent works across a wide spectrum, the events of history prevented his work from being evaluated as a whole because he did not have an integrated audience. His early journalistic and fictional works were directed to his cultural audience in Romania. His scholarly works, mostly published in French, were directed to a specialized audience. Although he continued writing fiction and wrote what is considered his most significant novel, *The Forbidden Trees*, during his years in Paris, he wrote it in Romanian. The audience for this book was cut off from him, locked behind a totalitarian and censoring government. He tried to publish fiction in French translation but was unsuccessful. The recent opening up of Romania came too late for him, and it remains to be seen if a wider audience for his works will emerge.

Approaching Eliade as an autobiographer is illuminating, for through the "personal myth" he establishes in his autobiographical writings, the reader can glimpse patterns of his total work. In this regard, too, his voluminous diary is more compelling than the two-volume autobiography. Written throughout almost his entire life, the diary had until recently been published only in excerpts. Some of his travel diaries had been published while he was still in Romania, but major excerpts from his later diaries were first published in 1977 and given the title *No Souvenirs*. The diaries of his later years have all been published in English. *No Souvenirs* and *Journal, Vol. I: 1945–1955* contain poignant reminiscences of his early exile. The title, *No Souvenirs*, refers to the fact that almost all earlier writings — journalistic articles, fiction, diaries, and notes — associated with his life in Romania were left there without his later access to them.

His study of Orientalism and India led him to explore the psychology and religion of archaic humans. Myth and symbol became paramount. To Eliade, human beings live in a network of interdependent connections that have symbology. In his diary he observes that modern man, like the man of archaic societies, cannot exist without myths, without exemplary stories. (Eliade, *Journal, Vol. I* 150). Life, even the life of an exile, means "an infinite series of intellectual adventures — I use the word adventure in its primary meaning of existential risk" (Eliade, *No Souvenirs* 74). For Eliade, every "exile is a Ulysses traveling toward Ithaca," traveling toward the center. It is incumbent on the exile to penetrate "the hidden meaning of his wanderings, and [to] understand them as a long series of initiation trials." The individual must decode the "hidden meanings, symbols, in the sufferings, the depressions, [and] the dry periods in everyday life" (Eliade, *No Souvenirs* 85).

In his Parisian period, Eliade overcame the "terrors of history" by interpreting the results of historical upheaval in his life through the regenerative power of myth. Battling "vagatonia" (melancholic depressions during which work was impossible), periods of poverty, and a new language, he pursued his journey to the center of the labyrinth. Once challenged that he saw symbols where others did not, he responded, "I see such symbols because they are there. If another person doesn't see them, it doesn't mean they don't exist but simply that he can't see them" (Eliade, *Journal, Vol. I* 8). For Eliade, the resonance of the ancient myths takes on a personal meaning. The experience of exile is surmounted with the sustaining meaning of a present, individually interpreted myth.

Eliade was keenly aware of the criticism leveled against his emphasis on the modern power of myth. In his diary, he articulates the objections to his views: "I idealize the primitives, I exaggerate the importance of their myths, instead of demystifying them and emphasizing their dependence on historical events (colonialism, aculturalization, etc.)" (Eliade, *No Souvenirs* 121). He emphasizes his need to respond to the world transhistorically and to contend with the criticism this engendered from colleagues. He sees his mission as trying to communicate with archaic man, for he believes that "Western culture must rediscover and proclaim all of man's modes of being. My duty is to show the grandeur, sometimes naive, sometimes monstrous and tragic, of archaic modes of being" (Eliade, *No Souvenirs* 179).

Eliade is an unique figure in the critical debates of autobiography. His two-volume autobiography, written at the end of his life, shows a well-formed persona. In it, the autobiographical shaper of reality constructs his life as an avant-garde thinker, an intellectual leader of Romanian culture, and a man of erudition. He also reveals himself to be a dynamic individual who provides meanings for his lapses in behavior and refuses to hide his monumental ambition. Although the second volume included the diary of his trip to Germany in 1937, it is, like volume I, by and large an autobiography with privileged authority in Benstock's terms.[5] On the other hand, Eliade's long-term diary shows a different persona — a discontinuous persona, an engaging thinker whose zest for knowledge and understanding is overpowering. As is to be expected from the diary form, Eliade's voice in the diary is passionate, exploratory, anguished, insistent as well as hesitant and questioning. His diary displays a questing mind which searches for meaning in a confusing and disintegrating world. Though the diary does not present a finished persona, I found it more captivating. Eliade's use of the form exalts it. For the most part he leaves out mundanity, instead exploring ideas and confronting larger issues.

Eliade's overarching symbol of the engaged life, the labyrinth, suffuses both forms of his autobiographical writings. In both, his wide-ranging mind challenges modern critical theories of Marxism, poststructuralism, and feminist thinking. Delineating the modern world through the focus of these theories sheds a penetrating and meaningful light on the social construction of societies, past and present. And in this intellectual world, archetypal and myth criticism is considered intellectually bankrupt. Eliade, however, discounted critics who insisted that he bind himself to the sociological-historical moment. He sought and found meaning in myth, which he perceived transhistorically or "eternally." Personally and professionally, he reminded his audiences that myth and the archaic human being have a message for the modern desacralized world.

But if Eliade sought and used the power of myth and symbol to gain personal distance from the "terrors of history," he still could not totally shake his acculturation. Though he once wrote that exile was only a "change of perspective," his diary contradicts that he found the transition easy. In the diary, he repeatedly records the painful episodes of remembering his homeland and all that he had lost in leaving it behind. As with Miłosz, though, Eliade came to a time when the rawness of the exile experience receded. In Paris during those troubling years after the war, he had a revelation while walking up to Sacre-Coeur: "Our exile from the homeland is a long and difficult initiatory order, destined to purify and transform us [the Romanian diaspora]. The distant, inaccessible country will be like a paradise to which we return spiritually, that is in spirit, in secret" (Eliade, *Journal, Vol. I* 145). He overcame the hardships of exile by finding solace in a personal myth.

chapter nine

The Currency of Language

I have been trying to learn English, but it
won't stick in this old brain.
  Albert Einstein, *The Muses Flee Hitler*

It has always been the fate of countless emigrants and exiles to
become stranded, as it were, between languages, so that in the end
they cannot find words to describe adequately even the most
common experiences.
  Sidney Rosenfeld

It is an ancient evil of emigration that language is,
in effect, refrigerated. At best it can be preserved.
  Ernst Weiss, *Gesammelte Werke*

In making the transition from one foreign culture to another,
perhaps the hardest task for any exile is mastering a new language.
A few — artists, film directors, musicians, for example — could at
least continue their careers after some adjustment, but for writers
and actors the loss of audience for their native language was devastating. Exiles' ability to master a second language many times made
the difference between personal disaster or their successful integration into a new culture. The German exile community in Hollywood bore this out.[1] For Thomas Mann and Bertolt Brecht, the
German language was their medium of artistry, and the "Hollywood scene" was alien. Neither author could nor would seriously
use English in place of German, so each remained isolated within
the new culture. Lion Feuchtwanger, in contrast, became one of
the most successful émigrés in California, precisely because he
accustomed himself so easily to Hollywood's culture. His works,
translated and published in English, were even offered in book
clubs.

Being able to adopt a new language frequently depended on
age, resiliency, and language background. Exiles such as Hannah

Arendt, Mircea Eliade, and Arthur Koestler adapted well into new languages and were able to continue their writing careers in their new languages. Others did not fare so well. Mastering a new language well enough to write and speak it with authority takes time and perseverance. Vladimir Nabokov was one of the few writers who published fictional works successfully in English and wrote about American culture. *Lolita* stands out as an American classic. Before Nabokov's exile, he was tutored in Russian, English, Latin, and French. He was educated at Cambridge and gave lessons in English and Russian during his exile years in Berlin (Nabokov 258). His early training in foreign languages clearly helped him master English well enough to write novels in this second language. For some, the lack of language-learning ability completely changed their lives. For others, adapting to a new language was an arduous and sometimes unsuccessful project. For most exile autobiographers, however, language plays a major role in their exile accounts.

Exiles trying to break language barriers were beset with myriad problems. Initially the need to survive in the new culture gave them great impetus to learn to understand and speak a new language. Clearly, exiles whose education and background had included long-term study and use of foreign languages adapted best. But writers needed not only to conquer the rudiments of the new language but also to be able to manipulate its nuances. Learning to use a second language at this level is a time-consuming and complex process. They also needed an audience. A general lament from exile authors is the loss of their native-speaking audiences. Gaining a new audience demanded new focuses. Moreover, writers needed new publishers willing to take a chance on their work. Those who wanted to continue using their mother tongue found publishers reluctant to accept their works unless they were well-established authors. Their audiences in the foreign settings were frequently too small to make publication worthwhile. Even Thomas Mann had his work translated almost immediately. *Doctor Faustus* appeared first in English.

Additionally, writers' command of their mother tongue sometimes suffered. Cut off from their cultural roots, they no longer had the ongoing nourishment of their native language. As Czesław

Miłosz noted, some genres of literature — the realistic novel, for example — are not conducive to being written in exile. ("Notes" 282). Nevertheless, exiles were usually highly motivated. An astonishing number did adapt to their new working environment. In *Escape to Life*, Erika and Klaus Mann briefly portray their struggle to conquer English so that they could conduct a lecture tour in the United States. Trying to bring refugee and exile problems to the attention of Americans meant being able to speak fluently in English. Carl Zuckmayer paints a painful picture of learning English so that he could lecture. After he decided to leave Hollywood, he worked briefly for Erwin Piscator's Dramatic Workshop at the New School for Social Research. He chose to lecture on "Humor in the Drama" but quickly realized that while he could write comedies, he couldn't theorize about humor, particularly not in a new language. Working in English became sheer torture for him:

> To this day I fall into a cold sweat whenever I think of my initial lecture. Laboriously, I wrote out the manuscript, and my translator, Elizabeth Norman-Hapgood, who was as fluent in German and Russian as she was in her native language and who had translated all the writing of Stanislavski into English, devoted no less labor to remodeling my involutions into a halfway speakable American. Then she coached me in the pronunciation of the same and tricked out my manuscript with all sorts of accents and curlicues to help me read it properly. (Zuckmayer 353)

While he found the students "kind and friendly," he recognized that the language barrier was too severe. In addition, the intellectual mentality at the school did not suit him. He then tried to collaborate on a play with Fritz Kortner for Broadway, but he "realize[d] fully and finally that synthetic literary products and artistic abortions would bring [him] neither inner satisfaction nor outward success" (Zuckmayer 355). This painful realization helped him decide to move to Vermont and become a farmer during the remaining war years.

Alfred Döblin also felt the grief of trying to cope with a new language:

> I had entered France as a foreigner, of course, but I happily would have liquidated — at least externally — all of what was foreign in my character, just as the Nazis had liquidated me by forcing me to expatriate. The only way would have been to speak French. And if I could not penetrate to the heart of the language, I would at least learn it superficially. That was difficult enough, but understandable in someone who continued daily to write in the German language. (*DJ* 93)

As we saw in chapter 1, Döblin could not remain in France, so the problems of language continued when he arrived in the United States.

By contrast, Arthur Koestler, perhaps the best example of an exile for whom changing languages was the least traumatic, quickly adapted. He notes in the first volume of his autobiography, *Arrow in the Blue*, that he always had a "conflict of languages in his head" (122). Born in Hungary, he grew up speaking German at home and Hungarian at school but used German more when he moved to Vienna at age fourteen. German began to get "the upper hand" and finally became his major language when he began his career as a correspondent for the Ullstein papers (Koestler, *Arrow* 122). His travels and his predilections gave him an impetus to use other languages well. During his last school year at the University of Vienna, he suddenly tore up his student book and decided to go to Israel to join the Zionist movement. In order to go, he had to pass an exam in Hebrew, which he had never studied: "The Hebrew examination was the easiest part of the preliminaries; I had learnt to speak the revived language of the Bible with tolerable fluency, by a kind of pressure-cooker method, in a few weeks" (Koestler, *Arrow* 133). Unfortunately for interested foreign language teachers, he doesn't elaborate on this "pressure-cooker method." He also spent several years living in France and presumably spoke French tolerably well. He traveled in Russia for over a year, "picking up" that language, and spent several months in a Spanish jail, where he also learned a smattering of Spanish. When he left the continent at the beginning of the French occupation, he switched into English, which became his new writing language: "In 1940 I had to change languages a second time, from German to English, this time abruptly and without transition. *Darkness at Noon* was the last book that I wrote in German: all my other books since have been written in English" (Koestler, *Arrow* 122).

Although he speaks glibly of changing languages, he does recognize that the process is not easy or without anguish. In the second volume of his autobiography, *The Invisible Writing*, Koestler describes writers' pains when they give up their native language and thus the nurturing soil of their native culture: "But to abandon his native language and traditions means in most cases death to the writer, and his transformation into a nondescript, cosmopolitan journalist or literary hack" (173). He also admits that the transition to a new language is almost never complete. "When awake, I now think in English, when asleep, in Hungarian or German or French. As I am a chronic sleep-talker, my wife is often awakened by my polylingual gibberish" (Koestler, *Arrow* 122).

Koestler's ready adaptability into a new language stood him well during his years of upheaval and change. It also gave him great insight into the capabilities of various languages. Although he spoke Hebrew in Israel, he thought it inappropriate to the development of that country:

It was a petrified language which had ceased to develop and been abandoned by the Jews long before the Christian era — in the day of Christ, they spoke Aramaic — and had now been revived by a *tour de force*. Its archaic structure and vocabulary made it totally unfit to serve as a vehicle for modern thought, to render the shades of feeling and meaning of twentieth century man. By making Hebrew their official language, the small Jewish community of Palestine cast itself off not only from Western civilization, but also from its own cultural past. (Koestler, *Arrow* 205)

Like Koestler, many exiles were able to continue their careers in a new language. Hannah Arendt, according to her biographer,

Elizabeth Young-Bruehl, was "a student of Greek, Latin, and French" and a "well-equipped language learner" (164). She quickly found her way first in French and then in English, unlike her husband, Henry Blücher. Having helped to support her husband and mother in France because she adapted so quickly to using French, she set out immediately to learn English when the family came to America in 1941. She took the practical step of applying for and receiving a two-month placement with an American family to learn English. She began teaching at the New School for Social Research and later wrote her treatises on totalitarianism and other works in English.

Mircea Eliade also quickly perceived that a language change was necessary if he was to continue his career. Early in his life, he understood the advantages of knowing other languages. He learned to read other languages primarily to be able to read important works in the original. Although he failed to learn French through the school methodology, he set out to read his favorite authors, Balzac and Voltaire, in French and calculatedly impressed his arrogant French teacher. He learned Italian to read Papini, Russian to read Dostoevsky, and German to read Goethe. When he became captivated by the ancient Orient, he studied Persian and Sanskrit. During his three-year sojourn in India, he continued to study Sanskrit and worked on learning to speak Bengali. In India, however, he realized he did not "enjoy the linguistic genius of a Tucci or Paul Pelliot," so he gave up the goal of becoming a Sanskrit scholar (Eliade, *Journey* 177). His wide study of foreign languages helped him to make the crucial transition from writing in Romanian to writing in French.

Eliade thoroughly catalogs his impressions of making this change. In September 1945, he noted, "What a strange feeling, to imagine myself writing in another language! I'll have to begin to write in French before I know it well. But the thing that bothers me most is, I don't know at all the public I'll be addressing" (Eliade, *Journal, Vol. I* 1). On December 16 of the same year, Eliade complains, "But how can I write anything in a language I don't know well, one that resists me as soon as I try to imagine, to dream, to play in it?" (*Journal, Vol. I* 11). Mastering the poetic dimension of a second language becomes a prime motivation for writers like Eliade, Nabokov, Anaïs Nin, and Eva Hoffman. But although Eliade went on to master French well, writing volumes of scholarly works in his new language, he never succeeded in writing creative works in French. Even after he moved to the United States, he primarily wrote his scholarly works in French and his creative works in Romanian. Like Zuckmayer, Eliade articulates his discovery that a writer's language develops from his immersion in his native culture. In Paris in 1946 he confronted the possibility of failure:

> For several hours, I had the feeling that these last six years of living abroad have separated me from the sources of my creativity, have diverted me from the course predestined for me, and that whatever I may do from here on, those six years are irretrievably lost. Moreover, that they have set me on a road from which I cannot return. The terror of the irreversible? for the first time in my life I could see and accept myself as a failure. (Eliade, *Journal, Vol. I* 33)

Elias Canetti: German, His Belated Mother Tongue

Elias Canetti, winner of the 1981 Nobel Prize for literature, published three volumes of autobiography in his late seventies. These works cover the period of his life from his early childhood in Ruschuk, Bulgaria, through his years in Vienna, which ended when he fled to England in 1937, where he lived until his death in 1994. *The Tongue Set Free: Remembrance of a European Childhood, The Torch in My Ear,* and *The Play of the Eyes* loosely cohere around the imagery alluded to in the titles — the tongue, the ears, and the eyes. The first volume centers on Canetti's coming to language. The second concerns the effect of voices in his writing, particularly the voices of Vienna and specifically that of Karl Kraus, editor of the fiery journal *Die Fackel* (The torch) in the twenties and thirties. The title of the third volume, focusing on his later, productive years in Vienna when his career as a writer began to take form, refers to the intriguing eyes of Anna Mahler, the talented sculptor and famous daughter of Gustav and Alma Mahler. The play of her intense eyes becomes the symbol of his passion for Anna and her subsequent rejection of him. *The Tongue Set Free* is the most engrossing of the three volumes, although *The Play of the Eyes* with its sometimes biting critique of the Viennese ambience in the thirties also closely engages the reader. In all three volumes, however, major themes weave in and out: Canetti's obsession with language and "words and letters" and his intellectual development through his teachers, friends, and family, most notably his mother. He also discusses major subjects in his writing — the crowd, the underside of life, evil, misogyny, and acoustic masks. The overriding emphasis, however, is his passion for the German language, the medium of his creativity. After the early moves from Ruschuk to Manchester, England, he lived in Lausanne, Vienna, Zurich, and Frankfurt before settling as an adult in Vienna. During his later years when he no longer lived in a country where German was spoken, he saw the German language as his exiled home.

Like Nabokov and Eliade, Canetti grew up with many languages. In his hometown lived Bulgarians, Turks, Spanish Jews (the Sephardim), Albanians, Armenians, Gypsies, Romanians from across the river, and the occasional Russian. Knowing several languages was not only usual but in some cases necessary: "People often talked about languages; seven or eight different tongues were spoken in our city alone, everyone understood something of each language. Only the little girls, who came from villages, spoke just Bulgarian and were therefore considered stupid. Languages could save the lives of the people" (Canetti, *Tongue* 27).

Canetti's first language was Ladino, the language spoken by his Sephardic relatives in Ruschuk. This language, a derivative of Spanish, became for him, as he says later, "a stunted language for children and the kitchen" (Canetti, *Torch* 91). He first recorded his childhood memories of the "loud and fierce" life in Ruschuk in Ladino. Later he recognized that its swiftness compared to the "slower languages of English and German" gave him the impetus for excelling intellectually (Canetti, *Tongue* 205). Nevertheless, he initially dismissed Ladino. Only later, on a trip back to Ruschuk when he heard his cousin use the language to persuade Sephardic Jews to emigrate to Israel, did Canetti realize its possibilities: "I was amazed to discover that it was possible to use this language [Ladino] . . . to speak about universal matters, to fill people with such passion that they earnestly considered dropping everything, leaving a country in which they had been settled for generations, a country which took them seriously and respected them" (Canetti, *Torch* 90). Finally, some years later, he noted that he "put away [his] distrust of Ladino culture and viewed it with respect" when he was persuaded by his friend Dr. Sonne that a man cannot overlook his ancestry (Canetti, *Play* 295).

Canetti notes a peculiar language transfer he experienced as a child stemming from his Ladino background. His "worst [childhood] terrors" were retained in Ladino, but most of his childhood memories were "rendered into German within [him]." As a matter of fact, he refers to this unconscious translation as perhaps the "oddest thing he has to tell about [his] youth":

> I cannot say exactly how this happened. I don't know at what point in time, on what occasion, this or that translated itself. I never probed into the matter; perhaps I was afraid to destroy my most precious memories with a methodical examination based on rigorous principles. I can say only one thing with certainty: The events of those years are present to my mind in all their strength and freshness (I've fed on them for over sixty years), but the vast majority are tied to words that I did not know at that time. It seems natural to me to write them down now; I don't have the feeling that I am changing or warping anything. It is not like the literary translation of a book from one language to another, it is a translation that happened of its own accord in my unconscious. (Canetti, *Tongue* 10)

Although Canetti learned German as a second mother tongue, his psychological allegiance to it was ferocious.

Canetti's introduction to German is very idiosyncratic. His parents, who met and fell in love in Vienna while at school, spoke

German to each other, a practice that made the young Canetti jealous. As he said, he had "good reason to feel excluded when [his] parents began their conversations" (Canetti, *Tongue* 23). His two grandfathers originally did not approve of his parents' marriage, and their school days in Vienna became a secret time for them and the language that "fed their love." The child Canetti noticed the transformation of his parents when they talked to each other in their secret language, and he became obsessed with learning this magic language, German:

> I believed that they were talking about wondrous things that could be spoken of only in that language. After begging and begging [to be taught the language] to no avail, I ran away angrily into another room, which was seldom used, and I repeated to myself the sentences I had heard from them, in their precise intonation, like magic formulas; I practiced them often to myself, and as soon as I was alone, I reeled off all the sentences or individual words I had practiced — reeled them off so rapidly that no one could possibly have understood me. But I made sure never to let my parents notice, responding to their secrecy with my own. (*Tongue* 24)

The next stage of the young Canetti's language acquisition occurred when he was about six years old and the Canettis moved to England so that his father could go into business there. He learned English at home and in school, but he continued to hear Ladino and French spoken by his mother's Arditti relatives and of course German from his mother and father.

The sojourn in England, however, ended abruptly when his father died suddenly. Years later, Canetti blamed his mother for his father's death. His mother had just returned from a long visit at a German spa where she had received the attentions of a doctor, supposedly because he liked the way she spoke German. Because his father was stricken, presumably by a stroke, while she was telling him about her stay at the spa, young Canetti believed that she had betrayed his father, not that she had sexually betrayed him, but she had betrayed him by using their secret love language with someone else: "Her infidelity had consisted in speaking German, the intimate language between her and my father, with a man who was courting her. All the important events of their love life, their engagement, their marriage, their liberation from my grandfather's tyranny, had taken place in German" (*Play* 224). To him the German words they used with each other were sacred. She had profaned these words, this language (Canetti, *Play* 227).

Canetti's father's death disrupted their lives. His mother took him and his two brothers, Nessim and George, to Vienna, the place where she had been the happiest. Canetti as the oldest son became her companion, but first he had to learn the magic language, German: "On the way to Vienna she stopped in Lausanne and hit me over the head with the language which up until then I had not been allowed to understand" (*Play* 227).

Coming from a rather large, well-off family, Canetti's mother was a sophisticated, intelligent, and well-educated woman who spoke several languages and seemed to be at home in any of the larger European cities where there was a Sephardic community. As a widow with three small children, she did not initially suffer economically, only emotionally. She became a major force in Canetti's education as his first instructor in German language and literature. But as a German teacher she was unique, succeeding wildly but using diabolical methods. Canetti claimed that she needed to be able to speak German, her language of intimacy, with him after his father died, so she set about teaching him the language overnight. "So, in a very short time, she forced me to achieve something beyond the strength of any child, and the fact that she succeeded determined the deeper nature of my German; it was a belated mother tongue, implanted in true pain" (Canetti, *Tongue* 70).

It is worth a detailed look at how she instructed him:

We sat at the big table in the dining room, I on the narrower side, with a view of the lake and the sails. She sat around the corner to my left and held the textbook in such a way that I couldn't look in. She always kept it far from me. "You don't need it," she said, "you can't understand it yet anyway." But despite this explanation, I felt she was withholding the book like a secret. She read a German sentence to me and had me repeat it. Disliking my accent, she made me repeat the sentence several times, until it struck her as tolerable. But this didn't occur often, for she derided me for my accent, and since I couldn't stand her derision for anything in the world, I made an effort and soon pronounced the sentence correctly. Only then did she tell me what the sentence meant in English. But this she never repeated, I had to note it instantly and for all time, Then she quickly went on to the next sentence and allowed the same procedure; as soon as I pronounced it correctly, she translated it, eyed me imperiously to make me note it, and was already on the next sentence. I don't know how many sentences she expected to drill me in the first time; let us conservatively say a few; I fear it was many. She let me go, saying: "Repeat it all to yourself. You must not forget a single sentence. Not a single one. Tomorrow, we shall continue." She kept the book, and I was left to myself, perplexed. (Canetti, *Tongue* 67–68)

If he didn't know the sentences, she then complained that he was not her son, because no son of hers could not learn languages quickly. Or she called him an idiot, a particularly distressing epithet for him, since he had a retarded cousin that the family called an idiot.

Some of Mrs. Canetti's methods were very forward-thinking for 1913. Teaching languages orally is customary today but was not then. On the other hand, she transgressed a real taboo, teaching languages in an atmosphere of fear and dread. She gave him much too much material at one time and demanded a superhuman response. He felt that he was stupid. Eventually, the governess interceded for him by telling his mother that he needed the book because he wanted to learn Gothic script. After he had the book to study by, he made rapid progress indeed, once again renewing her faith in her son.

Despite his odd introduction to German, the language became a deep source of inspiration for him. Throughout his life he was superconscious of the varying forms of German spoken around him — the Swiss German he practiced secretly away from his mother's prying ears, the "hard contours" of the Frankfurt German heard on the streets during the period of inflation in the twenties, and later the varying forms of Viennese German. One of the attributes he praises most in his friend Wotruba, the sculptor, was the strength of his language:

> [Wotruba] always expressed himself in the idiom of the Viennese district with whose cobblestones he had played as a child, and one was amazed to find that everything, literally everything, could be said in that language. It was not the language of Nestroy, which had shown me long ago that there was a Viennese idiom full of startling possibilities, an idiom that fostered delightful bursts of inspiration, an idiom both comical and profound, inexhaustible, varied, sublime in its acuteness, which no man of this hapless century can completely master. Perhaps Wotruba's language had only one thing in common with Nestroy's: its hardness, the exact opposite of the sweetness for which Vienna is famed and ill-famed throughout the world. (Canetti, *Play* III)

In another place, he elaborates on his aversion to the subversion of language by the Viennese.

> The way people dither with words, trot them out only to take them back, the way their contours are blurred, the way they are made to merge and melt though still present, to refract like prisms, to take on opalescent colors, to come forward before they themselves want to; the cowardice, the slavishness that is imposed on them — how sick I was of seeing words thus debased, for I took them so seriously that I even disliked distorting them for playful purposes, I wanted them intact, and I wanted them to carry their full force. (Canetti, *Play* 98)

As this passage suggests, the German language was sacred ground for Canetti. Canetti's learning German as he did made him a careful observer of language. His fascination with the German voices he heard in his life becomes a strength in his writing.

When Canetti returned to England, he went back to a country and a language he already knew, but he took German with him. From his friend Dr. Sonne he learned that

> [n]o part of a life must be lost. What a man touched upon, he should take with him. If he forgot it, he should be reminded. What gives a man worth is that he incorporates everything he has experienced. This includes the countries where he had lived, the people whose voices he has heard. It also takes in his origins, if he can find out something about them. (Canetti, *Play* 297)

For Canetti, this meant Ladino and the Ladino culture and the other languages he learned as a child, but most important, it meant his belated mother tongue, the German language. He recognized that "the story of a banishment must include everything that happened before it as well as the right subsequently claimed by the victims" (Canetti, *Play* 297). Dr. Sonne, the mentor Canetti saw as a prophet of the coming disaster in Europe, entreated Canetti to take his entire history with him into exile: "[H]e enabled me to take a language with me and to hold on to it so firmly that I would never under any circumstances be in danger of losing it" (*Play* 297). In England the German language became his homeland.

chapter ten

Reconstructing the Self:
Identity and Reflections of
the Postmodern

It is the person who remembers — not memory.
  Christa Wolf, *Patterns of Childhood*

A new thought. The end of the world didn't mean one's own death.
  Christa Wolf, *Patterns of Childhood*

Autobiographies written by those who experienced exile as children or those who are emotionally fragile are particularly illuminating, for their dramatic experiences involved changing allegiances, languages, and cultural definitions. Adding to these problems was significant psychological alienation, personal as well as social. These autobiographers frequently coped with loss or change of name, disruption of memory, loss of language on the most intimate level, and loss of the active symbolic formation that Robert J. Lifton calls "psychic numbing," as I discussed in chapter 5.

Lifton describes psychic numbing as the process of "decentering" and a "loss of grounding" that leads to the inability to create inner (symbolic) form. It is a complex, disorienting process:

> Impaired grounding inevitably leads to desymbolization, a state in which one can no longer re-create (give form to or symbolize) at least certain kinds of experience. Loss of centering and desymbolization are likely to follow upon extremely intense imagery of separation, disintegration, and stasis in a losing struggle to give psychic form to internal and external environments. (Lifton, *The Life* 79)

The holocaust situations Lifton studied included war, social disruption, and ideological change as well as life-threatening accidents or even mind-numbing everyday situations. Any of these experiences can cause psychic numbing. They "may be identified whenever there is interference in the 'formative' mental function" (Lifton, *The Life* 38). Exile autobiographers in particular illustrate Lifton's conclusions.

In *Lost in Translation* (1989), Eva Hoffman, writing in her early forties, recalls how she felt on the first day of school in Vancouver when teachers Anglicized her and her sister's Polish name:

> Nothing much has happened, except a small, seismic mental shift. The twist in our names takes them a tiny distance from us — but it's a gap into which the infinite hobgoblin of abstraction enters. Our Polish names didn't refer to us; they were as surely us as our eyes or hands. These new appellations, which we ourselves can't yet pronounce, are not us. They are identification tags, disembodied signs pointing to objects that happen to be my sister and myself. (105)

The alienation that Hoffman illustrates is typical of exiles' brutal process of integrating into a new culture. Hoffman, Saul Friedländer in *When Memory Comes* (1979), Christa Wolf in *Patterns of Childhood* (1980), Gregor von Rezzori in *The Snows of Yesteryear* (1989), and others write autobiographies that demonstrate this process, imaging the (re)construction of a new, provisional self that can be called postmodern.

In her article "*The Woman Warrior* as Postmodern Autobiography," Marilyn Yalom describes the tendencies of postmodernism as "openness, pluralism, marginality, difference, discontinuity, incoherence, fragmentation, absence, skepticism, irony, playfulness, ambiguity, chance, popular culture, heterogeneity, circularity" (108–109). The far-reaching social disruptions caused by the rise of fascism and its defeat irreparably changed the lives of these exiles. When Friedländer's family left Prague when he was about five years old, he suffered a disruption of memory that he only recovered as an adult. He felt compelled to write about his life as a way to recover the memories of himself as a child and his relationship with his parents (Friedländer 72). During Christa Wolf's yearlong journey of deprivation on the refugee trek westward, she begins at age sixteen to realize the ramifications of the past twelve years of the Third Reich, which for her had been a "normal" child-hood and adolescence. Publishing *Patterns of Childhood* in her for-ties, Wolf as the adult narrator forces herself to face the wider im-plications of that "normal" childhood. Eva Hoffman's loss of the Polish language, the intimate language of her identity, causes her the most pain, and she only feels comfortable with her restruc-tured identity when she has mastered her new language, English, on this same level.

The structure of these autobiographies clearly reflects the post-modern aesthetic. These interesting but problematic works de-pict discontinuous selves and seem to demand forms that symbol-ize this discontinuity, as Paul Jay observes in his discussion of the evolution of autobiographical forms. Of the works cited above, none is a straightforward narrative. All move back and forth from the present to the past, with frequent interruptions by the autobiographer.

But even if these autobiographers use a disjointed form to con-vey psychological destruction, it is clear that writing down these experiences helps them redefine their selves in their new cultural homes. Psychologically, then, the writing of an exile autobiography becomes a strategic part of the healing process in overcoming the rifts of their selfhood. Before turning to the main focus of this chap-ter, the reconstruction of identity through the renewal of language, I would like to discuss three unusual autobiographies which reflect Yalom's definition of postmodern autobiography — Rezzori's *The Snows of Yesteryear*, Jacov Lind's *Counting My Steps*, and Charlotte Salomon's visual autobiography of 762 watercolors, *Life? or Thea-ter?* These postmodern autobiographies present powerful but very different coping strategies that succeeded in allowing the autobi-ographers to survive exile and psychological uprooting.

Psychic Displacements

In Rezzori's *The Snows of Yesteryear*, his postmodern self emerges only in portraits of the five *others* in his life — his father, mother, nursemaid, sister, and governess. To protect his scarred identity, formed in his childhood and youth, he adopts this strategy of distancing himself from the reader by carefully placing the others in his life in the foreground. Rezzori, who grew up in a German family in "erstwhile" Romania, writes that his childhood, characterized by the disintegration of his dysfunctional, anti-Semitic family, precedes "by two decades the disintegration of Europe" (*Snows* 49), as we saw in chapter 6. His identity only asserts itself within the refracted memory of the other actors in his world, appearing like a jagged mosaic that in turn suggests the disparate pieces of the leftover Austro-Hungarian Empire. For Rezzori, there is no center where the security of family, home, and country can envelop the young boy. He survives a dysfunctional family but remains hidden and remote. He refers to himself as cold, unemotional, and therefore not appropriate subject material of an autobiographer. To tell his story of his autobiography — or perhaps his personal memoir? — he chooses warm memories of his sister, nursemaid, and governess, as well as the disturbing memories of his father and mother. He survives by holding his emotions in check, living in partial "psychic numbness," if you will. He allows himself to be glimpsed only in the lives of others. The narratives of these other lives bring him succor but not wholeness.

In contrast, Lind, a teenage Jewish boy who survives the war living in Holland and Germany, preserves his identity by distancing himself from the strong emotions of family and ethnic ties. On purpose, he deadens his soul so that he can move through his uprooted world as a survivor. And he makes it. He eludes the Nazis, the Allies' bombs, the transit and death camps, but when it is over, he has lost all connection: "In 1945 existence and identity were still a dubious affair. . . . I noticed I had nothing left but my bare skin. Everything else had gone. No Zionism, no idealism. No lover and no hatred and no language. Worst of all — no language" (Lind 177). To become the writer he wanted to be, he first had to find language and the meaning of what language can say. "I needed the understanding of an entire world from which I had seceded on 20 June 1943" (Lind 180). On that day he alone escaped the bomb which destroyed the barge and its crew on which he worked. To get through this ordeal, he used irony and sarcasm to keep from feeling his own loss and the horror of the world around him. After the war, he had somehow to find renewal. He succeeded in getting to Palestine, where his family had gone, and partially reconnected to the Jewish community that he made himself "hate" during the war to stay alive, as he put it. He stayed there for several years. In the end, however, he recognized that he needed to write, but his languages — his mother tongue of German, which he didn't like and which had all but disappeared, his "bargeman's" Dutch, even Hebrew — could not provide the medium for his need. He returned to Europe, settling in England, where the English language at first enticed him. His autobiographies were written in English, but later he recaptured his mother tongue and began to use that language for his work. At the war's end, he felt his mind was "burnt-out," his familiar mother tongue an inadequate medium to describe the unfamiliar world around him: "I needed a new language to express feelings and ideas I hardly knew how to formulate" (Lind 223). Lind needed the sustenance of a new language to re-create his self, a self that he had purposely submerged in order to survive a world most absurd. He survived by living once removed, "psychically numb" to the absurdity around him.

The artist Charlotte Salomon created one of the most incredible autobiographies among exiles. She titled her work *Life? or Theater? An Operetta*. In completing over 760 watercolors of the scenes of her life, she was able to survive exile and the torments of a family history of suicide. Her unique work, now housed in the Jewish Historical Museum in Amsterdam, has been most recently and lovingly highlighted by the meticulously researched, sensitive biography by Mary Lowenthal Felstiner, *To Paint Her Life: Charlotte Salomon in the Nazi Era* (1994). In this interpretative biography, Felstiner passionately delineates the artist's life: Salomon's life within her dysfunctional family, the pressures on her as a Jewish artist from the rising Nazi menace, and her exile to the south of France. Salomon's coping strategy was to survive her own psychological demons by painting and commenting on the scenes of her life, essentially creating a play in watercolor. That strategy succeeded in keeping her from choosing the route of others in her family — giving in to suicide. Her personal survival is short-lived, however, for she and her new husband were caught by Nazis in the Jewish roundups in France, taken to the transit camp Drancy, and subsequently shipped to Auschwitz, where Salomon presumably died on arrival.

Salomon was the daughter of a Jewish surgeon-physician, Alfred Salomon, and Fränze Grünwald. Her parents met during the war in 1915 when Fränze was a volunteer. Charlotte was born in 1917, and the family set up housekeeping in the Charlottenburg district of Berlin. In the winter of 1925–26, Charlotte's mother, Fränze, sank into a depression and eventually jumped to her death from her apartment window. Salomon was told that her mother died of influenza. She did not know that her mother had committed suicide, nor did she know that her mother's sister, her namesake, Aunt Charlotte, had earlier done the same. In exile, when she learned that six women and two men in her mother's family chose to end their lives, she was devastated. Her painting of this discovery shows the heads of her relatives. She captions it: "One two three four five six, does this mean we have a hex?" (Felstiner, *To Paint* 11).

Her mother's early death significantly affected the young Charlotte, causing her to become withdrawn and shy. Her father remarried a popular Jewish opera singer, Paula Lindberg, who became a real mother to Charlotte and helped to draw her out. According to Felstiner, however, Salomon was never very outgoing or emotionally strong. She left the Fürstin Bismarck school in 1933 when the Nazis came to power. In 1935, she succeeded against great odds in getting into the Berlin Art Academy, although only a fraction of the school's population was Jewish. Here she practiced her skills and learned to draw. At this point in her life she met Alfred Wolfsohn, a musician friend of her stepmother. The many, many paintings depicting their relationship reveal what an impact this man had on Salomon. Felstiner portrayed him as an almost cultish figure in Berlin who had an enormous effect on women. For the impressionable Charlotte, he became almost a god. Paula Salomon-Lindberg described him fifty years later. "He was a really gifted man but a dangerous dilettante. He missed his education in the war [World War I], he lost his memory, even his name, for a year. His method of singing did damage, because he made conclusions about other voices from his own. But with the young ladies he was an angel" (Felstiner, *To Paint* 52). Salomon's apparently very brief affair with him became a major act in her pictorial play.

In 1938, after Kristallnacht, Salomon's parents decided to send her to her grandparents, who had emigrated and were then living with an American, Ottilie Moore, in her villa, L'Ermitage, in Ville-franche on the Côte d'Azur. Mrs. Moore took in refugees and or-phaned children, including Salomon's grandparents, Ludwig and Marianne Benda. When Salomon arrived in France, she was ap-parently very unhappy with the way her grandparents took advan-tage of Mrs. Moore's hospitality. Her grandmother, as Felstiner points out, was beginning to feel "useless, female, and foreign" (*To Paint* 104). She finally succumbed to the family depression, as had her two daughters. Salomon and her grandparents took rooms in Nice, a short distance away, when Mrs. Moore closed her house. One day in September 1939, Salomon found her grand-mother hanging with a noose around her neck, "just short of dead" (Felstiner, *To Paint* 104). At this point Charlotte began to paint her life in scenes. Her grandmother's suicide attempt marks the period when Charlotte learned about the history of her mother's family. Her grandmother descended into madness, and one day, briefly unattended, she hurled herself through a window, like her daughter Fränze, Charlotte's mother.

For the next two years, in exile and confronted with the knowl-edge of the suicidal tragedies of her family, Charlotte painted to save herself from going mad. She created a volume of watercolors which she then edited, numbered, and finally taped over with trac-ing paper on which she wrote captions. She boxed them up, la-beled them property of Ottilie Moore, gave them to a friend, and survived her family's madness but not Hitler's.

Salomon's autobiography primarily reflects the psychological alienation she felt from her family because of their history of de-pression. As a child and young adult in Berlin, she was withdrawn, isolated within the family apartment. Living with her grandpar-ents in France, she experienced severe emotional conflict. But the context of a larger, even more alienating world is never far away.

From her window in Berlin, she painted marching Nazi groups and recorded the terror of Nazi youths smashing windows during Kristallnacht. Even the picture of Salomon and Daberlohn, presumably her and Wolfsohn, which represents an interlude of her young womanhood recorded outside the pressing walls of her family's apartment, cannot be seen as a respite if taken at face value. Felstiner reminds us of the subtext: the bench the lovers sat on would have had the words "For Aryans Only" (NUR FÜR ARIER) written on the back (*To Paint* 48–49). When Salomon was living in France she knew only too well the escalating danger for Jews, even in the false security of exile on the Riviera. Before long the reality of her situation intruded. Along with her grandparents, she was sent for a brief time to Gurs, the women's internment camp in the south of France. She returned to Nice, where she barely missed being picked up in one of the first roundups. As the external danger edged ever closer to her, she felt compelled to finish her work, to leave a record.

Salomon chose to tell her story in captioned scenes of a pictorial play that focused on the question, Life or theater? She depicted her psychic pain through distorted and repetitive figures in the hundreds of scenes. The snaking captions put into words her fears for herself and her world. The movement expressed in the distortion and fluidity of words and pictures conveys her inner storm. The postmodern form is uniquely suited to her anguished life. Paramount are the questions she asks about herself — will she too go mad? But the stage, increasingly subject to Nazi terrors, provides the backdrop for her turmoil.

The autobiographies of Rezzori, Lind, and Salomon reveal the coping strategies these three devised to survive their own particular demons as well as the disruptive forces around them. Their particular psychic realities were only exacerbated by the times they lived through. Salomon did not survive the Holocaust, but she survived her own demons, leaving a unique autobiography on the exile experience. Lind and Rezzori continued to live with their exile. Their autobiographies add another piece to the puzzle of this identity-altering experience.

Alienating Language

In chapter 9, I focused on the important role that learning a new language played in the lives of exiles. In the jargon of the pedagogy of language learning, the process is called second language acquisition. The preceding chapter's focus, however, promotes language as a tool, a currency in the new culture, or, in the case of Elias Canetti, first a tool and then a defended refuge. In this chapter, I want to focus on another aspect of language, what John Paul Eakin calls the "second acquisition of language" (*Fictions* 9). In his study, he asserts that autobiographers redefine their identity through the process of writing autobiography. According to Eakin, the language the autobiographer creates changes the autobiographer's identity. For exile autobiographers in particular, a life in a new language necessarily redefines the dislocated self, for the process of integrating into a new language and culture is time-consuming and overwhelmingly psychically uprooting. And it is here that exile autobiography becomes so potent. Revealing a reconstructed identity in language, particularly if it is a new language, throws a psychological light on the theoretical supposition of the self as an "intersection of discourses," as I have discussed in chapter 5.

During the "second acquisition of language" the exile autobiographer hammers out a new definition of self, leading to a refocusing of symbolic forms after the numbness of exile. In this section I concentrate on the reconstruction of self through the autobiographical journeys of those exiles for whom the experience is, on the one hand, the most psychologically disruptive and self-questioning and, on the other, the most self-affirming. To overcome the devastating numbness and loss of active symbolic formation that Robert J. Lifton describes, these exile autobiographers need to re-create themselves. Their painful journeys add new dimensions of meaning to the word identity. At the same time, they refine a form of autobiography — the postmodern autobiography.

In shaping his new identity through the act of writing his autobiography Saul Friedländer pursues the meaning of who he is by delving into the fragmentary memories of his previous life. He stops at one point in order to consider if he should go on:

> When I leaf through these pages I often feel deeply discouraged: I will never be able to express what I want to say; these lines, often clumsy, are very far removed, I know, from my memories, and even my memories retrieve only sparse fragments of my parents' existence, of their world, of the time when I was a child. . . . Should I go on? (Friedländer 134)

He recognizes that for most people, memories of childhood and youth follow a path that naturally fits into the continuous path of generations in a family. The ones remaining can explain to the children about the ones who have departed. But for him continuity of family was abruptly broken. He did not have the opportunity to learn about his family and his roots in the normal way. He must write to explain the few remaining artifacts of his previous life — a few letters and "two or three yellowed photographs." These "traces" and his shards of memory are his only remaining ties to his family and the roots of who he is (Friedländer 134).

In his autobiography, Friedländer, who was born Pavel Friedländer in 1932, depicts the wrenching task of recapturing the identity he lost when his parents were sent to Auschwitz. Friedländer was five years old when his German-speaking parents fled Prague for France. After a two-year sojourn in France his parents, realizing that they were about to be sent to a concentration camp, placed Pavel in a French Catholic orphanage and changed his name to Paul-Henri Ferland. Friedländer grew up French Catholic but ultimately reclaimed his Jewish heritage, renaming himself Saul Friedländer. Only slowly was he able to piece together what had happened.

Like Hoffman, Friedländer talks about the confusion and estrangement of his changing names:

> "Paul-Henri." I couldn't get used to my new name. At home I had been called Pavel, or rather Pavlicek, the usual Czech diminutive. . . . Then from Paris to Néris I had become Paul,

which for a child was something quite different. As Paul I didn't feel like Pavlicek any more, but Paul-Henri was worse still; I had crossed a line and was now on the other side. Paul could have been Czech and Jewish; Paul-Henri could be nothing but French and resolutely Catholic, and I was not yet naturally so. What was more, that was not the last of the name changes: I subsequently became Shaul on disembarking in Israel, and then Saul, a compromise between the Saül that French requires and the Paul that I had been. In short, it is impossible to know which name I am, and that in the final analysis seems to me sufficient expression of a real and profound confusion. (94)

It took years for Friedländer to sort out these name changes and what they meant to him. Each change meant trying to negotiate the culture that the name implied — German, Czech, Jewish, French, Catholic, Israeli. But, illustrating yet again how adaptable humans can be, he found ways to cope.

After his parents were sent out of France, he more or less adjusted to the Catholic orphanage, Montneuf, and eventually found solace in the rituals of the Catholic religion. The identity of Paul-Henri Ferland surrounded him like a cloak, and he began to envision himself as a priest. His life in a Catholic boys school continued after the war, even after he learned about his parents' death. Eventually, however, he learned from a priest, Father M., about the practices of Auschwitz and the other concentration camps. This knowledge galvanized him to learn all he could about his background. He no longer repressed memories of his early days but allowed memories of his parents to surface. During this period, he also began to study what it meant to be Jewish, an endeavor that became his lifelong occupation as a historian of the Holocaust. He gained a patron, a rich French Jew, who paid for his schooling and wanted him to continue his education. But his ties to his background, to his Jewishness took hold of his imagination. Shortly before he was to graduate from the *lycée* and enter the university, he found himself so much under the sway of Zionism that he ran away to Israel. But not even this radical change left him in peace: "It took me a long, long time to find the way back to my own past. I could not banish the memory of events themselves, but if I tried to speak of them or pick up a pen to describe them, I immediately found myself in the grip of a strange paralysis" (Friedländer 102). His paralysis was broken by becoming acquainted with some autistic youngsters whom he worked with at Tulsa, the mental institution his uncle directed in Sweden. From these youngsters who wanted to speak but could not he learned that he needed to speak, to articulate his story.

From Friedländer's association with these tortured children came the compulsion for him to write his autobiography, thus to connect the fragments of his history, harking to a "need for synthesis, for a thoroughgoing coherence that no longer excludes anything" (114). Following these insights, he was merciless in recovering his unique past identity and forging a new present one. The writing process reconnects his present and past selves, thereby healing the fissures of his memory. Through the writing, he confronts the discontinuities of his life and surmounts them.

*   *   *

More than any other exile autobiographer, Eva Hoffman illuminates the process of reconstructing identity through language. First characterizing the breakdown of the language that damages her feeling of identity, she then follows with the long second acquisition of the language of a new identity. Early in her autobiography, she writes of her love of words: "I love words insofar as they correspond to the world insofar as they give it to me in a heightened form. The more words I have the more distinct, precise my perceptions become — and such lucidity is a form of joy" (Hoffman 28). But once she begins to unpack the deadening of exile, it quickly becomes apparent that it is precisely this capturing of the world in words which is breaking down for her.

As she was leaving Poland, members of her homeroom class accompanied her and her family to the train. The moment they left, her world drained of color: "Then they are told to leave the train, and I stop crying, as if the fluid current of life had suddenly stopped flowing. For the rest of the trip, I am overcome by dullness that is like Lethe" (Hoffman 89). Numbness and dullness followed her to Canada. Her inquisitive mind pushes her to learn this new language, English, but her emotional self makes this task difficult. Daily she added new words to her vocabulary, but she speaks of developing allergies to certain turns of phrase. "'You're welcome,' for example, strikes me as a gaucherie and I can hardly bring myself to say it — I suppose because it implies that there's something to be thanked for, which in Polish would be impolite" (Hoffman 106). The emotional coloring of language arising from the conflict of the two cultures causes her to see even an innocuous, conventional phrase as a "prick of artifice." She also takes an irrational liking for certain words, mostly learned from reading, such as "enigmatic" and "insolent." The postmodern autobiographer interjects and describes the problem, the "signifier had become severed from the signified" (Hoffman 106). Like her new name, the new words she learns do not automatically refer to the same objects "in the same unquestioned way" as they did in Polish:

"River" in Polish was a vital sound, energized with the essence of riverhood, of my rivers, of my being immersed in rivers. "River" in English is cold — a word without an aura. It has no accumulated associations for me, and it does not give off the radiating haze of connotation. It does not evoke.

The process, alas, works in reverse as well. When I see a river now, it is not shaped, assimilated by the word that accommodates it to the psyche — a word that makes a body of water a river rather than an uncontained element. The river before me remains a thing, absolutely other, absolutely unbending to the grasp of my mind. (Hoffman 106)

This process of language estrangement necessarily impinges on the continuity of identity and brings about psychic numbness: "[T]he radical disjoining between word and thing is a desiccating alchemy, draining the world not only of significance but of its colors, striations, nuances — its very existence. It is the loss of a living connection" (Hoffman 107).

Hoffman's description of what happened to her after she got to Canada almost defines Lifton's clinical view of psychic numbing and loss of symbolization:

The worst losses come at night. As I lie down in a strange bed in a strange house — I wait for that spontaneous flow of inner language which used to be my nighttime talk with myself, my way of informing the ego where the id had been. Nothing comes. Polish, in a short time, has atrophied, shriveled from sheer uselessness. Its words don't apply to my new experiences; they're not coeval with any of the objects, or faces, or the very air I breathe in the daytime. In English, words have not penetrated to those layers of my psyche from which a private conversation could proceed. This interval before sleep used to be the time when my mind became both receptive and alert, when images and words rose up to consciousness, reiterating what had happened during the day, adding the day's experiences to those already stored there, spinning out the thread of my personal story.

Now, this picture-and-word show is gone; the thread has been snapped. I have no interior language, and without it, interior images — those images through which we take it in, love it, make it our own — become blurred too. (Hoffman 107–108)

The process of assimilating everyday events, of transposing them through language into the mind stuff of consciousness, is truncated, thus blocking the perception of ongoing identity. The people she meets and the events of the day defy description by her blocked mind. She cannot interpret reality because she has no meaningful words with which to do so. In trying to describe a Canadian couple she and her mother meet, nothing fits. These two people are unlike any people she has ever met. Polish words "slip off of them without sticking," and "English words don't hook onto anything." She tries to come up with some English words, but "they float up in an uncertain space. . . . They come up from a part of my brain in which labels may be manufactured but which has no connection to my instincts, quick reactions, knowledge" (Hoffman 108). It is as if she is falling through "a black hole." She laments, "I'm not filled with language anymore, and I have only a memory of fullness to anguish me with the knowledge that, in this dark and empty state, I don't really exist" (Hoffman 108).

For Hoffman, it is an ongoing inner conversation that allows her to interpret the world, to make sense of her environment while she is creating a self-identity, a self-story. Without the necessary words, and here she means meaningful words, those that take on her own emotional coloration, she doesn't exist. She is struck psychically numb. She is at ground zero of the expanding self.

In chapter 6, I noted that Nabokov, as well as Hoffman, described the exile's world as dull and flat, as a world drained of color and vitality, a world benumbed. Both these exiles sometimes experienced severe internal dislocation and consequently expressed the emotional flatness of the exile's world. But neither experienced the physical, emotional, and psychological deprivations of the Holocaust victim or the battered refugee. The particular experience of the Holocaust creates a suffering necessarily apart from the experiences of exiles, and thus I have not included autobiographies of camp victims in the scope of this study, for as Wolf says, "For all eternity, an insurmountable barrier separates the sufferers [of the Holocaust] from those who went free" (*Patterns* 233). The harrowing experiences of displaced peoples and refugees, however, do present a boundary situation in Lifton's sense that causes "psychic numbing." Christa Wolf's autobiographical heroine in *Patterns of Childhood*, Nelly, joined the trek of refugees from the East. As we will see, she, too, experienced this numbing. Nelly, too, hits ground zero of the psychic self.

Unlike Friedländer and Hoffman, Christa Wolf does not undergo the change from one national culture to another and thus from one national language to another, but she does change cultures. As her comfortable childhood in the Third Reich dissolves, she begins a year as a refugee, a chaotic transition to her new home, East Germany, during the cold war. Friedländer's overwhelming task was to connect his memory threads into a coherent identity. Hoffman's task was to cope with the loss of meaningful language and her Polish identity. For Wolf the task was quite different, but the effects of the events she suffered are similar to effects Friedländer and Hoffman and even Lind, Rezzori, and Salomon experienced. For Friedländer and Hoffman, the memory, even if fragmentary, becomes the lifeline to rebuilding the self. While Friedländer at first suppresses his memory fragments defensively, his investigation of memory allows him to break through his paralysis and shape a self-story. For Hoffman, the "memory of the fullness of language" prods her to rebuild her identity in a new language. For Nelly, the breakdown of the German way of life during the war and, particularly, letting go of the idea of the Third Reich calls for another strategy, forgetfulness.

Toward the end of her retelling of Nelly's story, Wolf asks poignantly, "What are we to do with the things that are engraved in our memories?" (*Patterns* 309). The reality of the Third Reich unfolds before Nelly, causing a gap to occur in her own perception of reality. She absorbs the shocks first of learning that her world is collapsing and then coming to understand that her beloved world is one of degradation. She lives through the chaos the Germans referred to as ground zero, the period between the collapse of the German bureaucracy and the establishment of the occupation. Nelly's strategy for survival is psychic numbing and amnesia. The narrator, Wolf, notes that a physician who worked in a camp recognized that his patients could only survive by becoming automatons, by not associating what they were going through with despair.

Lifton sees psychic numbing as a continuum:

> The first pole suggests breakdown of the formative process, or at the very least some impairment and desymbolization in response to what is perceived as a threat to physical or psychic existence. The other pole suggests an enhanced capacity for function and symbolization, within which whatever internal threat exists becomes transmitted and at least managed. Psychic numbing, then, is by no means always a bad thing. (*The Life* 80)

His examples of the positive effect of psychic numbing include the "surgeon who operates the more skillfully for not permitting himself to feel the potential consequences of failure" and the "pilot who lands his plane more safely by focusing on technical details rather than on the beauties of the sunset" (Lifton, *The Life* 80).

The numbing that Nelly undergoes and the amnesia she gives in to can be seen as coping mechanisms in the extremity of the situation she lives through. But for the narrator, this amnesia that Nelly developed became so total for her (and many of her fellow Germans) that she is compelled to tear it away. Finding a reference in the *General Anzeiger*, the newspaper in her former hometown, to the establishment of Dachau on 21 March 1933, she asserts, "Anyone who later affirmed that he had not known about the concentration camps had completely forgotten that their establishment had been reported in the papers. (A bewildering suspicion: They really had forgotten. Completely. Total war: total amnesia.)" (Wolf, *Patterns* 39).[1] Recognizing that so many had succumbed to amnesia about the war's events, the narrator admonishes herself by saying to the child Nelly, who has been hiding, "You're going to talk" (*P* 48). Up to that point, Nelly had refused to talk, but the narrator will no longer allow her to remain silent.

Nelly's descent into psychic numbing began before she left Landsberg an der Warthe. After the attempt on the Führer's life, all students wore their Hitler Youth uniforms to school to show their loyalty. But the everyday life in the Reich was already beginning to break down. Large groups of refugees streamed through the town, and Nelly began to deny what she saw with her own eyes. She described the "strange look" in the refugees' eyes "only as a sign of exhaustion" (*P* 278). She couldn't absorb what was happening. "Her inner memory, which forms opinions about an event, had to remain mute. Nothing but mechanical notetaking" (*P* 279). She saw the activities around her "as if a wall had been punched between her observations and her attempts to interpret them" (*P* 278), but her "external memory" preserved scenes "the way a piece of amber preserves a fly: dead" (*P* 279). Like everyone else, she quit school to help tend to the refugees, but she collapsed, an individual episode that foreshadows the collapse of the country, what the narrator describes as a "collapsed horizon of events" (*P* 296). Once her own family became part of the refugee flow, the deadening worsened. But Nelly was not ready to give in to the belief that "final victory" would not be possible. "Better to escape into absurd thinking than to give in to the unthinkable" (*P* 296). Although she hissed at her grandfather when he said that "the war was a 'lost game'" (*P* 296), a moment of reckoning came to her when her twelve-year-old brother, Lutz, informed her he no longer believed in "Germany's victory":

> If Nelly had ever been in danger of going off the deep end, it must have been that night. Desperation was not the proper expression for it, because to be able to despair indicates a connection with the cause of the desperation. Nelly was no longer connected with anything. The road on which she was walking . . . was the outermost edge of reality. The circumference of the thoughts she was still allowed to think had shrunk to a dot: to get through. (*P* 313)

She adhered to her inner compulsion to focus on the dot, for since "all outside commands had broken down," if the dot disappeared, she would go insane. She did not acknowledge her brother's statement.

What Nelly was registering only mechanically was an "unbelievable disorder" (*P* 319):

> What she saw, smelled, tasted, felt, heard — distorted faces, people dragging themselves along, the reek of the different overnight quarters, the lukewarm, thin coffee served by Red Cross helpers from their tin coffeepots, the sack of bedding that had turned into a solid rock from her sitting on it, the curses and invective over the distribution of places to sleep — it all registered, but she was by no means allowed to convert it into emotions, such as despair, discouragement. (*P* 296)

She learned that "emotional numbness" could be mistaken for courage, for she was praised for her courage: "She's really courageous for her age" (*P* 296). The narrator reminds the reader that this inner deadening was later called the "black box": "The brain as a black box, incapable of taking in images, let alone forming words" (*P* 281). The narrator observes too that the refugees' "inner sense of time stopped" (*P* 319):

Finally, Nelly begins to stop taking in images at all. When does a person stop picturing things? (Does everyone stop doing it?) Bardikow is the last place preserved in your memory as a series of images. If it's true that the good Lord is to be found in details — and the devil, too, of course — then both withdraw more and more from memory in the years to come. : . . Not that there are no more pictures: flash photos, also sequences. But their luminosity has diminished, as if the colors of reality no longer had the same quality as before. Instead, other mementos — flashes of perception and insight, conversations, states of emotion, thought processes — are becoming noteworthy. (P 336)

Richard Rorty and Daniel C. Dennett have noted how much humans depend on visual perception for their understanding of their world.[2] It's not as if Nelly no longer absorbed visual images, but she stopped coloring them with her own emotions. They no longer played a role in her own self-story. Nelly, alienated by becoming a refugee and by the upsetting events she experienced, learned the tricks of the survivor: "To be inconsiderate — without looking back — as a basic requirement for survival; one of the prerequisites that separate the living from the survivors" (P 334). The narrator breaks in and elaborates on how far-reaching this psychic numbing was for Nelly, herself, and her contemporaries:

Love and death, illness, health, fear and hope left a deep impression in your memory. Events that have been run through the filter of a consciousness that is not sure of itself — sieved, diluted, stripped of their reality — disappear almost without a trace. Years without memory which follow the beginning years. Years during which suspicion of sensory experience keeps growing. Only our contemporaries have had to forget so much in order to continue functioning. (P 387)

Nelly becomes estranged and alienated from her former self. This process intensified as she learned more about the despicable practices of the Nazi government. On their trek from the East, Nelly's mother invited a concentration camp evacuee to join them for their soup around the campfire. The family's introduction to his stories of Nazi practices helped pull the blinders from Nelly's eyes. Nelly's mother naively retorted to the man's admission that he was a communist, "But that wasn't reason enough to put you in a concentration camp." Nelly was interested to see that even though the man could no longer show "anger," "perplexity, or mere astonishment" (psychic numbing), his face could "change expression." He commented, almost as if to himself, "Where on earth have you all been living?" This statement, uttered by the concentration camp victim "without special emphasis," later became a motto for the narrator (P 332).

As the reality of the Third Reich suffuses her life, Nelly (and, of course, the narrator) begins to cope with new perceptions of that reality. She is first disabused of her pledge "to keep absolute, lasting faith in the Führer" (P 304). When Nelly goes back to school, she and her classmates "bitterly" denied their teacher's pronouncement that Schiller's *Don Carlos* had not been taught "in German schools during the final years of National Socialism because of a single sentence: 'Give us freedom of thought, Sire!'" (P 388). She begins to understand the pejorative use of the term "Nazis" (P 389) and learns that she had "been living under a dictatorship for twelve years, apparently without noticing it" (P 394). Nowhere does this jarring of perception and reality become more meaningful than in regard to language, and particularly the language of the self, the language one uses in defining the self.

Early in the book, the narrator discloses that "[e]very sentence, almost every sentence, in this language [German] has a ghastly undertone, which the ear, that simple hollow muscle, signals obstinately" (P 48). A great part of the narrator's expressed estrangement revolves around this phenomenon of alienating language. Like Hoffman, the narrator is fascinated by language and its power. When Nelly was a child, she recognized that certain words were "glitter words" because "[w]hen adults pronounced them, their eyes began to glitter" (P 57). Many of these words were glitter words for all children at all times, but some became glitter words because of the historical time. "Oversexed is a glitter word. Consumption is another glitter word, although a weaker one" (*P* 58). Glitter words of the Third Reich have a more ominous meaning: "Alien blood was another glitter word. The law for the prevention of genetically unfit offspring. Or sterilization which, as the paper stressed, was not to be identified with castration" (*P* 60). Words that might have been glitter words for young Nelly become almost unendurable for the narrator. As the narrator begins to unlock the suppressed memories, the difficulties of facing this estrangement of language haunts her. Words then become her salvation as well, although the temptation to quit and once again allow amnesia to take hold is strong:

> What do you do when unfit words work themselves into the text: is it a warning? To pay close attention or to quit? To wait until you'll have returned to the place where there's no exact equivalent of "fair"; where it may mean "impartial, honest, blond, light-skinned"? Where concentration on one's work will not be impaired by bewilderment about a language that doesn't hesitate to declare only the blond, the light-skinned, among its users to be impartial, honest, decent. And beautiful.
>
> Irritation. A single word, never before part of your vocabulary, passes the board of control without objective. The filters, which at first strictly held back, for critical evaluation, all that was unfamiliar, now seem to have become more porous. Where will it all lead? (*P* 254)

The writing process mirrors the excavation of her soul. Pulling away the protective layers causes her work to stop and her language to break into fragments. The defensive amnesia is beginning to break down in the writing process, but it is deeply ingrained and vitally protective:

> Where Nelly's participation was deepest, where she showed devotion, where she gave of herself, all relevant details have been obliterated. Gradually, one might assume. And it isn't difficult to guess the reason, the forgetting must have gratified a deeply

insecure awareness which, as we all know, can instruct our memory behind our own backs, such as: Stop thinking about it. Instructions that are faithfully followed through the years. Avoid certain memories. Don't speak about them. Suppress words, sentences, whole chains of thought, that might give rise to remembering. Don't ask your contemporaries certain questions. Because it is unbearable to think the tiny word "I" in connection with the word "Auschwitz." "I" in the past conditional: I would have. I might have. I could have. Done it. Obeyed orders. (P 229–230)

Deep in the psyche, in the juncture where I and self meet, there is a chasm covered over with amnesia. Looking into this chasm is the scariest, most threatening task. How can she or anyone contemplate the unthinkable? How can she face her devotion as a young girl to a government that created Auschwitz? And to be faced with the ultimate question — could she have? Done it? Obeyed orders? Over the years, like her contemporaries she has defended herself against the chaos of these thoughts with strong imperatives beginning with don't, avoid, suppress. But in the end she stands face to face with the thoughts that annihilate her soul. I would. I might have. I could have. Done it. Obeyed orders.

At one point, Wolf almost allows Nelly to remain hidden, not to bring that darkest portion of her story to life through words. Ironically, the narrator thought of this when she was visiting her former hometown, now in Poland. There a foreign language surrounded her:

During the night, in the foreign town with its foreign-language noises, you realize that the emotions which you have suppressed will take revenge and you understand their strategy to the last detail: They apparently withdraw, taking related emotions with them. Now it's no longer just the sadness, the pain, that are nonexistent but regret and, above all, memory, as well. Memory of homesickness, sadness, regret. Taking the ax to the root. Emotions are not yet fused with words; in the future emotions will not be governed by spontaneity but — no use avoiding the word — by calculation. . . . To live between echoes, between the echoes of echoes . . . What you're permitted to find difficult, and what not. What you're permitted to know, and what not. What must be talked about, and in what tone. And what must be buried in silence forever. You wouldn't be able to write this book, and you knew why. (*P* 275–276)

Despite this turn in thinking, when the morning comes, she is ready once again to pick up the task. She reaches down to that level where she again fuses the picture with its emotional covering.

Patterns of Childhood has a unique narrative structure. This autobiographical novel employs three time frames and voices in the second, third, and, finally, first person. There are also three stages of action: Nelly's childhood, the ongoing historical events at the time of writing (1972 to 1975), and what one critic has called the "almost diaristic account of the writing process" (Frieden 475). Having failed to write the novel in the first person as the narrator tells the reader at the beginning (*P* 5), she unfolds Nelly's story in the third person, objectifying her earlier self but simultaneously revealing her current self in the inner dialogue she narrates in the German familiar form of *du* (you). In the end she fuses the two voices and speaks briefly from the "I" voice: "And the past, which can still split the first person into the second and the third — has its hegemony been broken? Will the voices be still? I don't know" (*P* 406). This autobiographical novel, so indicative of the postmodern era, constructs the narrator's and in turn Wolf's transitional, provisional self.

What emerges from Wolf's and Hoffman's autobiographical turnings is a way to understand and to absorb the shock of their disrupted lives and a way to continue living with this cleft in their selfhood. Wolf achieves a tenuous unity of her disparate voices but leaves the reader feeling that keeping this fragile unity will be hard work, and it may not last. Hoffman, too, recognizes that "there's no returning to the point of origin, no regaining of childhood unity" (273). She, too, will have to contend with voices competing in two languages: "[W]hen I speak Polish now, it is infiltrated, permeated, and inflected by the English in my head. Each language modifies the other, crossbreeds with it, fertilizes it. Each language makes the other relative" (Hoffman 273). She even sees this state as "translation therapy" where, as she says, "I keep going back and forth over the rifts, not to heal them but to see that I — one person, first-person singular — have been on both sides" (Hoffman 273). Both Wolf and Hoffman cling to their newly reconstructed, fragile "I."

chapter eleven

The End of the Journey

I keep going back and forth over the rifts, not to heal them but to see
that I—one person, first-person singular—have been on both sides.
Eva Hoffman, *Lost in Translation*

In a 1946 interview, Erich Maria Remarque, then living in
New York, gave his fellow émigrés advice on how to be a refugee:
"[H]ave a phonograph and books if possible; take a room as near
the center of a great city as you can get; be on friendly terms with
a large number of people who are not refugees and who do not
speak your native language; avoid the temptation to write an autobiography" (Van Gelder 3). As we have seen, a great number of exiles did not resist this temptation. The resulting autobiographies
offer us an authentic view of this experience of physical and emotional uprooting. These autobiographers wanted their audiences
to understand the journeys they have taken. They testify to these
brutal events of history and speak of flight, despair, survival, transformation, and healing. And like Hoffman, they keep going back
and forth over the rifts of their lives.

The exile literature critic Sidney Rosenfeld points out that the
end of the war could be seen as the end of exile for émigré artists:
"Though the period of exile could have been terminated in a formal sense after 1945, it remains true that for many refugees and
émigrés exile had become a permanent inner state of being" (339).
The continuing publication of autobiographies for decades after
the war is affirmation that he is right. The exile experience irrevocably alters the vision of those who made the journey. Sometimes it strengthened and deepened understanding, sometimes it
destroyed.

Nelly Sachs, a German poet who found refuge in Sweden in
1940, wrote many poems imbuing this devastating experience with
striking images. In 1966 she shared the Nobel Prize for literature

with Samuel Joseph Agnon, the Israeli novelist. She recited the
following poem at the award ceremony.

Fleeing
what a great reception
on the way—

Wrapped
in the wind's shawl
feet in prayer of sand
which can never say amen
compelled
from fin to wing
and further—

The sick butterfly
will soon learn again of the sea—
This stone
with the fly's inscription
gave itself into my hand—

I hold instead of a homeland
the metamorphoses of the world.[1]

In this poem of flight and transformation, Sachs captures the buf-
feting forces of exile. The security of one's homeland is traded in
for the stones of one's destiny. But the eternal evidence of change
and transformation is imprinted also on the stone in the ancient
body of the fly. The exile who undergoes the perilous journey has
the resiliency to survive and join the continuing metamorphosis of
the world.

Notes

1 After he came to the United States, Arnold Schoenberg changed the spelling of his name from Schönberg to Schoenberg.
2 See Rosenfeld for further support for extending the arbitrary dates of German exile literature.

I. ESCAPE TO LIFE

1 During the two years he spent in Amsterdam, Klaus Mann started an exile literary journal, *Die Sammlung*. The politics of this journal shows how the exile community could not sustain attacks on Hitler. An agreement to publish literary pieces in the journal became difficult for four famous authors: Thomas Mann, Stefan Zweig, René Schickele, and Alfred Döblin, all of whom were still publishing in Germany in 1933 and had not yet been blacklisted by the Nazis. The Nazis monitored exile publications closely, and after the first edition of *Die Sammlung* came out, they apparently put pressure on the publishers of these writers to censure the exiles' efforts. The publishers in turn requested disavowals from the writers. Thomas Mann telegraphed his German publisher, S. Fischer, to renounce the journal by stating he "could only confirm that the character of the first issue of *Die Sammlung* does not conform to its original program" (Krispyn 36). Thomas Mann's statement as well as those from Stefan Zweig, René Schickele, and Alfred Döblin found their way into the Nazi press, an action seen as a propaganda victory for Joseph Goebbels, Hitler's minister of propaganda. At the same time it confused the exile community. While eventually all these writers unabashedly spoke and wrote for the exile cause, incidents such as these marred the impact of the exiles' overall effectiveness in countering Nazism.
2 In *The Devil in France*, Feuchtwanger consistently refers to the internment camp as Les Mille. Les Milles is the proper name.
3 Albert Stone refers to the apology as testament.
4 In 1994, Steven Spielberg set up the Survivors of the Shoah Visual History Foundation. This foundation is making video interviews of

survivors of the Holocaust using the most up-to-date technology. The foundation sets as its aim "to videotape eyewitness accounts of the Holocaust and to develop the largest multimedia archive of survivor testimonies ever assembled" (http://www.vhf.org/More_Informaton. html). The foundation intends to capture in a structured video interview as many of the living Holocaust survivors as possible. These interviews will be made available through technical networks to scholars and interested parties.

2. THE FALL OF FRANCE

1 At the end of the war, Fersen-Osten and her sister were sent first to a Jewish camp and then to their grandmother in Cardesse. Both her mother and father survived and returned to France much changed. Eventually, Fersen-Osten emigrated to the United States.
2 Döblin, *Destiny's Journey* 23. Hereafter cited in text as *DJ*.
3 Nazi Germany and Italy sent support for the war to the Nationalists, led by Franco. The U.S.S.R. supported the Loyalists, and the Comintern organized leftists and liberals to lead volunteer groups called International Brigades to fight against fascism. Gustave Regler recounts his experiences in Le Vernet in his autobiography, *The Owl and Minerva*.
4 Feuchtwanger notes in *The Devil in France* that he could not divulge his saviors, but he was rescued by Frank Bohn, who had been sent to France by the American Federation of Labor to help European labor leaders escape the Nazis. See *Assignment: Rescue* for information about Bohn.

3. THE PERSECUTION AND FLIGHT OF THE JEWS

1 Jesus was a Jew child! Jesus was a Jew child!
2 Yehuda Nir changed his name from Grünfeld.
3 Nir frequently mentions that the three always believed that they had better chances with the Germans. They understood that the many anti-Semitic Poles could easily recognize them as Jewish and would turn them in, as indeed some did. To the Germans, however, they were only other Poles.
4 After he went to England, Clare Anglicized his name from Georg Klaar to George Clare.
5 Clare's father and mother did not survive the war. His mother joined Clare's father in France, and after France's capitulation, the Vichy government sent them to a small village, St. Pierreville, to live. This action

was a part of a program called *résidence assignée*, in which Jews were housed in villages where the population could watch their activities. A local government official added their names to a list of Jews going to Auschwitz.

6 Many Jewish Poles in Germany were deported to Poland, but Poland chose not to reinstate their citizenship. Thus, these unfortunate people were stuck at the Polish border for an extended period. The Poles countered by sending German Jews back to Germany. Eventually a compromise was reached. Some were allowed in Poland, some went to concentration camps, and some returned to Germany.

4. AFTER THE WAR

1 Anthony Heilbut's *Exiled in Paradise* discusses the German community in Hollywood in detail.

2 The television documentary *The Exiles* portrays Eisler's story as well as changes in the lives of other exile composers and writers.

3 *The Muses Flee Hitler* and *The Sea Change: The Migration of Social Thought 1930–1963* assess the European émigrés' contributions to the American intellectual community.

5. CROSSING BOUNDARIES

1 Donald Prater in his article "Stefan Zweig" quotes this passage from a "copy in Friderike Zweig's *Nachlass* [literary estate]" (317–318).

2 Film and other visual media can be interpreted as autobiographical texts. See chapter 10 for a discussion of the exile autobiography by Charlotte Salomon, *Life? or Theater?* — an autobiography primarily composed of paintings.

3 See Paul John Eakin's book *Touching the World* for arguments reclaiming referentiality for autobiography.

4 Albert Stone admonishes autobiography critics of the dangers of fictionalizing autobiography without stressing the "complex processes of historical re-creation, ideological argument, and psychological expression" (*Autobiographical Occasions* 19). See chapter 1 for my discussion of the connections of history and autobiography.

5 Eakin points out, however, that "students of psychoanalytic procedure . . . insist on the radical differences between autobiography and autoanalysis." In their view, writing functions many times as a defense mechanism. They also point out that the process of writing an autobiography does not include the "crucial relationship between patient and

analyst that is the source of the therapeutic value of psychoanalysis" (*Fictions* 59).

6 In *Touching the World*, Eakin reiterates his views concerning the "autobiographical act . . . understood as an extension of a lifelong process of identity formation" (52) as he had developed them in *Fictions of the Self*.

6. CHILDHOOD AND THE MYSTERY OF ORIGINS

1 In a recent speech "Parting from Phantoms: The Business of Germany" given on 27 February 1994 at the Dresden Staatsoper and published in English in *PMLA*, Wolf sums up her conflicting views and feelings regarding not only the Germany of her childhood but also the GDR era and the current era of unification. Although her defensiveness about her youthful associations with the East German Communist government causes her to remark that all East Germans are "considered Stasi accomplices, government supporters, or collaborators," she basically grapples with what it has meant in her life to be a German writer. Although she "learned to see herself as a German writer," the politics of all the Germanies she has known still seem problematic for her.

2 For an interesting feminist and postmodernist view of the fascist implications for Nelly's and Wolf's subjectivity, see Marie-Luise Gättens's discussion of *Patterns of Childhood* in her book *Women Writers and Fascism*.

7. THE INTELLECTUAL RESPONSE

1 Hereafter cited in text as *NR*.

2 GG refers to the General Government, the area of Poland that the Nazis occupied and where they placed most of the death camps.

3 See chapter 3 for Yehuda Nir's tale of surviving as a Jew in the GG.

4 Gombrowicz, *Diary* 159. Hereafter cited in text as *D*.

5 The above translation is published in *A Kind of Testament*. In the 1988 edition of *Diary*, the translation is much stronger.
Monday: Me
Tuesday: Me
Wednesday: Me
Thursday: Me. (3)

6 See essays by Georg Iggers, Wilma Iggers, and particularly Leo Botstein's essay "Stefan Zweig and the Illusion of the Jewish European," in *Stefan Zweig*.

7 See, for example, some of Zweig's letters to Friderike from 1935 to 1937.

8 Prater notes, for example, that "the unfortunate Friderike became more and more the scapegoat" during the period when Zweig was vacillating between his marriage to Friderike and his new relationship with Lotte. "Without telling her [Friderike], he had begun to make arrangements for the sale of a great part of his collection of manuscripts . . . which she had so carefully maintained for him over the years. . . . He blindly told himself, however, that she alone was at fault, believing her still unwilling to uproot, and continued to blame her for his own inability to settle into the new life. Yet at the same time he wanted her to be on hand in Austria, to be near his mother" (Prater, *European* 244–245).

9 Prater notes that Klaus Mann met him on the street in New York in 1941 and saw a "strange and wild Zweig . . . he was unshaven, and deep in thought, clearly not very pleasant thought." When Zweig saw Mann, he "pulled himself together . . . and in a trice was once again the old Stefan Zweig, the elegant and worldly man of letters, friendly and interested" (Prater, *European* 300). Zuckmayer as well as Friderike also noticed his pessimism about this time.

10 It is important to remember that Zweig died in 1942, thus before the most heinous crimes against Jews in Poland and Russia had been reported widely. Nevertheless, he lived through the escalation of harassment against Jews and found his own works disparaged and censored by the Nazis.

11 According to Egbert Krispyn, in 1936 Mann had still not demonstrated his "commitment to the antifascist cause" to exile writers. He did eventually and strongly demonstrate his support for exile writers with an open letter to Eduard Korrodi, a Swiss journalist. Because of Mann's silence, Korrodi had tried to suggest that Mann held no sympathies for the exiles. In his letter, Mann condemned the Nazis categorically and "taunted that for the past three years they had been unable to decide whether to revoke his German citizenship" (Krispyn 51–52). This letter brought him prominence as one of the leading outspoken exile writers. The Nazis did revoke his citizenship.

12 See Mann, *Thomas Mann, Teil III*, for the letters specifically relating to the reception of *Doctor Faustus*.

13 English translations from "Deutschland und die Deutschen" are my own.

14 See Bergsten for details about the sources of these two groups.

15 See particularly the views of Helmut Koopmann, Manfred Dierks, Egon Schwarz, and Ehrhard Bahr and the responses to their perspectives.

16 Ein einsamer Mann faltet seine Hände und spricht: Gott sei euerer armen Seele gnädig, mein Freund, mein Vaterland.

1 Interestingly, Anaïs Nin in her multivolume diary also creates a self-mythology and specifically uses the labyrinth as one of her consistent images, not only in the diary but also in her fiction. Like many others, Nin fled Europe just before Hitler came into Paris. But although she was lucky enough to travel the same route through Lisbon that many refugees did, Nin is not so much an exile as an expatriate and thus fits into the scope of this study only tangentially. She was returning to the United States, where she had grown up and where she had visited in 1934 and 1935. She viewed life in the United States as a place bereft of myth: "I ask myself where I am now? In a place which denies myth, and sees the world in flat, ordinary colors" (Nin 77).

Nin, who was born in Cuba, came to the United States as a young girl when her mother brought her and her two brothers to the United States from Europe after the break-up of her marriage to the concert pianist Joachim Nin. Nin considered this rupture an exile and sought refuge in beginning a diary to send back to her father, still in Europe. As a young teenager she also began her lifelong occupation with the image of the labyrinth. Although the metaphor has many permutations in Nin's works, she mostly used it in her adult years as a symbol for the interiority of woman's psychic space. Most Nin readers agree that she interpreted personal traumas as well as social or political calamities through the focus of her own interiority. Like Eliade, her metaphor for these shifting internal patterns is the labyrinth.

2 See Olsen for an understanding of Eliade's quest to reach the "center" and how this relates to his overall work.

3 In 1994, Maitraye Devi published her own account of this love affair in *It Does Not Die*. Eliade's account appears in English as *Bengal Nights*.

4 In his autobiography, Eliade does not deny his association with Nae Ionescu and Ionescu's ideological support of the Legionnaires but insists that his view was humanistic, not fascist. Ricketts in his biography of Eliade maintains that although Eliade did write supportive periodical articles of the Legionary movement, Eliade's intentions were primarily humanistic, not political. Ricketts notes, however, that Eliade in his sincere effort to create the "culture" of his Romanian homeland was very nationalistic, and he did support the Legionnaires. See chapter 22, "Nationalism and the Primacy of the Spiritual" (Ricketts 881–930).

5 Like many men of his generation, Eliade reveals a strong sexist view of women. The journals, in particular, have several sexist comments.

9. THE CURRENCY OF LANGUAGE

1 See Heilbut for an in-depth view of the Hollywood German community during World War II.

10. RECONSTRUCTING THE SELF

1 Hereafter cited in text as *P*.
2 See *Philosophy and the Mirror of Nature* by Rorty and *Consciousness Explained* by Dennett for their views on the importance of the visual.

11. THE END OF THE JOURNEY

1 This poem is in the cycle "Flight and Metamorphosis." See Bahr for a close reading of this poet's exile poetry. The poem was translated and published in Sachs, *O the Chimneys*.

Bibliography

PRIMARY SOURCES

Adorno, Theodor. *Minima Moralia: Reflections on a Damaged Life*. Trans.
E. F. N. Jephcott. London: New Left Books, 1974.

Bell, Susan Groag. *Between Worlds: In Czechoslovakia, England, and
America*. New York: Penguin Books, 1991.

Breznitz, Shlomo. *Memory Fields: The Legacy of a Wartime Childhood in
Czechoslovakia*. New York: Alfred A. Knopf, 1993.

Canetti, Elias. *The Play of the Eyes*. Trans. Ralph Mannheim. New York:
Farrar, Straus and Giroux, 1985.

———. *The Tongue Set Free: Remembrance of a European Childhood*. Trans.
Joachim Neugroschel. New York: Farrar, Straus and Giroux, 1979.

———. *The Torch in My Ear*. Trans. Joachim Neugroschel. New York:
Farrar, Straus and Giroux, 1982.

Clare, George. *Last Waltz in Vienna: The Rise and Destruction of a Family,
1842–1942*. New York: Avon Books, 1980, 1983.

Döblin, Alfred. *Destiny's Journey*. Ed. Edgar Pässler. Trans. Edna
McCown. New York: Paragon House, 1992.

———. *Schicksals-Reise: Flucht und Exil, 1940–1948*. Munich: Piper Verlag,
1980.

Domin, Hilde. *Aber die Hoffnung: Autobiographisches aus und über
Deutschland*. Munich: Piper Verlag, 1982.

Eliade, Mircea. *Autobiography, Vol. I: 1907–1937: Journey East, Journey West*.
Trans. Mac Linscott Ricketts. Chicago: University of Chicago Press,
1981.

———. *Autobiography, Vol. II: 1937–1960: Exile's Odyssey*. Trans. Mac
Linscott Ricketts. Chicago: University of Chicago Press, 1988.

———. *Journal, Vol. I: 1945–1955*. Trans. Mac Linscott Ricketts. Chicago:
University of Chicago Press, 1990.

———. *Journal, Vol. III: 1970–1978*. Trans. Teresa Lavender Fagan.
Chicago: University of Chicago Press, 1989.

———. *Journal, Vol. IV 1979–1985*. Trans. Mac Linscott Ricketts. Chicago:
University of Chicago Press, 1990.

———. *No Souvenirs Journal, 1957–1969*. Trans. Fred H. Johnson, Jr. New
York: Harper & Row, 1977.

Erikson, Erik H. "Autobiographic Notes on the Identity Crisis." *Daedalus* 99. 4 (1970): 730–759.

Europa Europa. Dir. Agnieszka Holland. Les Films du Losange (Paris)/CCC Filmkunst (Berlin), 1991.

Exile. Dir. Alexis Krasilovsky. Rafael Film, 1984.

Fersen-Osten, Renée. *Don't They Know the World Stopped Breathing? Reminiscences of a French Child during the Holocaust Years*. New York: Shapolsky Publishers, 1991.

Feuchtwanger, Lion. *The Devil in France*. Trans. Elisabeth Abbott. New York: Viking Press, 1941.

Friedländer, Saul. *When Memory Comes*. Trans. Helen R. Lane. New York: Farrar, Straus and Giroux, 1979.

Fry, Varian. *Assignment: Rescue*. New York: Scholastic, 1968.

Furst, Desider, and Lilian R. Furst. *Home Is Somewhere Else: Autobiography in Two Voices*. Albany: State University of New York Press, 1994.

Gombrowicz, Witold. *Diary: Vol. I*. Ed. Jan Kott. Trans. Lillian Vallee. Evanston, Ill.: Northwestern University Press, 1988.

——. *A Kind of Testament*. Ed. Dominique de Roux. Trans. Alastair Hamilton. Philadelphia: Temple University Press, 1973.

Grosz, Georg. *A Little Yes and a Big No: The Autobiography of Georg Grosz*. Trans. Lola Sachs Dorin. New York: Dial Press, 1946.

Hoffman, Eva. *Lost in Translation: A Life in a New Language*. New York: Viking Penguin, 1989.

Koestler, Arthur. *Arrow in the Blue: An Autobiography*. New York: Macmillan Company, 1952.

——. *The Invisible Writing: An Autobiography*. Boston: Beacon Press, 1954.

——. *The Scum of the Earth*. New York: Macmillan Company, 1941.

Kokoschka, Oskar. *My Life*. Trans. David Britt. New York: Macmillan Company, 1974.

Lind, Jacov. *Counting My Steps: An Autobiography*. London: Macmillan Company, 1968.

Mann, Golo. *Reminiscences and Reflections: A Youth in Germany*. Trans. Krishna Winston. New York: W. W. Norton and Company, 1990.

Mann, Heinrich. *Ein Zeitalter wird besichtigt*. Hamburg: Rowohlt, 1973.

Mann, Katia. *Unwritten Memories*. Ed. Elisabeth Plessen and Michael Mann. Trans. Hunter and Hildegarde Hannum. New York: Alfred A. Knopf, 1975.

Mann, Klaus. *The Turning Point: Thirty-five Years in This Century*. New York: Markus Wiener Publishing, 1942, 1984.

Mann, Klaus, and Erika Mann. *Escape to Life*. Boston: Houghton Mifflin Company, 1939.

Mann, Thomas. *Autobiographisches*. Frankfurt am Main: Fischer Bücherei, 1968.

——. "Deutschland und die Deutschen." *Politische Schriften und Reden*. Vol. 3. Frankfurt am Main: Fischer Bücherei, 1967. 161–178.

——. *Diaries: 1918–1939*. Trans. Richard and Clara Winston. New York: Harry N. Abrams, 1982.

——. *Doctor Faustus: Das Leben des deutschen Tonsetzers Adrian Leverkühn erzählt von einem Freunde*. Moderne Klassiker. Frankfurt am Main: Fischer Bücherei, 1967.

——. *Doctor Faustus: The Life of the German Composer Adrian Leverkühn as Told by a Friend*. Trans. H. T. Lowe-Porter. New York: Vintage Books, 1947.

——. *Schriften und Reden zur Literatur, Kunst und Philosophie*. Vol. 3. Frankfurt am Main: Fischer Bücherei, 1968.

——. *A Sketch of My Life*. New York: Knopf, 1960.

——. *The Story of a Novel: The Genesis of Doctor Faustus*. Trans. Richard and Clara Winston. New York: Alfred A. Knopf, 1961.

——. *Thomas Mann: Teil III, 1944–1955, Dichter über ihre Dichtungen*. Vol. 14/III. Ed. Hans and Marianne Fischer. Germany: Ernst Heimeran Verlag, 1981.

——. "The Years of My Life." Trans. Heinz and Ruth Norden. *Harper's* 10 (1950): 243–264.

——. "What Is German?" *Atlantic Monthly* (May 1944): 78–85.

Miłosz, Czesław. *Native Realm: A Search for Self-Definition*. Trans. Catherine S. Leach. New York: Doubleday and Company, 1968.

Nabokov, Vladimir. *Speak, Memory: An Autobiography Revisited*. New York: Vintage International, 1967.

Nin, Anaïs. *The Diary of Anaïs Nin: Volume III, 1939–1944*. Ed. Gunther Stuhlmann. New York: Harcourt Brace Jovanovich, 1969.

Nir, Yehuda. *The Lost Childhood: A Memoir*. New York: Berkley Books, 1989.

Regler, Gustav. *The Owl of Minerva: The Autobiography of Gustav Regler*. Trans. Norman Denny. New York: Farrar, Straus and Cudahy, 1959.

Rezzori, Gregor von. *Memoirs of an Anti-Semite*. New York: Penguin Books, 1982.

——. *The Snows of Yesteryear: Portraits for an Autobiography*. Trans. H. F. Broch de Rothermann. New York: Vintage Books, 1989.

Sachs, Nelly. *O the Chimneys: Selected Poems*. Trans. Michael Hamburger, Christopher Holme, Ruth and Matthew Mead, Michael Roloff. New York: Farrar, Straus and Giroux, 1967.

——. *The Seeker and Other Poems*. Farrar, Straus and Giroux, 1970.

Salomon, Charlotte. *Leven? of Theater? Life? or Theatre?* Amsterdam: Joods Historisch Museum, 1992.

Seghers, Anna. *Transit*. Trans. J. A. Galston. Boston: Little, Brown, 1944.

Whiteman, Dorit Bader, ed. *The Uprooted: A Hitler Legacy: Voices of Those Who Escaped before the "Final Solution."* New York: Plenum Press, 1993.

Wolf, Christa. "Change of Perspective." Trans. Leslie Wilson. *German Women Writers of the Twentieth Century*. Ed. Elizabeth Rütschi Herrmann and Edna Huttenmaier Spitz. Oxford: Pergamon Press, 1978.

———. "Parting from Phantoms: The Business of Germany (Honorary Fellows Series)." Trans. Jan van Heurck. *PMLA* 3. 3 (1996): 395–407.

———. *Patterns of Childhood*. Trans. Ursule Molinaro and Hedwig Rappolt. New York: Farrar, Straus and Giroux, 1980.

Zeller, Frederic. *When Time Ran Out: Coming of Age in the Third Reich*. New York: Berkley Books, 1989.

Zuckmayer, Carl. *A Part of Myself*. Trans. Richard and Clara Winston. New York: Carroll & Graf Publishers, 1966.

Zweig, Friderike M. *Greatness Revisited*. Boston: Branden Press, 1971.

———. *Stefan Zweig*. New York: Thomas Y. Crowell Company, 1946.

———, ed. *Stefan Zweig/Friderike Zweig: Briefwechsel*. Bern: Alfred Scherz Verlag, 1951.

Zweig, Stefan. *The World of Yesterday: An Autobiography by Stefan Zweig*. New York: Viking Press, 1943.

SECONDARY SOURCES

Arendt, Hannah. *The Life of the Mind*. New York: Harcourt Brace Jovanovich, 1971.

Bahr, Ehrhard. "Flight and Metamorphosis: Nelly Sachs as a Poet of Exile." *Exile: The Writer's Experience*. Ed. John M. Spalek and Robert F. Bell. Chapel Hill: University of North Carolina Press, 1982. 267–277.

Barclay, Craig C. "Schematization of Autobiographical Memory." *Autobiographical Memory*. Ed. by David C. Rubin. Cambridge: Cambridge University Press, 1986.

Beddow, Michael. *Doctor Faustus*. Cambridge: Cambridge University Press, 1994.

Benstock, Shari. "Authorizing the Autobiographical." *The Private Self*. Ed. Shari Benstock. Chapel Hill: University of North Carolina Press, 1988. 10–33.

Bergsten, Gunilla. *Thomas Mann's* Doctor Faustus: *The Sources and*

Structure of the Novel. Trans. Krishna Winston. Chicago: University of Chicago Press, 1963.

Botstein, Leon. "Stefan Zweig and the Illusion of the Jewish European." *Stefan Zweig: The World of Yesterday's Humanist Today*. Ed. Marion Sonnenfeld. Albany: State University of New York Press, 1983. 82–110.

Brecht, Bertolt. *Bertolt Brecht Poems: 1913–1956*. Ed. John Willett and Ralph Mannheim with the cooperation of Erich Fried. 2nd ed. New York: Methuen, 1979.

Brewer, William F. "What Is Autobiographical Memory?" *Autobiographical Memory*. Ed. David C. Rubin. Cambridge: Cambridge University Press, 1986.

Broe, Mary Lynn, and Angela Ingram, eds. *Women's Writing in Exile*. Chapel Hill: University of North Carolina Press, 1989.

Bruss, Elizabeth. *Autobiographical Acts: The Changing Situation of a Literary Genre*. Baltimore: Johns Hopkins University Press, 1976.

———. "Eye for I: Making and Unmaking Autobiography in Film." *Autobiography: Essays Theoretical and Critical*. Ed. James Olney. Princeton: Princeton University Press, 1981. 296–320.

Carnegy, Patrick. *Faust as Musician: A Study of Thomas Mann's Novel Doctor Faustus*. New York: New Directions Publications, 1973.

Chandler, Marilyn R. "A Healing Art: Therapeutic Dimensions of Autobiography." *a/b: Auto/Biography Studies* 5. 1 (1989): 4–14.

Coe, Richard. *When the Grass Was Taller: Autobiography and the Experience of Childhood*. New Haven: Yale University Press, 1984.

Connell, Charles. *World-Famous Exiles*. Feltham: Odhams, 1969.

Couser, G. Thomas. *Altered Egos: Authority in American Autobiography*. New York: Oxford University Press, 1989.

De Man, Paul. "Autobiography as De-facement." *The Rhetoric of Romanticism*. New York: Columbia University Press, 1985. 67–81.

Dennett, Daniel C. *Consciousness Explained*. Boston: Little, Brown and Company, 1991.

Drews, Richard, and Alfred Kantorowicz. *Verboten und verbannt*. Berlin: Kindler Verlag, 1947.

Eakin, Paul John. *Fictions in Autobiography: Studies in the Art of Self-Invention*. Princeton: Princeton University Press, 1985.

———. *Touching the World: Reference in Autobiography*. Princeton: Princeton University Press, 1992.

Eliade, Mircea. *Bengal Nights*. Chicago: University of Chicago Press, 1994.

The Exiles. Narr. Arthur Cunningham and Sabine Thomson. Dir. Richard Kaplan. PBS. WNET, 1989.

Exner, Richard. *"Exul Poeta: Theme and Variations." Books Abroad* 50. 2 (1976): 285–295.

———. "Response to Brigitte Prutti." *Thomas Mann's* Doctor Faustus: *A Novel on the Margin of Modernism*. Ed. Herbert Lehnert and Peter C. Pfeiffer. Columbia, SC: Camden House, 1991.

Felstiner, Mary Lowenthal. "Artwork as Evidence: Charlotte Salomon's 'Life or Theater?'" *Remembering for the Future: The Impact of the Holocaust on the Contemporary World*. Oxford: Pergamon Press, 1988. 1739–1748.

———. "Charlotte Salomon's Inward-Turning Testimony." *Holocaust Remembrance: The Shapes of Memory*. Ed. Geoffrey Hartman. London: Blackwell, 1993. 104–116.

———. *To Paint Her Life: Charlotte Salomon in the Nazi Era*. New York: HarperCollins, 1994.

———. "Taking Her Life/History: The Autobiography of Charlotte Salomon." *Life/Lines*. Ed. Bella Brodzki and Celeste Schenck. Ithaca: Cornell University Press, 1988. 320–327.

Fleishman, Avrom. *Figures of Autobiography: The Language of Self-Writing in Victorian and Modern England*. Berkeley: University of California Press, 1983.

Frieden, Sandra. Autobiography: *Self into Form*. New York: Peter Lang, 1983.

Friedman, Susan Stanford. "Women's Autobiographical Selves: Theory and Practice." *The Private Self*. Ed. Shari Benstock. Chapel Hill: University of North Carolina Press, 1988.

Gättens, Marie-Luise. *Women Writers and Fascism: Reconstructing History*. Gainesville: University Press of Florida, 1995.

Geertz, Clifford. "'From the Native's Point of View': On the Nature of Anthropological Understanding." *Meaning in Anthropology*. Ed. Keith H. Basso and Henry A. Selby. Albuquerque: University of New Mexico Press, 1976. 221–237.

Gelber, Mark H., ed. *Stefan Zweig heute*. New York: Peter Lang, 1987.

Guillén, Claudio. "On the Literature of Exile and Counter-Exile." Books Abroad 50. 2 (1976): 271–280.

Gusdorf, Georges. "Conditions and Limits of Autobiography." Trans. James Olney. *Autobiography: Essays Theoretical and Critical*. Ed. James Olney. Princeton: Princeton University Press, 1981. 28–48.

Hamilton, Nigel. *The Brothers Mann: The Lives of Heinrich and Thomas Mann, 1871–1950 and 1875–1955*. New Haven: Yale University Press, 1979.

Hart, Francis Russell. "History Talking to Itself: Public Personality in Recent Memoir." *New Literary History* 11 (1979): 193–210.

———. "Notes for an Anatomy of Modern Autobiography." *New Literary History* I (Spring 1970): 485–511.

Heftrich, Eckhard. *Vom Verfall zur Apokalypse: Über Thomas Mann.* Vol. II. Frankfurt am Main: Vittorio Klostermann, 1982.

Heilbut, Anthony. *Exiled in Paradise: German Refugee Artists and Intellectuals in America from the 1930s to the Present.* New York: Viking Press, 1983.

Hoffman, Alice. "Reliability and Validity in Oral History." *Oral History: An Interdisciplinary Anthology.* Ed. David K. Dunaway and Willa K. Baum. Nashville: American Association for State and Local History, 1984. 67–73.

Hughes, H. Stuart. *The Sea Change: The Migration of Social Thought 1930–1963.* New York: Harper and Row, 1975.

Iggers, Georg. "Some Introductory Observations on Stefan Zweig's *World of Yesterday.*" *Stefan Zweig: The World of Yesterday's Humanist Today.* Ed. Marion Sonnenfeld. Albany: State University of New York Press, 1983. 1–9.

Iggers, Wilma. "The World of Yesterday in the View of an Intellectual Historian." *Stefan Zweig: The World of Yesterday's Humanist Today.* Ed. Marion Sonnenfeld. Albany: State University of New York Press, 1983. 10–19.

Jarrell, C. Jackman, and Carla M. Borden, eds. *The Muses Flee Hitler: Cultural Transfer and Adaptation 1930–1945.* Washington, D.C.: Smithsonian Institution Press, 1983.

Jay, Paul. *Being in the Text: Self-Representations from Wordsworth to Roland Barthes.* Ithaca: Cornell University Press, 1984.

Klawiter, Randolph. "The State of Stefan Zweig Research: An Update." *Stefan Zweig: The World of Yesterday's Humanist Today.* Ed. Marion Sonnenfeld. Albany: State University of New York Press, 1983. 324–340.

Kraszewsk, Charles. "Witold Gombrowicz." *Cyclopedia of World Authors.* Vol. II. Ed. Frank N. Mcgill. Pasadena, CA: Salem Press, 1989.

Krispyn, Egbert. *Anti-Nazi Writers in Exile.* Athens: University of Georgia Press, 1978.

Kurzke, Hermann. *Thomas Mann: Epoche — Werk — Wirkung.* Arbeitsbücher zur Literaturgeschichte. Munich: C. H. Beck Verlag, 1985.

Langer, Lawrence L. *Holocaust Testimonies: The Ruins of Memory.* New Haven: Yale University Press, 1991.

Lehnert, Herbert. "Thomas Mann, Bertolt Brecht, and the 'Free Germany' Movement." *Exile: The Writer's Experience.* Ed. John M. Spalek and Robert F. Bell. Chapel Hill: University of North Carolina Press, 1982. 182–202.

Lehnert, Herbert, and Peter C. Pfeiffer, eds. *Thomas Mann's* Doctor Faustus: *A Novel on the Margin of Modernism*. Columbia, SC: Camden House, 1991.

Lejeune, Philippe. *Le Pacte autobiographie*. Paris: Editions du Seuil, 1975.

Lifton, Robert J. *The Broken Connection: On Death and the Continuity of Life*. New York: Simon and Schuster, 1979.

———. *The Life of the Self: Toward a New Psychology*. New York: Simon and Schuster, 1976.

Lipsey, Roger. "We Are All Witnesses: An Interview with Elie Wiesel." *Parabola* 10. 2 (1985): 26–33.

Maitraye, Devi. *It Does Not Die: A Romance*. Chicago: University of Chicago Press, 1994.

Mason, Mary G. "The Other Voice: Autobiographies of Women Writers." *Autobiography: Essays Theoretical and Critical*. Ed. James Olney. Princeton: Princeton University Press, 1981. 207–235.

Mauron, Charles. *Des metaphores obsedantes au mythe personnel: Introduction à la psychocritique*. Paris: Librairie U. Corti, 1962.

McCabe, Cynthia Jaffee. "'Wanted by the Gestapo: Saved by America' — Varian Fry and the Emergency Rescue Committee." *The Muses Flee Hitler*. Ed. Jarrell C. Jackman and Carla M. Borden. Washington, D.C.: Smithsonian Institution Press, 1983. 79–91.

Miłosz, Czesław. "Notes on Exile." *Books Abroad* 50. 2 (1976): 281–284.

Misch, Georg. *A History of Autobiography in Antiquity*. Trans. E. W. Dickes. 2 vols. Cambridge: Harvard University Press, 1951.

Nussbaum, Felicity A. *The Autobiographical Subject: Gender and Ideology in Eighteenth-Century England*. Baltimore: Johns Hopkins University Press, 1989.

———. "Toward Conceptualizing Diary." *Studies in Autobiography*. Ed. James Olney. Oxford: Oxford University Press, 1988. 128–140.

Olney, James. "Autobiography and the Cultural Moment: A Thematic, Historical, and Bibliographical Introduction." *Autobiography: Essays Theoretical and Critical*. Ed. James Olney. Princeton: Princeton University Press, 1981. 3–27.

———, ed. *Autobiography: Essays Theoretical and Critical*. Princeton: Princeton University Press, 1980.

———. *Metaphors of Self: The Meaning of Autobiography*. Princeton: Princeton University Press, 1981.

———, ed. *Studies in Autobiography*. Oxford: Oxford University Press, 1988.

Olsen, Carl. *The Theology and Philosophy of Eliade*. New York: St. Martin's Press, 1992.

Pauker, Henri R. "Exile and Existentialism." *Exile: The Writer's*

Experience. Ed. John M. Spalek and Robert F. Bell. Chapel Hill: University of North Carolina Press, 1982. 82–94.

Prater, Donald. *European of Yesterday: A Biography of Stefan Zweig*. Oxford: Clarendon Press, 1972.

——. "Stefan Zweig." *Exile: The Writer's Experience*. Ed. John M. Spalek and Robert F. Bell. Chapel Hill: University of North Carolina Press, 1982. 311–332.

Proctor, Robert E. *Education's Great Amnesia*. Bloomington: Indiana University Press, 1988.

Reed, Donna K. *The Novel and the Nazi Past: Germanic Languages and Literature*. Vol. 28. New York: Peter Lang, 1985.

Reed, T. J. *Thomas Mann: The Uses of Tradition*. Oxford: At the Clarendon, 1974.

Ricketts, Mac Linscott. *Mircea Eliade: The Romanian Roots, 1907–1945*. Vols. I–II. New York: Columbia University Press, 1988.

Rorty, Richard. *Philosophy and the Mirror of Nature*. Princeton: Princeton University Press, 1979.

Rosenfeld, Sidney. "German Exile Literature after 1945: The Younger Generation." *Exile: The Writer's Experience*. Ed. John M. Spalek and Robert F. Bell. Chapel Hill: University of North Carolina Press. 333–341.

Rubin, David C., ed. *Autobiographical Memory*. Cambridge: Cambridge University Press, 1986.

Ryan, Judith. *The Uncompleted Past: Postwar German Novels and the Third Reich*. Detroit: Wayne State University Press, 1983.

Said, Edward. "The Mind of Winter." *Harper's* 269 (1984): 49–55.

"Schoenberg (Schönberg), Arnold." *Baker's Biographical Dictionary of Musicians*. 6th ed. Rev. Nicolas Slonimsky. London: Collier Macmillan Publishers, 1978. 1540–1543.

Seidel, Michael. *Exile and the Narrative Imagination*. New Haven: Yale University Press, 1986.

Simpson, John, ed. *The Oxford Book of Exile*. Oxford: Oxford University Press, 1995.

Sonnenfeld, Marion, ed. *Stefan Zweig: The World of Yesterday's Humanist Today*. Albany: State University of New York Press, 1983.

Spalek, John M., and Robert F. Bell, eds. *Exile: The Writer's Experience*. Chapel Hill: University of North Carolina Press, 1982.

Sprinker, Michael. "Fictions of the Self: The End of Autobiography." *Autobiography: Essays Theoretical and Critical*. Ed. James Olney. Princeton: Princeton University Press, 1981.

Strauss, Herbert A. "The Movement of People in a Time of Crisis." *The Muses Flee Hitler*. Ed. Jarrell C. Jackman and Carla M. Borden. Washington, D.C.: Smithsonian Institution Press, 1983. 45–59.

Steiner, George. *Extraterritorial: Papers on Literature and the Languages Revolution*. New York: Atheneum, 1971.

Stelzig, Eugene. "Is There a Canon of Autobiography?" *a/b: Auto/Biography Studies* 7. 1 (1992): 1–12.

Stone, Albert. *Autobiographical Occasions and Original Acts: Versions of American Identity from Henry Adams to Nate Shaw*. Philadelphia: University of Pennsylvania Press, 1982.

———. "Modern American Autobiography: Text and Transactions." *American Autobiography: Retrospect and Prospect*. Ed. Paul John Eakin. Madison: University of Wisconsin Press, 1991.

Tabori, Paul. *The Anatomy of Exile: A Semantic and Historical Study*. London: Harrap, 1972.

Thompson, Ewa M. *Witold Gombrowicz*. Boston: Twayne Publishers, 1979.

Van Gelder, Robert. "Erich Maria Remarque Lays Down Some Rules for the Novelist." *New York Times Book Review*, 27 January 1946: 3.

Vordtriede, Werner. "Vorläufige Gedanken zu einer Typologie der Exilliteratur." *Akzente* 15. 6 (1968): 556–575.

Voss, Lieselotte. *Die Entstehung von Thomas Manns Roman Doctor Faustus*. Tübingen: Max Niemeyer Verlag, 1975.

Wagener, Hans. "Erich Maria Remarque: Shadows in Paradise." *Exile: The Writer's Experience*. Ed. John M. Spalek and Robert F. Bell. Chapel Hill: University of North Carolina Press, 1982. 247–257.

Watts, Alan. *Beyond Theology: The Art of Godmanship*. New York: Vintage Books, 1973.

Weinstein, Fred. *The Dynamics of Nazism: Leadership, Ideology, and the Holocaust*. New York: Academic Press, 1980.

Wittlin, Joseph. "Sorrow and Grandeur of Exile." *Polish Review* 2. 2–3 (1957): 99–111.

Wyman, David S. *Paper Walls: America and the Refugee Crisis, 1938–1941*. New York: Pantheon Books, 1968, 1985.

Yalom, Marilyn. "*The Woman Warrior* as Postmodern Autobiography." *Approaches to Teaching Kingston's* The Woman Warrior. Ed. Shirley Geok-lin Lim. New York: Modern Language Association of America, 1991. 108–115.

Young-Bruehl, Elisabeth. *Hannah Arendt: For Love of the World*. New Haven: Yale University Press, 1982.

Zohn, Harry. "Introduction." *The World of Yesterday* by Stefan Zweig. Ed. Harry Zohn. Lincoln: University of Nebraska Press, 1964. v–xii.

Index

Adorno, Theodor, 53, 63, 141
Anschluß (Annexation), 28
Antifascists, 3, 6, 19
Apology, 10
Arendt, Hannah, xii, 53, 63, 160–161, 164
Arlen, Michael, 10
Article 19, surrender on demand, 21
Atonal music, xiii
Australia, 54
Austria, 4, 6, 28, 30, 41, 48
Autobiographical memory, 80–81
Autobiographical subject, 65–74
Autobiography: and "author," 66–68; and canon formation, 66, 67; and childhood, 84–86; collective, 30; and creative process, 63; and culture, 82–83; and feminism, 66, 98, 146; and film, 66; and genre, 66, 67; and history, 10–12, 15, 78; and identity, 77; and "life," 65–66; and mythology, 144, 145; and painting, 66; as personalized history, 11; and postmodernism, 66, 175–181, 196–197; and referentiality, 67, 73; and self, 63–64, 65, 66, 68; and self-definition, 77; and subjectivity, 64, 65; as therapy, 65, 74, 75–83; traditional, 54; and truth, 65. *See also* Exile autobiography; Memoir

Bahr, Ehrhard, 205n, 207n
Banishment, xiii
Barthes, Roland, 71
Bauhaus architecture, xiii
Beckett, Samuel, xv
Beddow, Michael, 131, 142
Belgium, 31, 32
Bell, Robert F., xi, xvi
Bell, Susan Groag, 94, 95, 96
Benjamin, Walter, 59
Benstock, Shari, 70, 146–148, 158
Berghahn, Marian, 29
Bergsten, Gunilla, 135, 137, 138, 140, 205n
Blücher, Henry, 53, 165
Bohn, Frank, 202n
Botstein, Leon, 128, 129, 204n
Brazil, 54
Brecht, Bertolt, xii, xiii, xiv, 3, 53, 132, 160
Brewer, William F., 80
Breznitz, Shlomo, 28, 35–36, 37
Britain, 6, 24, 32, 54
Broch, Hermann, xv
Broe, Mary Lynn, xv
Bruss, Elizabeth, 66, 72
Bulgaria, 57, 93

Camus, Albert, xv
Canada, 53
Canetti, Elias, xx, 57, 58, 81, 83, 91, 93–94, 166–173, 182; and Bulgaria, 93, 167; and German, 168–169, 170–173; and Ladino,

Canetti, Elias (*continued*)
167–168, 173; and Vienna, 166,
167
Carlyle, Thomas, 71
Carnegy, Patrick, 140
Chagall, Marc, 26
Chandler, Marilyn R., 75, 76
Childhood, xx. *See also*
Autobiography
Children's railroad, 43, 48
Chodorow, Nancy, 148
Cicero, 68
Clare, George, 41–43, 49, 202n
Coe, Richard N., 84–86
Concentration camps, 20, 31;
Auschwitz, 17, 35, 197; Drancy
(transit camp), 179; Westerbork
(transit camp), 39, 48
Confession, 10
Connell, Charles, xiii
Couser, Thomas, 70, 71
Czechoslovakia, 6, 35, 94, 95;
Czechoslovakian crisis, 41

Dante, xiii, xiv
De Man, Paul, 67, 68
Dennett, Daniel C., 192, 207n
Derrida, Jacques, 63
Des Pres, Terrence, 29
De Staël, Madame, xiv
Diary, 18
Dierks, Manfred, 205n
Die Sammlung, 201n
Displaced persons, xiv
Döblin, Alfred, 15, 17–19, 24, 27,
49, 52, 53, 54, 80, 163; and exile
experience, 27; and psychic
numbing, 18
Domin, Hilda, 50
Duchamp, Marcel, 26

Eakin, Paul John, 8, 10, 12, 64, 73,
76, 77, 83, 182, 203n, 204n

Einstein, Albert, xii, 4, 160
Eisler, Hanns, 53
Eliade, Mircea, xvii, 57, 83, 144,
145, 148, 149–159, 161, 165–
166, 167, 206n; and critics, 151,
157, 158; as diarist, 57–58, 156,
157–158; and Eranos, 155; and
Goethe, 149; and India, 150,
151, 152; and labyrinth, 151, 158,
159; and Nae Ionescu and
Legionary movement, 152, 153,
206n; and Paris, 157, 158, 159;
and personal myth, 152, 156,
157; and Romania, 149; and
Romanian exile community,
154; and Surendranath
Dasgupta, 150, 151; and time,
149; and United States, 155
Émigré(s), xiv, xvi, 6, 26
Enemy aliens, 7
Erickson, Erik, 50, 77–79, 81,
82
Europa, Europa, 38
Exile, xii; authorial responses to,
xvii; definition, xiii, xiv, xv,
xix; and existentialism, xv;
metaphor for alienation, xv;
and nostalgia, 86–87, 111;
self-imposed, xiv
Exile autobiography, xv, xvi;
classifications, xviii; and
identity, 82–83; and nostalgia,
86; and self-reconstruction,
80–82; as therapy, 76–77;
writing process, xviii
Exile community, 6, 13, 89–90,
160; *The Exiles*, 203n
Exiles, historical, xiii; influence of,
xii
Exner, Richard, xiii, 134

Fascism, xi, xiii, xv, 13
Felstiner, Mary Lowenthal , 178

Fersen-Osten, Renée, 16–17, 27, 36, 49, 202n

Feuchtwanger, Lion, 6, 7, 13, 15, 19, 21–23, 24–25, 27, 49, 51, 53, 80, 131, 160, 202n; and internment, 21–23; and refugee's plight, 24–25

Fleishman, Avrom, 145–146

Foucault, Michael, 63, 82

France, 6, 8, 15–27, 31, 32; free France, 16, 24; occupied zone, 21; phony war, 21

Frank, Bruno, 52

Freud, Anna, 78

Freud, Sigmund, 75, 78

Friedländer, Saul, 77, 80, 81, 88, 94, 96, 101, 175, 182–185, 188, 189; and Catholic orphanage, 184; and Czechoslovakia, 175; and Holocaust, 184

Friedman, Susan Stanford, 70, 146, 148

Fry, Varian, 26–27

Frye, Northrup, 145

Furst, Desider, 45–47

Furst, Lilian, 41, 45–47, 49, 57

Gätten, Marie-Luise, 204n

Geertz, Clifford, 69

German exile literature, xi, xvi; younger generation, xvi

Germans, 4, 6, 36; repatriated, 101

Germany, 4, 6, 15, 30, 35, 113; Hitler's Germany, 42, 48, 103

GG, 204n

Goebbels, Joseph, 5

Goethe, Wolfgang von, 70

Gombrowicz, Wittold, 83, 112, 117–121, 122, 130, 144, 204n; and Argentina, 118, 120; and exile, 120; and existentialism, 118, 119; and Poland, 117, 119, 121

Graf, Oskar Maria, 5

Grass, Günther, 142

Gropius, Walter, xii, xiii

Grosz, Georg, 50, 54–55, 95; and Dadaism, 55, 56; and United States, 54–55

Grynszpan, Herschel, 28

Guillén, Claudio, xvii, xviii

Gusdorf, George, 70, 84, 146

Hamilton, Nigel, 135

Hampl, Patricia, 10

Harrington, Michael, 11

Hart, Francis Russell, 10–11, 13

Hauptmann, Gerhart, 5

Heilbut, Anthony, 203n, 207n

Heine, Heinrich, xiii

Heraclitis, 80

Herr, Michael, 11

Herzfeld, Ernst, 4

Hesse, Hermann, 50

History, oral, 11–12; personal versions of, 49

Hitler, Adolf, xii, 3, 5, 6, 7, 8, 15, 16, 41, 95, 101, 105, 107, 124, 130, 131, 132, 137

Hoffman, Alice, 12

Hoffman, Eva, xi, xvi, xx, 83, 87, 88, 90–91, 94–95, 96, 103, 166, 175, 185–188, 189, 196, 197; and Kraków, 90, 95; and language and identity, 185, 186, 187; and nostalgia, 87–88; and psychic numbing, 186, 188

Holland, 31, 32, 39

Hollywood, German exile community, 51

Holocaust, 9, 11, 29, 75, 188, 201–202n

Horkheimer, Max, 53

House Un-American Activities Committee, 53

Hugo, Victor, xiv

Identity, 14, 57, 77, 176, 181, 182;
    Erikson, 50, 58, 77–79; and
    exile, 64, 77
Iggers, George, 122, 125, 204n
Iggers, Wilma, 125, 126, 204n
Immigrants, xiv, xvi
Ingram, Angela, xv
International Brigades, 19, 202n
Internment, 6, 7, 19–23; Gurs, 21;
    Les Milles, 7, 15, 21–23; Nîmes,
    23; Le Vernet, 19, 20, 21, 22

Jay, Paul, 66, 71, 72, 75, 76, 176
Jews, xii, 6, 13, 16, 17, 28, 29, 30,
    31, 33, 36; and circumcision, 38,
    40, 47; and Poland, 203n
Joyce, James, 71
Jung, Carl, 144, 145

Kafka, Franz, xv
Kindertransports (Children's
    transports), 32
Koestler, Arthur, 6, 13, 15, 19–21,
    24, 49, 54, 58, 80, 83, 161, 163–
    164; and internment, 19–21;
    and languages, 163–164; as
    typical Eastern European, 58
Kokoshka, Oskar, 50, 54, 55–56,
    144; and Albrecht Dürer, 55;
    and Rembrandt, 56
Koopmann, Helmut, 205n
Korngold, Ernst, 51
Korrodi, Eduard, 205n
Krispyn, Egbert, 201n, 205n
Kristallnacht (Crystal Night), 28,
    29, 30, 32, 34, 43
Kurzke, Hermann, 142

Lacan, Jacques, 73, 147
Lang, Fritz, 52
Langer, Lawrence L., 9, 12
Latvia, 41, 42
Lawrence, D. H., xiv

Lehmann, Lotte, 3
Lehnert, Herbert, 142
Lejeune, Philippe, 70, 71
Lessing, Theodor, 4
Lifton, Robert J., 18, 77, 79–80,
    81, 82, 91, 174, 182, 188, 189
Lind, Jacov, 36, 37, 38, 39–40,
    95, 176, 177–178, 181, 188;
    "apocalyptic . . . therapy,"
    40; and circumcision, 38; and
    no language, 177; survival
    strategy, 39
Lipchitz, Jacques, 26
Li Po, xviii
Lithuania, 42, 114
Lothar, Ernst, 130

Mahler-Werfel, Alma, 5, 26, 54
Mann, Erika, xii, 3–6, 131, 162;
    and émigrés, 3–6; and Gustav
    Grundgens, 5
Mann, Golo, xvii, xx, 92–93, 96,
    131, 136
Mann, Heinrich, 3, 26, 51, 52, 133,
    134
Mann, Katia, 135
Mann, Klaus, xii, xv, 3–6, 13–14,
    91–93, 96, 131, 162, 201n, 205n;
    and Die Sammlung, 201n; and
    émigrés, 3–6; and trope of lost
    paradise, 92
Mann, Thomas, xii, xiv, xx, 3, 4,
    50, 53, 83, 112, 127, 130–143,
    144, 160, 161; and Adorno,
    140; and Carla Mann, 135, 136;
    as exile spokesman, 130, 132;
    and Faust, 139; and Frido
    Mann, 135; and Germany,
    132, 133, 134, 137, 138, 139,
    140, 141, 142; as Germany's
    autobiographer, 130, 132, 138,
    142; and Julia Mann, 135; and
    Klaus Pringsheim, 136; and

montage techniques, 133, 140; and Nazi Germany, 131, 133, 137, 138, 139, 140; and Nietzsche, 136, 139; and Richard Wagner, 131; and United States, 132

Marcuse, Herbert, xii

Martinque, 26

Mason, Mary G., 98

Mauron, Charles, 145

McCabe, Cynthia Jaffee, 26

McCarthy, Senator Joseph, 53

Memoir, xix; exile memoir, 13–14; "focused," 13–14, 27, 58, 64; memoir and history, 8–13; memoirs of integration, 50; personal memoir, 8–13

Memory, 8–9, 12; and sense of identity, 73

Mexico, 24

Mies van der Rohe, Ludwig, xiii

Miłosz, Czesław, xx, 83, 112, 113–116, 117, 122, 130, 144, 158, 161–162; and exile, 64, 116; and Poland, 15–16

Misch, Georg, 70

Nabokov, Vladimir, xi, xv, xx, 81, 83, 86–90, 91, 96, 104, 161, 166, 167, 188; and Berlin exile community, 89; and trope of lost paradise, 86–87

Narrative discourse, 8; narrative strategies, 33, 76

Narratives: childrens', 31–33; escape, 13, 16–19, 40–48; personal, 8; survival, 13, 28–31

Nazis, xii, 3, 5, 7, 13, 15, 26, 105, 107, 108, 115, 131, 132; brutality, 33–35, 36, 39; Illegalen, 28, 29, 30, 33

Nazism, 17, 124

Nietzsche, Friedrich, xv, 72, 136

Nin, Anaïs, 166, 206n

Nir, Yehuda, 36–38, 202n, 204n; and circumcision, 37–38; Lala (sister), 38, 40, 49

Nostalgia, 84, 87

Nussbaum, Felicity, 66, 70–71, 72

Olney, James, xviii, 63, 70, 73, 145, 146, 148; metaphors of self, 64, 80

Olsen, Carl, 206n

Ossietsky, Carl von, 4

Ovid, xiii, xiv

Palestine, 31

Panofsky, Erwin, 4

Paucker, Henri R., xv

Personal myth, 145

Petrarch, xiii, 68

Pfeiffer, Peter C., 142

Poland, 6, 36, 37, 94, 95, 103

Portugal, 25, 27

Pound, Ezra, xv

Prater, Donald, 123, 125, 126, 127, 128, 129, 203n, 205n

Proctor, Robert, 68

Psychic numbing, 18, 22, 79, 102, 110, 174–175, 177, 178, 182, 188, 189, 190, 192

Ragland-Sullivan, Ellie, 147

Rainer, Luise, 3

Rath, Ernst vom, 28

Reed, Donna K., 142

Reed, T. J., 133, 142

Refugees, xiii, xvi, 24, 26; definition, xiii

Relief organizations: American Friends Rescue Committee, 25; Emergency Rescue Committee, 25–27; Red Cross, 25; Unitarian Service Committee, 25

Remarque, Erich Maria, 53, 198

Rezzori, Gregor von, xx, 81, 83,
    96–102, 104, 175, 176–177, 181,
    188; and Austrian empire, 97,
    98; and the Bukovina, 97, 100;
    and childhood, 97, 100; and
    dysfunctional family, 101, 102,
    177
Ricketts, Mac Linscott, 149
Rilke, Ranier Maria, xv, 127
Romania, 36, 58, 97, 98,
Rorty, Richard, 192, 207n
Rosenfeld, Sidney, 160, 198, 201n
Rousseau, Jean Jacques, 84, 85
Rowbotham, Sheila, 148
Russian Revolution, xiii

Sachs, Nelly, 198–199, 207n
Said, Edward W., xiv, xv, xvii
St. Exupéry, Antoine de, xv
Salomon, Charlotte, 176, 178–181,
    188, 203n; and dysfunctional
    family, 179–180; and exile in
    France, 180; and Nazis, 178–
    179; and paintings, 181
Sartre, Jean Paul, xv
Schickele, René, 131
Schiller, Friedrich, 70
Schoenberg, Arnold, xii, xiii, 51,
    53, 201n
Schuschnigg, Kurt von, 28
Schwarz, Egon, 205n
Seghers, Anna, 24
Seidel, Michael, xiv, xv, 86
Self, 9–10, 66, 67; fiction of, 73;
    historical definitions of, 68–
    70; and language, 72, 73, 83;
    postmodern, 70–73
Self-analysis, 75, 203n
Self-defined witnesses to history,
    xviii, 8–13
Self-reconstruction, xix, 80–82,
    182. See also Friedländer, Saul;
    Hoffman, Eva; Lind, Jacov;

Rezzori, Gregor von; Salomon,
    Charlotte; and Wolf, Christa
Self-schema, 80, 188
Self-story, 63–65, 76, 188
Shanghai ghetto, 31
Shoah Visual History Foundation,
    201n
Sinhuhe, xiii
South America, 24, 26
Spain, 25
Spalek, John M., xi, xvi
Spengler, Oswald, 54
Spielberg, Steven, 201n
Sprinker, Michael, 72
SS, 32
Steiner, George, xi, xv, 73
Stelzig, Eugene, 66
Stone, Albert, 8–9, 13, 201n, 203n
Strass, Herbert A., 31
Subjectivity, 64
Sudetenland, 6
Sweden, 32
Swift, Johnathan, xiv

Tabori, Paul, xiii, xv
Terkel, Studs, 11
Third Reich, 5, 102, 103, 104, 110
Toller, Ernst, 59
Trope of lost paradise, 86–92
Tucholsky, Kurt, 5

United States, 19, 23, 24, 25, 26,
    50, 53, 54; Hollywood exile
    community, 51

Virgil, Robert, xv
Visa: exit, 24; transit, 24
Vordtriede, Werner, xi
Voss, Lieselotte, 140

Walter, Bruno, 3
Watts, Alan, 69
Weinstein, Fred, xix

Weiss, Ernst, 59, 160
Werfel, Franz, 3, 4, 26, 51, 52, 131
Whiteman, Dorit Bader, 29, 32–33
Wiesel, Elie, xix
Wilder, Billy, xii, 51, 53
Wittlin, Joseph, 82, 86
Wolf, Christa, 82, 84, 96, 102–110, 142, 174, 188–196; and alienation of language, 194; and euthanasia program, 107; and Germany, 204n; and "glitter words," 194; and memory, 106, 108, 190; and postmodern style, 196; and psychic numbing, 190, 191, 192, 193; as refugee, 109; and Third Reich, 176, 188, 190, 191, 192, 193, 194
Wordsworth, William, 71
Wyman, David S., 24, 32

Yalom, Marilyn, 175
Young-Breuhl, Elisabeth, 53, 165

Zeller, Frederic, 28, 34–35, 37, 41, 43–45, 47; and family, 48, 49, 95, 108
Zinnemann, Fred, 52
Zohn, Harry, 129
Zuckmayer, Carl, xx, 50, 51–52, 53, 54, 56, 63, 162, 166; and Hal Wallis, 52; and Hollywood, 51–52; and language, 162
Zweig, Arnold, 52
Zweig, Friderike, 128, 204n, 205n
Zweig, Stefan, xx, 3, 4, 58, 83, 112, 121–130, 133, 144; and Austria, 122, 125, 127; and exile, 123, 128; and exile community, 124, 128; and Friderike, 122, 123, 125, 126, 127; and Lotte, 123, 126; and suicide, 121, 123, 130